THE GENESIS FLEET

FLEET

VANGUARD

THE GENESIS FLEET

VANGUARD

JACK CAMPBELL

TITAN BOOKS

The Genesis Fleet: Vanguard
Print edition ISBN: 9781785650406
E-book edition ISBN: 9781785650413

Published by Titan Books
A division of Titan Publishing Group Ltd
144 Southwark Street, London SE1 0UP

First edition: May 2017
2 4 6 8 10 9 7 5 3 1

A CIP catalogue record for this title is available from the British Library.

Printed and bound in Great Britain by CPI Group UK Ltd.

What did you think of this book? We love to hear from our readers. Please email us at: readerfeedback@titanemail.com, or write to us at the above address.

To receive advance information, news, competitions, and exclusive offers online, please sign up for the Titan newsletter on our website: www.titanbooks.com

*To Colonel Gary S. Baker, USAF. Veteran of Vietnam and the Cold War,
B-47 Navigator/Bombardier, AC-47 "Puff the Magic Dragon" pilot/
advisor to the VNAF, and midwife for the C-5 (including being pilot #5
to qualify for midair refueling, and command of C-5 56th Military Airlift
Squadron at Altus AFB).*

For S., as always.

1

There was something about breathing the air of a new world, something about knowing that the oxygen you inhaled had never before sustained any human being. It felt crisp and new and strange and exciting. Not like Earth, which he had visited once, where every molecule had cycled through countless generations of humanity, where the same old stories had played out endless times on land trod by untold numbers of people. Here, this spot, right there, had never before felt the weight of a person's foot. There, where trees with strange leaves and odd shapes marked where the grassland changed to forest, no person's eyes had ever before rested. Compared to this world, even the planets in the Alfar Star System felt like what they were now called, an Old Colony.

The sun overhead wasn't quite the right size for someone familiar with the sun that warmed the planets orbiting Alfar and looked a little too orange, but it was at the right distance from this world so that the heat it gave off allowed a person to walk about in shirtsleeves at this latitude and this time of the planet's year. The air had that fresh relish to it and could be breathed by humans. The green of the plants felt a little too blue, but that was all right.

A flock of small, birdlike creatures rose into the air with a thunder of wings and high-pitched, warbling cries. Like every habitable world that humanity had discovered so far, this one held an array of native life but nothing that could be considered sentient. If other intelligent species existed in the galaxy, they were still somewhere out there, beyond the current boundaries of human exploration.

Robert Geary knelt and touched the grass, grinning. Behind him, he could hear the rumble of machinery coming off the landing shuttles that had brought the devices down from orbit. Soon enough, those machines would begin constructing the first buildings of a city. Not an old city, with memories of generations of people and buildings, but also something new, not burdened with history but still awaiting history's first imprint.

A new world. A new beginning.

Unlike Alfar, the Old Colony he had come from. In human terms, a new place that had become Old in a few generations. Where "how we do things here" had fossilized rapidly into a society where no one was supposed to rock the boat because the rules set forth by the first colonists were the best and only imaginable ways to do things.

And if you could imagine other ways? If you wanted to try something different? Or, worse, change the way things were? Who do you think you are?

I think I am Robert Geary; therefore I am not going to put up with this when I can go somewhere new with other people who want to be able to breathe. Somewhere we can make our own rules.

"Rob Geary?"

The call from his comm unit jarred Rob from his reverie. He frowned at the worried tone of it. Why would the president of the colony's governing council be calling him? "Here. Is something wrong?"

"A ship arrived at the jump point from Scatha five hours ago. They sent a message as soon as they showed up, which we have now received."

"And?"

"They say this star system is under their 'protection,' and we owe them what they call residency and defense fees."

"That's ridiculous," Rob said. "I thought we were granted full ownership here by the Interstellar Rights Authority."

"We were, and we intend on telling them that. But what if they don't listen?"

"Why are you asking me? I'm not on the governing council."

"Because that new arrival is a warship. And the warship is heading toward this world."

He gazed upward, where the blue of the daylight sky drowned out sight of the countless stars. Somewhere up there was . . . what? A warship belonging to some other recent colony? A private corporation wanting to sell security services in a new part of space? A pirate, absurd as that seemed? "What does the council expect me to do about it?"

"We need advice, Rob. Advice from someone who knows something about this kind of thing. And in this colony, that's you."

Rob Geary touched the place on his collar where he had once worn the insignia of a junior officer in the small fleet of Alfar Star System. He had thought he had put that part of his life aside forever.

But maybe not. Whether whoever controlled that other ship called themselves pirates or privateers or security professionals or part of whatever fleet Scatha had, they were playing a very ancient game. It looked like humanity had brought some old, bad habits along with it to new stars and new worlds. And as someone who had chafed at not being able to make changes, to make a difference, Rob wasn't in a very good position to refuse to help when asked.

Fortunately, a shuttle had been about to lift back up into orbit to the ship, saving Rob time that could be valuable.

"What have we got?" Rob asked as he entered the command deck. The elderly passenger and bulk-cargo carrier *Wingate*, called the *Wingnut* by everyone, had been built to haul people and materials in a single star system, then had a new jump drive added on and instantly became an elderly interstellar transport. Aside from the up-to-the-minute jump control panel, the rest of the command deck was taken up by displays and controls that had been in service for decades—and showed it.

The main display flickered erratically until the *Wingnut*'s captain, a woman apparently as old as the ship, slammed her fist against a control unit in a spot already dented by many similar blows. As the display steadied, Rob squinted at the information about the ship that was demanding protection money. "It's a Buccaneer Class cutter?"

"Yep," the captain said. "Not good for much in the Old Colonies but still handy where there's not much else to threaten them."

"You don't seem to be very worried," Rob told her, not bothering to hide his irritation at her attitude.

"You already paid me," the captain said, "and those guys from Scatha won't give me a hard time because I already paid them a license fee to operate in this region."

"License fee? You mean extortion?"

The captain spread her hands. "Call it what you want. Do you have a better idea? You going to fight that Bucket with your fists?"

Frustrated, Rob took another look at the display, then stormed off in search of the colony's governing council.

Half the council were already gathered, crammed into *Wingnut*'s grandly named recreational room, which was just a compartment with several aging displays built in. The men and women of the rest of the council, still on the surface of the planet, could be seen on one of the displays. As Rob entered the compartment, a storm of argument dwindled as everyone looked at him. Council President Chisholm, looking unhappy, nodded at Rob. "Thank you for getting back up here quickly. What's your assessment?"

He didn't waste time asking why the leaders of the colony were calling on a lowly former lieutenant for his opinion. The Old Colonies tended to have really small military forces, which was why ex–junior officer Rob Geary was the most senior veteran among the initial group of roughly four thousand colonists settling this world.

"They have an old Buccaneer Class cutter," Rob told the council. "It arrived at the jump point from Scatha, about five light hours from this planet we're orbiting and colonizing. The information we have is still almost five hours light-delayed, but they were headed on an intercept for us at that time, and there's no reason to think they'd change vector. Their velocity is point zero five light speed, and they can't afford to push it any faster even if they had newer technology for their propulsion system. That means they'll get here in a little more than three and a half days."

"What can you tell us about the Buccaneer? How dangerous is it?"

Rob made an indecisive gesture with one hand. "Back home? Not very dangerous at all. The Buckets are nearly a century old, not very fast or maneuverable, and fairly small. They were built for law-enforcement duties like stopping smuggling and for search and rescue. All of the Old Colonies have retired and sold their Buckets, which is how a new colony like Scatha could get its hands on one for what was probably a cheap price. But in this star system, as the only ship equipped to fight, it's as dangerous as it needs to be. The sensors on the *Wingnut* are too badly maintained to tell us any details about the Bucket that showed up here, but it's probably got the standard weapons. That would be a single grapeshot launcher and a single pulse particle beam projector. Those are both close-in weapons. They'll have to be right on top of us to hit us, and their particle beam is probably early second-generation equipment, which means its hitting power is limited."

"But what can it do with those weapons?" Chisholm pressed.

Rob paused to think. "They could destroy our shuttles, preventing us from landing any more people or equipment, and stranding anyone up here in orbit. They could also decide to target this ship directly despite the owner's having paid them off earlier. Destroying the *Wingnut* would take a lot of work, but hitting critical areas like access hatches, air locks, and shuttle docking sites could cripple us."

"I kept saying we should invest in a warship of our own!" Council Member Kim complained.

"We didn't come out here to fight wars!" Chisholm snapped at Kim. "We went out to find the freedom and the room to follow our dreams! It's easy to say now what we should have done, but when all of us here decided where to put the money for this colony, we found that we couldn't afford even one warship like this Buccaneer cutter."

"We can't afford to lose any of our shuttles or pay this extortionate demand, either!" Kim tapped his comm pad furiously. "If we pay this, we'll barely be able to proceed with building the colony."

"According to the message from the warship, Scatha Star System says we need to be protected," another council member said. "Shouldn't we learn more before making a decision to reject their, um, offer?"

"They are not making an offer," Chisholm said. "Scatha is making a demand. That is not the action of someone seeking to help us."

"Do we know anything about Scatha?"

"All we know," Chisholm said, "is that the name they chose for their star system, Scatha, appears to be derived from that of an ancient warrior goddess. That and the fact that their first interaction with us is a demand that we pay them a very large sum."

"Appeal to Old Earth!" Council Member Odom urged. "When they hear—"

"They won't hear for months," Chisholm said. "And then what will they do? Old Earth has made it clear that while they love having their children spreading colonies among the stars, that love does not extend to actually helping them when they run into trouble."

"Old Earth got badly beaten up during the last Solar War," Kim grumbled. "They're still trying to rebuild. We can't expect them to help us. Which is why I wanted to buy our own protection!"

"Can't the police force do anything?" Council Member Odom asked plaintively.

"Twenty men and women with nonlethal weaponry?" Kim asked, his voice dripping with sarcasm.

"We have some weapons," Odom insisted.

"Hand weapons for hunting." Chisholm looked to Rob again. "What can we do?"

"I don't know," Rob said. "There are two other veterans among the current batch of colonists, and they're both former enlisted specialists from Alfar's fleet. They might know something about the Bucket that could help."

"You were an officer," Kim pointed out. "Surely you know more than any enlisted."

"Being an officer meant I knew enough about the systems on my ship to know how to best employ them," Rob said. "Most officers are generalists. The real equipment experts are the enlisted. I'll ask them. But regardless of what they tell me we *can* do, I need to know what we're willing to do."

Chisholm looked around, most of the other council members avoiding her gaze. "I know how criminals work," she told them all. "They'll take as much as they can, returning to hit us up repeatedly, while still leaving us enough to survive and generate more loot for them. We can't afford to give in to that. I need options beyond refusal and hoping they don't carry through on their threats," she finished, gazing at Rob once more.

"I'll see if we've got any," Rob told her.

Lyn "Ninja" Meltzer was still aboard the *Wingnut*, naturally enough. Also, naturally enough, she wasn't where the colony's individual locator software said she was on the ship even though that software was supposedly hack-proof. Rob punched her ID into his pad, hoping she would accept his call. "Ninja, where are you? We're dealing with a reality-bites situation."

Her reply came in moments later, showing her head against the top of her bunk. He had only met Ninja a few times, but she smiled in welcome at seeing him. "Hey, Lieutenant! Reality for real?"

"Yeah. Break time is over. Do you know anything about the old Buccaneer cutters?"

"I might."

"What about Torres? Do you think he's familiar with them?"

Meltzer grinned. "Corbin Torres served six years on a Bucket."

"How do you know that?" Rob asked.

"He's the only other fleet vet with this mob. Who else am I going to swap stories with?" Meltzer eyed Geary. "I heard there's another ship in-system. We're dealing with a Bucket?"

"Yes. Let's you and me and Torres get together and brainstorm this."

"Corbin isn't going to want to play."

Rob exhaled slowly. "Tell Corbin he either meets with me and you in the break room on the third deck in ten minutes, or the police will show up in fifteen minutes and drag him there."

"We're not being recalled, are we?" Meltzer asked. "Because I wouldn't like that, either."

"No one is being recalled. But the council, and all the other people with us, need you and me and Torres to figure out if there's anything we can do about that Bucket. If you and Torres want to go walkabout after we've hashed over the problem, I won't try to stop you."

Fourteen minutes later, as Rob was getting ready to call the council, Torres shuffled into the break room and sat down heavily in the seat next to Meltzer. In a colony group made up primarily of young people looking for a start in life and middle-aged people seeking a new start, Torres stood out for being older, his face bearing the lines of experience and the resentment of someone who thought life had not dealt out the rewards expected for a long life of work.

Acutely aware that his authority over Torres was limited, Rob tried not to talk like the lieutenant he had been. "You two know the problem, right? And you both appear to know more than I do about Buckets. What can we offer the council as alternatives to surrendering and paying the protection money being demanded?"

Ninja made a face. "If they haven't upgraded their systems, they're probably still running on HEJU."

Corbin shook his head, speaking grudgingly. "Unless they gutted the systems, they're still using HEJU. Those things were designed around the operating system. That's why everybody sold their Buckets instead of upgrading them."

"HEJU," Rob commented. "Is that the one where you have to input commands backward?"

"Yeah," Ninja said, smiling.

"No," Torres insisted. "HEJU is designed to make you think through the entire process and your end goal before starting, so you have to enter command sequences in the reverse order you want them executed."

"Same thing," Ninja said. "That means their firewalls must be extremely obsolete. No one has coded in HEJU for at least twenty years, so there couldn't have been any upgrades in ages."

"The crew codes HEJU," Torres corrected again. "They have to. The operating system needs patches and repairs. But they're probably not any good at it, just stuff they learned on the job, so the patches and repairs are probably just able to get by."

"Do you think there's any way we can deal with that Bucket?" Rob asked him.

Torres paused, eyeing Rob as if trying to judge the sincerity of his outward respect for the former sailor's knowledge. "If we had anything better, and just about anything would be better, that

Bucket would be toast. Even an old Sword Class destroyer could take it without breaking a sweat. But this old tub," he said as he kicked the deck of the *Wingnut* with his heel, "is useless. They didn't bring any weapons?" he demanded.

Rob shook his head. "No. Just hand weapons."

"Then you got a boarding party. That's something."

"A boarding party?" Ninja laughed. "Like some old pirate vid? We swing across to the Bucket with knives in our teeth? How do we get them to open a hatch for us?"

"Can't you do that, Ninja?" Rob asked her.

She paused to think. "You mean hack their systems? I don't know. If we had some stuff on HEJU aboard—"

Rob held up his pad. "I just checked. We do. In the colony library."

"Cool. Yeah, I can hack them. Just tell me what you want me to do."

"Can you disable their weapons?"

"Permanently?" Ninja frowned in thought.

Torres shook his head. "HEJU is an obsolete and gnarly system, but it's easy to patch. That's its only good feature. No matter how you hacked the weapons, they could do a work-around if they had time."

Ninja raised one eyebrow at Rob. "I could try to jinx the power core. Cause an overload. They wouldn't have time to patch that."

"An overload?" That would certainly solve the problem of the Bucket. But . . . "How many people do they have aboard? The database says standard crew size is twenty-four."

"You can run it long term with six, as long as nothing big breaks," Torres said. "It'd be hard to handle a battle with that few, though. Or pack in as many as forty. What's the matter, Ninja? Don't want to have that many lives on your conscience? Don't worry. They're all just apes like us. Nobody important."

"Shut up, Corb," Ninja told him.

"I don't think we should blow it up," Rob said, trying to think beyond an immediate solution. One of the things that had frustrated him back on Alfar was the attitude that short-term solutions were fine because in the long term someone else would have to deal with the problem. "That would work for an immediate solution. But it would leave us without any defense against the next predator who showed up. If we could capture it—"

Torres glowered at Rob. "Don't even think about drafting me to help operate it!"

"I wasn't," Rob said, letting his voice grow cold and sharp. "I'd think you'd be interested in the idea of setting yourself up as a private contractor to help maintain the thing for the colony. Ninja, can you hack the systems on the Bucket to drop their shields and open a hatch? Without the Bucket's crew knowing right away, so they wouldn't try to override your hack?"

"Yeah," she said. "That should be doable. You're seriously thinking about a boarding operation? Does anybody with us know how to do that? And, just for the record, I don't."

Rob didn't bother asking Torres. "I went through a couple of drills. That's it. But it sounds like those are our two options. Either try to remotely override the controls on the Bucket's power core so it blows up or try to capture it."

"Or pay the money," Torres said.

"Yeah. Three options. Thank you," he said to both Ninja and Torres. "I'll let the council know and see what they say." He paused, once again having to focus on the fact that he could not give either

Ninja or Corbin Torres orders. "Please stay where I can get in contact with you again quickly if the council has more questions."

The council was still in session when Rob returned to brief them. They didn't bother hiding their lack of enthusiasm for either of the options. "There has to be something else we can do," Council Member Odom insisted.

"You asked me to look at military options," Rob said, trying to keep his voice level. "That's what I did, along with Lyn Meltzer and Corbin Torres."

"Why can't your IT person shut down everything else on the cutter except the power core?" Council President Chisholm asked. "Then they wouldn't be a threat."

Rob used his hands to illustrate the movement of ships as he spoke. "We could try that. Two things might happen. One is that the Bucket crew figures out how to get their systems working again, patches the damage done by Ninja, and comes back at us. Torres says they should be able to patch anything Ninja does if given enough time. The other thing that might happen is that the Bucket crew can't fix it, and their ship doesn't brake velocity before they reach us, instead being stuck on the same vector as they race past this planet and the star and onward out into the dark between stars, where they would slowly starve to death."

Council Member Kim smiled derisively. "Not a humane alternative, then?"

"The closest we have to a sure thing," Rob said, "is to task Ninja with trying to get the Bucket to blow up."

"But can she do that?" Chisholm asked. "I've met my share of programmers who say they can do what I need and end up delivering something far short of that."

"Ninja got asked to leave Alfar's fleet because she was too good at breaking and entering," Rob said. "I reviewed her case when she was getting pushed out. That's how we met back at Alfar. She got her nickname both because her code is so hard to spot that it can get into anywhere and because she never left footprints firm enough for anyone to nail her afterward. The service could never get enough evidence to charge her with anything, so finally they just pushed her out. If anyone can do it, Ninja can. But she hasn't promised she can do it. She needs to brush up on the programming language used on a Bucket, then probe their systems from long range to see what can be done."

"Then how can we know that she can support that other alternative, capturing the ship?" Odom complained.

"Supporting a boarding operation should be simpler," Rob said. "Power cores have a lot more safety interlocks built in. You've asked me for advice, so I think we should try to capture that Bucket and use it to defend this star system until we can get something better. I'm putting my money where my mouth is on this because I know I would have to lead any boarding effort. I'm the only one with our colony who knows anything about how to do it."

A long moment passed while the members of the council exchanged wordless glances. One finally spoke up. "There's a fourth option. Leave. If Scatha plans to prey on whoever occupies this star system—"

A furious eruption of voices drowned out the speaker.

"This star system is *ours*," Council President Chisholm said after she managed to silence the uproar. "We will not cut and run, leaving it to anyone who threatens us. So, Rob, you and this Ninja and Corbin Torres would be part of this boarding effort—"

"No," Rob said, shaking his head. "Ninja will be doing her thing aboard the *Wingnut*. Torres has no interest in participating and no training in that area. He's also not a young man, and a boarding operation can be extremely stressful physically. I was hoping the police force could assist."

"We'd have to ask for volunteers," another council member advised. "The contracts for the police force do not include this kind of thing. We have no authority to demand that they take part."

"We could ask for volunteers from everyone," Kim argued. "How many do you need?"

"Twenty," Rob said. "I'd only have three days to train them."

"Why are we even discussing this?" Odom said. "We don't have the means to take over that ship."

"Then I have to recommend that we try to blow it up," Rob said.

"We can't just decide to blow up another ship!" one of the members down on the planet protested.

"Self-defense," another chimed in.

Chisholm halted the babble of cross talk that followed. "We'll research this and consult with our legal team. We have almost three and a half days to make this decision and ensure that it is legally justifiable."

"Excuse me," Council Member Leigh Camagan said. Short in stature but with intense eyes, her two words commanded everyone's attention. "What happens if we can't blow it up? Physically cannot. Citizen Geary said that is a possibility. If all we do is prepare for causing that ship's power core to overload, and we find out it cannot be done, we will have no alternative but to pay the extortion."

Silence fell until Council President Chisholm spoke again. "What do you suggest, Leigh?"

"Prepare for all possibilities, not just the one we prefer. Have Mr. Geary recruit some volunteers and train them. If we don't need them, we haven't lost anything. But at least we might have another option if the power core overload does not work."

Kim nodded. "I think Council Member Camagan is right."

The vote went in favor of pursuing both plans.

"Mr. Geary needs some authority if he's going to do his part," Leigh Camagan pointed out.

Another vote was taken, and Rob Geary, formerly a lieutenant in the small space force of the Old Colony Alfar Star System, found himself temporarily a lieutenant once more.

"Really?" Ninja asked once he had found her again. "A temporary lieutenant in what?"

"The otherwise nonexistent defense forces of this star system," Rob said.

"So you're, like, the most senior officer, and the most junior officer, and you've got no enlisted? Who's going to do all the work?"

"Are you interested?"

"No way."

"I do have a budget, so there's money in it for you," Rob pointed out. "And a challenge to your skills."

"The money is enough," Ninja assured him, "if it's enough money."

It was.

He was pleasantly surprised when ten of the twenty-officer police force volunteered for the possible boarding operation. Those ten contacted friends who they thought might be interested, and in short order, Rob had the twenty volunteers he needed.

"I also need battle armor and military-grade weapons," he

commented to his new second-in-command.

Val Tanaka was a police veteran of the tough district around the largest spaceport on the surface of Alfar's primary world. She was at least ten years older than Rob, one of the middle-aged types looking for a change. Rob had met her once on Alfar while bailing some of his sailors out of jail after their night on the town had gotten seriously out of hand. "What you've got are survival suits and nonlethal shockers," Val commented. "Why exactly don't we have any lethal weaponry?"

"Because we wouldn't need lethal weaponry," Rob explained. "Or so they told me. Because we'd all get along, and everyone else would leave us alone because it's such a big universe."

"Did they ask anybody who actually lives in this universe whether that made sense?"

Rob shrugged. "It came down to money. They had other things that were regarded as higher priorities."

"Sure," Val said. "I bet they found enough money for insurance, though, didn't they?"

"You're right. Investing in some military forces would have been another form of insurance. But what would they buy? A full-on space combatant like that Bucket? Aerospace craft for defending a planet? Ground forces? Get them all, and that's really expensive for a new colony that has a lot of other things they need to spend money on." Rob gestured toward the outside of the *Wingnut*, where infinite space held uncounted stars. "But the main reason is because they're still thinking in Old Colony, pre–jump drive terms. Space is too big, so aggression between star systems is too hard, and even minimal defenses will prevent anyone's being tempted. And if anybody does try anything serious, Old Earth will jump in and put things right. The jump drive changed all that, but the jump drive is too recent, less than a couple of decades old, so a lot of decision makers are still caught in the past. Trips that required years between neighboring stars now only take a week or two. The same thing that made it affordable for us to plant this colony makes it profitable for somebody on Scatha to shake us down using an old warship."

"And because we can go so much farther, Old Earth is a long, long ways off. So what's our plan?" Val asked.

"We act pretty much helpless."

"We *are* pretty much helpless."

Rob grinned. "Then that ought to make our act believable, right?"

Space might have become much smaller in terms of human ability to travel between stars, but when floating in endless space, gazing at countless stars, it still felt very much like infinity. It was strange, Rob thought, that the human mind could not really grasp forever, but human emotions could feel it. Infinity felt cold and uncaring, too vast to even notice the insignificant gaze of humans, but also almost unbearably magnificent and beautiful, because humans were a part of all that and could sometimes sense a connection to something immensely greater than themselves. Perhaps that was just an illusion, but it felt real.

Drifting weightless and gazing on the universe from outside the protective shell of a ship or a world was humbling, Rob decided, no matter what other emotional responses it triggered.

Also humbling was trying to figure out the "intuitive" maneuvering controls for a thrust pack whose customer service was light years away. Instead of working pointer style, where you pointed one hand toward your objective and the thrust pack calculated and triggered the necessary push to get there, it used a look-style system, where you looked at your objective and the thrust pack used that input. But it was too sensitive, reacting to every twitch, which meant that every time Rob's eyes wandered even a little, the thrust pack took that as a new input command and adjusted its push. The constant small jolts and jerks were not only incredibly irritating, they also burned up energy at a ridiculous rate. His attempts to scroll through menus to change the sensitivity settings kept running into the software equivalent of blind alleys and bottomless pits.

It reminded him all too much of the reasons he had been happy to leave the small fleet that Alfar had maintained. Getting anything done had been almost impossible, and by the time he'd actually achieved something or gotten somewhere, he had a hard time remembering why he had wanted to go there in the first place.

But that in turn reminded him of one of his failures that had particular relevance right now. The one time he had actually led a boarding party in a drill, he had totally failed. The memory of that still stung, and added to that now was guilt that he hadn't mentioned it to the council.

Rob finally got the target positioned about half a kilometer out from the *Wingnut*. The target was simply a large panel with tethers on the corners to keep it from drifting away from the ship. He double-checked the data on the movement of the warship from Scatha that he had entered into his survival suit's very limited heads-up display, making sure that the bulk of the *Wingnut* blocked any view of what was happening here from where the Bucket was currently located. The Bucket was still a couple of light hours away, about two billion kilometers, but even the obsolete sensors on the old warship shouldn't have any trouble seeing clearly across such a distance, and the last thing Rob wanted was for the crew of the Bucket to see people near the *Wingnut* apparently practicing jumping from one ship to another.

He rejoined his waiting recruits at an air lock facing the target, nineteen men and women who had volunteered for the boarding operation despite none of them having even worn a survival suit before, let alone space jumped. "There are two things to remember," Rob explained. "One is to keep your eyes on where you want to go. Your suits don't have thrust packs like I have because the *Wingnut* only has two and wouldn't sell us both. But that's fine. For training, you've all got tethers tying you to the ship, so you can't get lost. Before you jump, keep your eyes fixed on the target and push toward it. Your body will automatically go where your eyes are looking. It's that easy." And that hard, because as the old saying went, everything was simple in space, but all of the simple things were difficult.

"The second thing is to remember that you won't slow down," Rob continued. "Whatever speed you jump off at is the speed you'll be going when you reach your target. You'll instinctively want to push off hard because that's how we learn to jump on planets. That's a bad idea. Jump off hard in space, and you hit hard when you get to the other ship. Think about if you're on a planet and you're going to jump straight at a wall right in front of you, how hard are you going to want to jump to be sure you can catch yourself on the wall without hurting yourself?"

"How strong are the tethers?" one of the volunteers asked,

unable to keep the nervousness from his voice.

"You can't break them," Rob said. "You'd need ten times your mass moving at a dozen times the velocity any human could manage using their own muscles. Even if you jump too fast and get hauled up hard at the end of your tether, the only thing that will hurt is your pride. I'll go first, with the thrust pack I'm wearing turned off, so you can see how it goes." He paused. "One other thing. Some people have trouble out in space, especially close to a planet. If you get out there and feel yourself panicking, lock your eyes on the *Wingnut* and keep them there. I'll pull you in, and you'll be fine."

He did a textbook jump from training because that was the only way he knew how. Rob didn't think his volunteers would be happy knowing that Rob himself had only made two space jumps prior to this, so he hadn't brought that up.

Fortunately, he got it all right, with a smooth, easy jump off, flying through space, eyes on the target as it quickly got closer, then the tether reaching its end and hauling him up just short of the target. He pulled himself back inside the *Wingnut*'s air lock.

Val Tanaka went next. She flew out smoothly, but at the end as her body swung around on the tether, she began flailing her arms and legs, her breathing suddenly harsh and heavy. Rob pulled her in quickly, cursing inside. Why did Val have to be one of those who panicked in open space? Not only would he lose his second-in-command, but the others would be unnerved by her experience.

"It's fine, you're fine," Rob said reassuringly as he steadied Val inside the air lock. She looked at him, her breathing slowing. Rob could feel everyone else staring at him as he tried to come up with an inspirational speech to get them past this.

Before he could say anything else, Val Tanaka turned, positioned herself, and jumped for the target again.

Once more she flew directly to the target, but this time when the tether halted her she hung calmly as Rob pulled her tether back in.

He could see through the visor of the survival suit helmet that her eyes were closed until the moment she touched the side of the air lock again. She grinned at him, the gesture tight with tension, her breathing still fast. "Piece of cake."

"How did you do that?" Rob demanded.

"I didn't give the fear time to get settled," Val replied. "Got back on the horse, you know?" She turned to the others. "Let's go."

Only one of the others panicked, but they felt obligated by Val's example to try again and managed it the second time. Rob stood back watching as everyone made additional jumps.

Val joined him, standing side by side. A tiny symbol appeared before Rob's eyes, telling him that she was calling on a different circuit than the one being used to speak with the other volunteers. "What's up?"

"I was just wondering what you were afraid of, sailor," she replied.

He paused, gazing out at the star-spangled dark of space. "What makes you ask that?"

"You've hesitated a few times when talking about this plan, and out here you've sounded a little less confident than you should and a little too much like you're trying to convince yourself."

"Do you think any of the others have picked up on that?"

"If they haven't already, some of the others will. So what's the story?"

Rob grimaced. "When I was with Alfar's fleet, I only did one serious boarding practice exercise. As an ensign, still new, but I'd gone through other training. And I failed. The scorers took me apart."

He was surprised to hear Val chuckle softly. "Didn't you have time to learn that there are two kinds of graded drills? The first kind are the ones where the grades directly affect the promotions and awards for the top bosses, whoever they are. People always get passing scores on those. Dead people could get passing scores on them. Because the bosses want to look good, you know? The second kind are the ones designed to show you how important the scorers are. People always fail those and get torn apart for all the things they did wrong."

Rob turned his head to look at her. "What about graded drills designed to give you experience doing it and identify critical errors?"

"In a perfect universe, that's how they'd all work. But in a universe run by humans, drills over time often become self-licking ice cream cones that justify whatever purpose those in charge of the drills are looking for." Val looked back at him with a mocking grin. "Were there other graded drills along with that one you failed? How'd the others go?"

"We failed all of them," Rob said. "You're saying that was the point?"

"That was the point, and my point is that it doesn't matter. You're still the one guy with us who knows how to do this and has done it enough to fail at it once."

"Thanks, Val."

"Now, you gonna get out there and lead like you know what you're doing?"

"I can fake it," Rob said.

He came out of a tired sleep that night when someone grabbed his shoulder. "Hey, Lieutenant!"

Rob blinked sleep from his eyes, keeping his voice low to avoid disturbing the other two men still sharing his cabin. "What's up, Ninja?"

"We're not blowing up the Bucket's power core. Can't be done," she whispered.

"Their firewalls are that good?"

"Pfft!" Ninja said. "Their firewalls are as easy to get through as wet cardboard. But that doesn't help us with the power core because they're running it on manual."

"What?" Rob stared at her. "How can you tell?"

"Because the auto controls are all disabled. Probably nonfunctional."

Rob sat up carefully, running one hand through his hair as he thought. "I didn't know you could run a power core on manual."

"I asked Torres. He said you could, but he wouldn't," Ninja said. "It's possible, but inefficient as hell. And if something goes seriously wrong, whoever they've got nursemaiding the core had better react fast and do the right things."

He nodded, blowing out an exasperated breath. "I'll tell the council they can stop debating whether or not to blow up the Bucket. Either we board it, or we pay up. You can get into the right systems so we can board that ship, right?"

"Oh, yeah. Easy." She glanced at him, then at his bed. "I wouldn't mind relaxing a little right now if you're in the mood."

Rob sighed again. "Ninja, a couple of days ago I might have taken you up on that. But, at the moment, I'm your boss. It wouldn't be right."

Ninja shook her head. "Why do I always go after guys who follow the rules?"

"Opposites attract?"

"That might be it." She paused, looking down. "So, you're going to do the hero thing? Jumping over to the Bucket with a knife in your teeth?"

"Metaphorically, yeah," Rob said. "I think the council is leaning heavily toward not just giving in to extortion."

"Try not to get hurt, okay?"

He gave her a surprised look. "I didn't know you cared, Ninja."

"Well, duh. Do you think I make an offer like that to just anybody?"

She left before he could say anything else.

Rob stared after her, startled that he had without realizing kept himself from thinking about Ninja that way. Probably because their first interactions back at Alfar had been him as an officer and her as an enlisted. And despite his dislike of Alfar's fixed way of thinking, he must have taken on some of that, not considering the possibility that circumstances had changed and so could how he thought about her. He had always liked Ninja, even when he wouldn't allow himself to like her more than he should. Maybe now . . . ?

If he didn't get himself killed trying to capture that Bucket.

He couldn't do anything about Ninja at the moment. All he could do was lie there in the dark, thinking of all the things that could go wrong when a barely experienced former junior officer led a bunch of inexperienced and poorly armed volunteers against a warship. And thinking of what would very likely happen if he didn't lead that mission.

Thanks to the distant protection of Old Earth, Alfar's small navy hadn't had much in the way of heroic traditions born of war. None, actually. But there had been other causes for sacrifice. Like the young sailor on Rob's ship whose mother had died a decade earlier on an asteroid habitat with failing life support because she gave her oxygen recycler unit to a child who would otherwise have died instead. "She left me a message," the sailor had told Rob. "She said she couldn't just stand by and let someone else die. Not if she could do something; because that kid might have been me, and she'd have wanted someone else to save me."

"Do you ever wish she hadn't?" Rob had asked.

"Every day. And every day I wonder how she would have been able to live with doing that. She made her choice, sir. That's all any of us can do, right? Try to make a choice we can live with."

The next morning, the council gave him his orders to try to capture that ship. He could have begged off, could have found numerous excuses not to lead such a risky effort, but instead Rob Geary saluted and said he would do his best.

2

A day and a half later, Rob waited with the rest of his optimistically named boarding party in one of the *Wingnut*'s main air locks. The air lock had already been cleared of atmosphere, but the outer hatch remained closed to prevent giving warning to the Bucket, which was now on final approach to its intercept of *Wingnut*'s orbit. The demands for protection money had been repeated twice, and each time the council had responded with references to space law and promises to report the incident to Old Earth. The crew of the Bucket hadn't seemed the least bit impressed by either argument, instead repeating their own "concerns" that if the colony didn't pay up "it would be unprotected against aggression."

As always, Rob found waiting harder than actually doing something. The survival suit he was wearing felt too flimsy for a combat mission because it was. Strong enough to protect humans from the hazards of space and cheap enough to serve as a space equivalent of a life jacket at sea, the suit wouldn't stop any weapon. He tugged at one armpit, the suit feeling even more one-size-fits-all than normal. The air being recycled through the suit was fine according to the readouts, so Rob concentrated on controlling his breathing and ignoring a persistent worry that it smelled off.

He looked at the men and women who would follow him aboard the enemy ship. They were gazing back at him, their expressions hard to see but their body postures tense. At least during his time in Alfar's fleet he had learned how to give a pep talk before a difficult task. *Keep it simple, keep it short.* "The rest of the people in this colony are counting on us to stop these guys. We can do this. I have every confidence in all of you. The people on that warship won't be expecting trouble, so they're going to be very surprised when we give them more trouble than they imagined possible. Stay cool and stay sharp, and we'll get the job done."

"Lieutenant Geary."

He switched to the comm channel for private communications. "Here."

"This is Council Member Leigh Camagan. I wanted to inform you that under pressure the council has finally agreed on a name for this colony. It will have to be confirmed by a vote of all citizens of the colony, but I have no doubt of the outcome. Let those you are leading know that they are now defending the people of the Glenlyon Star System. Good luck."

"Thank you." Rob passed the news on to the rest of the boarding party, all of whom seemed happy to be defending newly named Glenlyon.

"How does it look, Ninja?" he asked over the coordination circuit.

"Smooth," she replied, her voice confident and cheerful. "I've got control of every automated system on that ship, but I inserted a shell that makes it look to the crew like everything is normal.

They'll find out different in about one minute, but even then they'll think the problem is confined to their maneuvering systems."

"Sensors are hacked?"

"Absolutely! All they'll see is the *Wingnut* looking like it was a couple of minutes ago, hatches sealed and nobody doing nothing."

Rob gave the rest of the boarding party a thumbs-up. "We've got effective control of the Bucket's systems. Ninja is about to order the Bucket to brake velocity and come to a stop relative to us. That will finally alert the crew of that ship that something is wrong, but their sensors have been hacked, so they won't see this air lock hatch opening and their displays won't tell them that their ship is dropping its shields. They'll be focused on trying to figure out what happened to their ship's maneuvering systems while we get aboard and get down to business." *I hope*, he added to himself.

"Ninja accessed the crew files to confirm there are twenty-three of them aboard that Bucket," Val Tanaka reminded the others. "There are twenty of us. But almost all of their crew will be in small groups at duty stations, so we can overwhelm them at each spot. Everybody double-check your shockers and make sure the safeties are engaged until we reach the other ship and you're told to ready them."

"Once we get control of the bridge and the power core, we've won," Rob added as the air lock's outer hatch swung open.

Buccaneer Class cutters were a lot smaller than the *Wingnut*, only about one hundred twenty meters from bow to stern, and the warship had been coming in fast for an intimidating firing run. It was still far enough off that Rob could only spot it because of the flare from the main propulsion unit, which was facing toward *Wingnut* as the warship braked velocity to engagement speed so the Bucket could threaten to fire on *Wingnut* or one of the colony shuttles, or put a precise shot into part of the *Wingnut* to encourage the colony to pay up before more damage was inflicted.

Any moment now, the crew of the Bucket would realize that something was wrong, as their main propulsion kept going past when it should have shut off, and the warship kept slowing until it came to a stop relative to the *Wingnut*.

"Their sensors are going to tell them that they're stopped fifty kilometers away from the *Wingnut*," Ninja reported gleefully.

"How close can you really get them to us?"

"You asked for one hundred meters, and you're getting one hundred meters."

"Have you maneuvered ships before, Ninja?"

"In simulators. I'm using the Bucket's own maneuvering systems to do this, though. Don't worry! I don't want anything happening to you!"

It was a bit comforting to realize that Ninja really did like him and had extra motivation to get everything right as a result, but Rob felt his breathing speeding up and his heart racing as the start of the attack approached. He concentrated on controlling both despite the memories of that failed drill when he was an ensign filling his mind. He was facing an actual combat situation for the first time, something else that Val Tanaka had advised him not to share with the rest of the boarding party. Feeling fear of both failure and of personal injury or death, Rob hoped that he could power through the fear and make the right decisions at the right times.

Because these others were counting on him.

The Bucket came sliding in along a gentle arc, matching the orbit of *Wingnut* and coming to a stop relative to the other. Both spaceships were now actually orbiting the planet beneath them at about seven kilometers per second, fast on a planet but a snail's pace in space, and since both were going exactly the same direction at the same speed they appeared to each other to be unmoving.

Ninja had done exactly as promised, directing the Bucket's maneuvering systems to position the warship hanging in space about one hundred meters from where Rob waited. This close, the hull of the Bucket almost filled the view of space from the air lock hatch. Unlike the boxy shapes of large cargo ships, warships more closely resembled oceangoing predators. The chunky Buccaneers, though, looked less like sharks or barracudas than they did bloated trout, one of the reasons why they had been nicknamed Buckets.

"The Bucket's door is open!" Ninja announced. "Mind the gap!"

Rob saw a patch of light appear on the Bucket's hull as the outer hatch opened for the warship's largest air lock amidships. "Follow me," Rob told the others, trying to sound calm and authoritative, aiming for what even this close looked like a far-too-small target against the immensity of space. Knowing that any hesitation on his part would unnerve his boarding party, he took a deep breath and jumped off.

Despite his own experience, his inbred planetary instincts kept insisting that either he must be slowing down due to air resistance and gravity as he crossed the one-hundred-meter gap of emptiness, or increasing speed as if he were falling. The last thing his mind wanted to accept was that he was gliding along at an unvarying rate, the side of the Bucket growing steadily larger.

He felt an absurd sense of accomplishment as he reached the Bucket close enough to the air lock to grab onto the side of it as he hit the other ship with a bit more force than he had planned on.

Rob looked back, reaching out to grab other members of the boarding party as they came flying toward him. Some of the impacts when they slammed into him were hard enough to cause bruises, but everyone made it safely even though a few hit the side of the Bucket and had to stick, then crawl along to the air lock using the gecko gloves on their survival suits.

The Bucket's air lock could only hold ten at a time. Rob sent Val Tanaka through with the first ten, hanging on to the side of the warship and hoping the crew wouldn't figure out what was happening despite their sensors being hacked. "How's it look, Ninja?"

"The guys on the bridge are seriously upset, but they're still trying to fix what they think is a main-propulsion control problem," she told him. "Do you want an audio feed? Their captain isn't too good at swearing, but he makes up in volume for what he lacks in variety."

"No, I'm good. Nobody suspects what we're doing?"

"One of the other officers is trying to tell the captain that it's really suspicious they came to a stop relative to us, but nobody is listening because it looks to them like they're still fifty kilometers from us. Oh, hell, she's trying to run a diagnostic on the other systems on the ship. I need to deal with that. Talk to you later."

"Thanks. The air lock is cycling open. I'm going in."

The air lock was a tight fit with ten of them inside. It ambled through its cycle at a sluggish pace, but Rob finally led the rest of the boarding party into the ship, into a nondescript passageway running fore and aft. Without consciously thinking about it, his eyes ran across the nearby piping, conduits, auto-sealing vents, fire suppression features, and other equipment, evaluating how well they had been maintained and kept clean. Not up to Alfar fleet standards but good enough as far as he could tell from the brief scan.

"Everyone arm your shockers and ensure the safeties are off. Make sure you don't point them at anyone else in this boarding party! Like we planned," he told Val. "Go." She gestured to nine others, and that group headed aft for the power core control compartment. Neither she nor Rob had ever been on a Bucket before, but the standard deck plans for a Buccaneer Class cutter had been available in the colony's vast database, and the route on such a small ship hadn't been too hard to memorize.

Rob turned toward the bow, leading the remaining nine members of the boarding party still with him toward the bridge buried inside the ship farther forward.

They hadn't gone more than five meters before reaching an airtight hatch sloppily left open during what should have been a combat readiness situation. At the same moment, two crew members of the Bucket arrived on the other side, coming aft. The crew members were actually jumping through the hatch before they realized Rob and the others were standing there, and barely had time to begin to stare in disbelief before a half dozen shockers went off, the impacts of the charges knocking the two flying before they hit the edges of the hatch and fell unconscious.

"Didn't you tell us they'd be wearing survival suits, Lieutenant?" one of the men with Rob asked.

"They should be," Rob said. "But they're so confident that they're ignoring basic precautions. That's good for us."

Their route had been planned to go past the local control station for the Bucket's pulse particle cannon. Rob led the group in a rush to the hatch giving access, finding it, too, hanging open and four crew members lounging around the powered-up weapon consoles as they traded jokes. Their survival suits lay draped across the backs of their seats.

Rob didn't give them a chance to give up. Too much depended on speed and silence. He and the rest of his team fired, and the four weapons crew members jerked and fell as multiple shocker charges hit each of them.

"That's going to hurt," one of the boarding party commented.

"Maybe it'll hurt enough that they'll realize they need to wear their survival suits in a potential combat situation next time," Rob replied. He waited impatiently for the few seconds required for those of his party who were members of the colony police force to expertly and swiftly bind the hands and legs of the unconscious crew. "Elliot and Singh, you two stay here and make sure no one else from the crew shows up and tries to use that cannon. Seal the hatch and use the panel here to see anyone who tries to open it."

"Got it," both Elliot and Singh replied.

Rob led the remaining members of his group back out into the passageway, heading forward, then almost immediately inward toward the bridge. Worry nagged at him, that he had taken a wrong turn or misread something, but then he spotted a ready response compartment just where it should be if he was on the right route.

Six more crew members were lying around the ready response compartment, supposedly prepared to rush out and reinforce or fix any place or anything that needed either. But the six were all engrossed in whatever was on their individual handhelds, none of them noticing the arrival of Rob and his team until shock charges knocked them out and fried their handhelds.

As these six had their hands and legs bound, Rob looked around the compartment and saw something with familiar markings that had probably been standardized on Old Earth centuries before.

"That's an arms locker. One of these guys might have a key to it." It would take time to search for that key, if any of these crew members had been entrusted with one. Time they couldn't spare. But if the locker contained anything useful . . . Rob hesitated, trying to decide.

"They might have some good hand weapons in there," one of Rob's team suggested.

"We don't know that," Rob said, making up his mind, "and even if they do, and even if we can find a key fast, that locker door might be alarmed so the bridge would know if we opened it. Our best weapon is still surprise."

He paused again, not happy at the idea of further diminishing the size of his force but knowing he couldn't leave these crew members and an arms locker unguarded. "Safwat and Watson, you two stay here," he ordered. "That arms locker has to be watched. Don't hesitate to use your shockers again on any other crew members who come by, or any of these six who wake up and cause any trouble."

Rob gripped his shocker tightly as he ran the final stretch to the bridge through empty passageways, followed closely by the five other boarding party members left with him. There was the hatch to the bridge, helpfully identified by absurdly ornate letters spelling BRIDGE that had been painted above it. He nodded to the five with him, then tugged at the hatch, cursing as he discovered that it was locked. Finally, someone on this ship had done something right, and just where it was least needed.

"Ninja?" he called over the coordination circuit. His signal shouldn't be able to transmit through the warship's hull, but if Ninja had control of the Bucket's internal comm system she might be able to—

"Whatcha need?" Ninja called back. "Oh, got a locked hatch?"

Spotting the tiny red light that marked the active surveillance camera by the bridge hatch, Rob nodded toward it, knowing that Ninja must be remotely controlling that system as well. "What are things like on the bridge? Can you see there?"

"Yeah. The captain is still screaming at everybody, and everybody is looking at him because if they look away, he screams at them personally. He's wearing a sidearm. I don't think it's a shocker, so don't take any chances with him."

"Understood. Thanks. Can you pop the lock on this hatch?"

"Stand by. Three, two, one, go."

Rob tugged again, and the hatch swung open.

He led his team onto the bridge. As Ninja had reported, everyone on the bridge was standing at attention and facing inward toward the captain, who was so busy yelling at them all that he didn't even notice Rob's arrival.

Rob aimed and fired his shocker.

The captain's latest angry shout changed to a strangled garble as the charge hit and knocked him senseless into the nearest other member of the bridge crew.

A woman officer spun to look, one hand reaching for where her sidearm would have been holstered. But she broke off the motion as if realizing she didn't have a weapon and raised her open hands in surrender. The others on the bridge also raised their hands, staring at Rob in disbelief.

"Are you the second-in-command?" Rob asked the female officer, using his survival suit's external speaker.

She shook her head. "The captain sent him back to engineering to yell at the techs there."

"Ninja? Can you tell how Val Tanaka is doing?" Rob asked.

"She's got the power core," Ninja confirmed. "They just knocked out some officer who came charging in as if he were being chased by rabid dogs. Here. I'll link you through the ship's internal comms."

"Val?"

"Here. We're in full control, but I'd recommend getting that Torres character aboard so he can fix up the controls on the power core. One of the guys with me, Snee, has a little experience with gear like this, and what he can see of their control setup has him scared. Yeah, I see, Snee. Duct tape. Who the hell fixes a power core backup control link with duct tape?" she asked Rob.

"I've seen stranger uses of duct tape," Rob said. "But I agree with Snee. We'll bring the Bucket in closer to *Wingnut* and get some reinforcements aboard."

The female officer was gazing at Rob with a wondering expression. "How the hell did you jump fifty kilometers?"

"We hacked your sensors," Rob said. "You're actually only a hundred meters from our ship."

"Oh. I thought the problem was a lot bigger than it looked, but Cap'n Pete was too busy yelling at us to fix things to listen to what we thought might be broken." She sighed. "If you have the power core and the bridge, we've lost. What do you intend doing with the crew?"

Rob shook his head. "That's up to the colony council, but I assume we'll put you all aboard the *Wingate* and let her carry you back to her next destination. I don't know what they'll do with you there, but as long as you never come back here, I don't care."

"All right. Let me use the general announcing system, and I'll tell everyone aboard to surrender. There's no sense anyone else's getting hurt."

One of Rob's group had removed the captain's sidearm. "Look at this, Lieutenant. Ground forces issue. Anybody he hit with this would have been badly wounded or killed. These guys weren't playing around."

Rob gave the woman officer a hard look. "How many colonies have you guys shaken down for protection money?"

"I don't know," she replied. "This is my first run with them. I got recruited out of Earth Fleet by a bunch of assurances that turned out to be as worthless as a Red's promise."

"Earth Fleet?" Rob asked, startled and looking at her with new eyes.

"Yeah, I'm former Ensign Danielle Martel of Earth Fleet, now a former lieutenant in Scatha's fleet because you just gave me a chance to get out of a bad contract." She shook her head at him. "You should know that Scatha isn't going to be happy about this."

"Too bad," Rob said. "We've got this ship, and we'll use it if they try anything else."

"Do you really think this is over? Scatha has two other warships, both better than this one, and its leaders are not nice people. Ever since I got to Scatha, I've been hearing pronouncements from those leaders about how Scatha is going to be a new Earth but with teeth. They want what they call order and safety, and to do that they intend to be the big dog in this region of space, whether the neighboring star systems want it or not. You'd better be planning on how to handle whatever they try next."

Rob gave Danielle Martel a grim look, the glow of victory fading within him. This had just been the first skirmish in what looked to be a war rather than an isolated raid.

"Can't Old Earth do something?" Ninja asked over the comm circuit.

"Not out here," Rob replied. "Not anymore. We're on our own."

Many light years away from the star now named Glenlyon, Carmen Ochoa stood glaring out a window at an ancient landscape that countless other human eyes had looked upon. "Earth was the center of the universe. Now, we're irrelevant."

Her boss favored Carmen with a weary look. "What is it now?"

She kept her gaze on the scene outside. An impact crater from the First Solar War still marked the site of the original spaceport outside of Albuquerque, the new port spreading out to the south. Clusters of trees and closely trimmed grass designed to reclaim battered land provided welcome carpets of color. The remnants of the old city, and the newer structures built to look like early structures and so strangely seeming older than the original buildings, filled the valley beyond the port and the crater. Beyond them, rough mountains and hills rose toward a daytime sky that had looked down uncaring on human activities for thousands of years.

Make the low-lying sun a lot smaller, make the mountains and hills a little redder, and it would look very much like the sort of landscapes that Carmen had grown up seeing on Mars. The buildings, though . . . not like here at all. Put up in a rush, on foundations of idealism that proved to be as sturdy as shifting sand, sagging under the burdens of age, makeshift repairs, and the voracious dust of Mars. Unbidden, Carmen's mind summoned up memories from when she was little, huddled into one corner of a small room hiding from gang battles outside, or from the searching eyes of gang recruiters.

Promising herself that someday she would keep other places from ending up like Mars had. Doing whatever she had to in order to make it off Mars and to the one place that had the power to make a difference.

As if to mock that old vow, from here a large piece of public art was visible, globes shining reddish golden in the sunlight fixed to swooping, silvery metal shafts. In the center hung the globe representing Sol, the sun of Earth. Spreading outward in an irregular sphere were the other globes, each marking a star where humanity had planted colonies.

Old Earth, it was called now, and those colony worlds were increasingly known as the Old Colonies as new worlds were settled after the explosion of humanity into space as the new jump drives made interstellar travel much faster and easier. The sculpture was obsolete, a relic of the past. Like her job. "I am thinking," Carmen said, "that I just wasted more of my time and effort for nothing."

Her boss shrugged. "You got the cease-and-desist order approved and sent."

"Yeah. You know what's funny? When ships tried to push light speed and spent years getting to one of the Old Colonies or back to Earth, they listened to Earth. They respected Earth. But now that ships can use jump space to make the same journey within weeks, the Old Colonies pay less and less attention to Earth."

Another shrug. "Nothing funny about it," her boss said. "Familiarity breeds contempt. When we were the incredibly distant home that took years to reach, we were wrapped in myth and memory. But when anybody can get from there to here in a few weeks? Then we're just another planet, one with dozens and dozens of independent governments ruling independent states that often refuse to cooperate. A planet that has seen a lot more mistakes and stupidity than any of the Old Colonies have gotten around to yet."

Carmen shook her head. "Everyone is talking about how much smaller the galaxy is with jump drives. But it took four months for that request for a cease-and-desist to reach us, on ships jumping from star to star, then four more months for me to work it through the bureaucracy and get the order approved, and it will take another four months for that order to get back to the star Derribar, where a colony has now existed for eight months. And what will happen when the colony at Derribar presents that cease-and-desist order to the nearly-as-new colony at Cathal? Nothing. Because Cathal knows they can ignore it. Assuming that in the year since the request was first made by Derribar that it hasn't already been overtaken by events."

"What do you want, Ochoa?" her boss asked. "For Earth to build a fleet big enough to force colonies in a sphere hundreds of light years across to do what we want?"

"I know that's impossible, even if enough of the governments in the solar system agreed on something like that." Carmen gritted her teeth. "You know that I grew up on Mars. I saw firsthand how ugly things can get when there is no such thing as effective government or respect for law."

"And, for a Red, you're a really decent person. But most of the Reds seem to like it that ugly, at least until their terraformed ecology begins to collapse again due to neglect and they beg the organized governments on Earth to step in and fix it." Her boss sighed. "Humanitarian crises shouldn't be so predictable."

"You're a really decent person . . . for a Red." Even her boss on Earth couldn't forget where she had come from. "I didn't like it that ugly.

So I left to try to make things better. And instead, it's happening all over again! Just like when Mars was colonized, only this time it's happening on countless worlds. The sheep are scattering in pursuit of places with no shepherds, and the wolves are sharpening their knives." Carmen shook her head, turning away from the window. "I can't make any difference here. I'm resigning. Heading out. Maybe out there I can do something that matters."

"I'm sorry to hear you're leaving," her boss said, sounding almost sincere but also too tired and worn-out to care. Like most of Earth, he had seen too many wars and too many half-failed efforts to save people who stubbornly refused to cooperate in their own deliverance. "You're not going to try heading up the spiral arm, are you? The colonies in that direction are still refusing to let any new people move in."

"I wouldn't go up even if they'd take me," Carmen scoffed. "Them and their Original Blood of Terra nonsense. No, I'm going down the spiral arm, where the colonies are expanding as fast as ships can jump to new stars. There's a ship leaving for one of those new colonies next week."

"Which colony?" her boss asked, not even trying to sound as if he were actually interested.

"Kosatka."

"Never heard of it."

"You will." Carmen had been preparing for this moment for a long time, not knowing when she would finally make the leap but knowing it would happen. She powered down her system, logged out for the last time, swept the few personal items allowed on her desk into her backpack, and nodded good-bye to her boss. "Farewell."

Her boss rubbed his face with one hand, nodding back, his own attention already shifting back to processing the next interstellar court order that would very likely be ignored by every party involved. "Good luck, Carmen. You'll need it."

Many light years down the spiral arm of the galaxy that contained Earth, Lochan Nakamura helped one of the other survivors off the lifeboat, then stood gazing around at the plain metal walls and overhead of the enclosed surface docking station. Having gotten this far, he wasn't sure where to go next.

The star humans had named Vestri was a red dwarf, about a third the size of Earth's sun, putting out a fraction of the light and heat of brighter stars, puttering along as it had for billions of years and would continue doing so for much longer. Vestri had no worlds worthy of the name orbiting it, just several airless asteroids that were not quite large enough to be labeled planets and countless smaller rocks that had mostly formed into two impressive belts about the star. Fortunately for Lochan and the others who had been passengers aboard the merchant freighter *Brian Smith*, one of those large asteroids held a way station and had been within range of the lifeboat from the ship.

One of the way station employees, wearing coveralls and a smile, stuck a pad in front of Lochan. "Thumbprint, bio-scan, and signature," she requested.

"For what?" Lochan asked, still bemused from his escape.

"Agreement to pay for rescue services, lodging, provisions, and life support until someone picks you up," the local said cheerfully. "You've still got your universal wallet, right? Great. You'll need to compensate the station for everything you receive."

Wondering at her attitude in the wake of the hijacking of the freighter, Lochan scrolled through the document he was being asked to sign. "These rates are ridiculously high."

Her smile widened. "You're welcome to get your food, water, heat, and air from another place, sir."

"And you're the only source for those things in this star system, aren't you?" Lochan asked, finally understanding why the woman was so happy.

"That's right. And we've got bills to pay."

Having left the Old Colony at Franklin in part because he was tired of paying taxes for government services he didn't think he needed, Lochan took a moment to savor the irony of his situation. In Franklin's star system, this station would have been run by the government and provide rescue and aid without charge. "Are you going to report that pirate who took the freighter and dumped us here?" he asked as he pressed a thumb to the pad.

"Of course," she said absentmindedly as she checked to make sure everything had been done right.

As the local went off to put the screws to another castaway, a young woman paused beside Lochan. He had seen her on the freighter but hadn't spoken with her before. Even if her bearing and attitude hadn't proclaimed her a veteran, the small brass sword-and-shield clipped to one earlobe would have given her away as having once been part of Franklin's tiny force of Marines.

"She didn't seem too upset about that pirate," Lochan commented.

The woman smiled. "I'll bet you that pirate hits ships passing through Vestri all the time and shares profits with this station. Why do you think the pirates let us all keep our wallets?"

"That's why they let us go so easily?" Lochan shook his head. "Nice scam."

"Who's going to stop them?" The woman nodded to him. "I'm Mele Darcy."

"Lochan Nakamura. What's a Marine doing out here?"

"Former Marine," Mele said, her eyes studying the crowd. "Force reductions to save money, so I decided to give the new colonies a try."

"What do you think so far?"

"It sucks." She grinned. "Where are you headed?"

"Down and out. I haven't decided exactly where, yet. What about you?"

"Same. Figured I'd go until I found a place worth staying." Mele looked around. "I can already tell that Vestri ain't that place."

"You got that." Lochan and Mele followed the rest of the group as they were led down stairs toward the station's accommodations beneath the surface.

"You know what I am. What are you?" Mele asked as they trudged along bare-walled corridors mined from the rock of the asteroid.

"Me?" Lochan shrugged. "Failed business owner, failed politician, failed husband."

"Oh? What are you planning on doing down and out?"

"Find something else to fail at, I guess."

Mele laughed. "I think you can do better than that. Stick with me. We'll watch each other's backs until we get off this rock."

Lochan had been wondering why the Marine had attached herself to him. He knew he wasn't the sort of man that younger women gravitated toward. But self-interest. He could understand that.

The room the former passengers were brought to proved to be a single large space lined with bunks. The only privacy was offered by a bathroom. Several vid screens were on the walls, but as Lochan suspected, the first involuntary guests who tried them discovered that they had a per-minute viewing charge. "This is what a cash cow looks like," Lochan said to Mele.

A nearby way station employee looked offended. "We're providing a service. Where would you be if this station hadn't been here?"

"Probably still on the *Brian Smith*, approaching the jump point for the next star," Lochan said.

The employee glared at Lochan. "You'd better be careful what you—" He paused in the act of raising a fist, looking to the side where Mele stood with her arms crossed and her eyes fixed on him, then lowered his hand and walked away.

Lochan nodded to Mele. "Thanks. I've got a big mouth."

"You did say you'd been a politician." Mele gestured toward the rest of those from the freighter, who were milling about in various states of despair and distress. "How about using those skills to organize these people? The vultures running this station will pick them clean if we don't all look out for each other."

Startled, Lochan looked over the group. "Are you going to help?"

"That depends on how you work. I'm feeling a need to stay in the background, and I've learned to listen to my instincts. But show me a good leader, and I'll follow."

Lochan nodded once more. He couldn't explain why, but he didn't want to let Mele Darcy down. Maybe it had just been too long since anyone, himself included, had thought he could do anything right. Or maybe he was already tired of trying to run away from past failures. Sooner or later, he would have to stop running and start trying again. "I'll give it a shot."

She gazed at him, then abruptly pulled him close in a tight hug, burying her face next to his ear and whispering so low he could barely hear. "They've probably got these rooms bugged. If we need to pass on serious warnings to each other, use this old code." One finger tapped the back of his neck three times quickly, three times with a slight pause between each, then three times quickly again.

Mele stepped back, looking sheepish for the benefit of onlookers. "Sorry. I get physical sometimes."

"No problem," Lochan said, wishing she had held the hug a little longer and wondering if she would be interested in something more later.

But she smiled again and shook her head slightly at him, answering that unspoken question before Lochan could build up any false hopes.

He turned to the others and raised his voice to command attention. "Hey, everybody! I've got a couple of suggestions."

Carmen Ochoa hadn't been in space since leaving Mars for Earth, but the experience hadn't changed all that much in a decade. Take the regular shuttle up to the orbital station, then transfer to the ship, in this case a large, newly built craft whose boxy lines contained enough room for hundreds of passengers in conditions ranging from luxurious to cramped, as well as plenty of freight compartments holding goods that would be snapped up by the growing colonies on the edges of human expansion.

Her walk through the orbital station was hindered by the presence of a lot of Earth Fleet sailors. Men and women in uniform were seemingly everywhere, some of them lined up to get into crowded bars but most standing around in somber groups. Whatever was happening didn't seem to be a celebration.

"What's going on?" Carmen asked one small gathering of sailors.

An older man with several service stripes on the sleeve of his uniform gestured toward space beyond the station. "The fleet just decommissioned the last three Founders Class destroyers."

A woman about the same age nodded morosely. "The *George Washington*, the *Simon Bolivar*, and the *Joan of Arc*. The ceremonies ended about an hour ago. I spent three years on the *Bolivar*. Now the only people aboard her are contractors shutting down all the systems before the ships get hauled to join the ghost fleet at Lagrange 5."

"Are you going to other ships?" Carmen asked.

"There aren't enough other ships left in the active fleet. Most of us are being let go," the older man said. "Early retirement or just kicked out as surplus."

"They're talking about demilitarizing the solar system," the woman sailor said, sounding both bewildered and angry. "Getting rid of the fleet completely. Who's going to defend Earth? Who's going to help the Old Colonies if they need it?"

An officer passing by stopped to partially answer the question. "The Old Colonies up and out have cut themselves off from us already. The colonies down and out will have to help themselves. There are rumors that Earth gov is trying to set up an arrangement for the Old Colonies to protect *us*," he finished.

"Maybe we can get positions in their fleets," the woman sailor said.

"You can try," the officer agreed. "But the Old Colonies don't have much because they've depended on our forces if things got really bad."

Carmen spoke up. "There are all the new colonies. They're going to need something."

The sailors looked at her with various degrees of curiosity and skepticism. "Where are the new colonies going to get ships?" the older sailor asked. "It takes a while to develop shipyards."

"They can probably get our old ships cheap," the officer remarked. He fixed a tired, cynical gaze on Carmen. "Are you going down and out? Let them know Earth has a lot of warships with plenty of light hours of sailing time left on them just drifting in the ghost fleet."

"They can recruit crews when they buy the ships, too," the woman sailor said. "There will be plenty of us sitting around wishing we had a deck under our feet again. I'd rather be part of something growing than wait until I'm the person who turns out the last light and locks the last hatch for good in the Earth Fleet."

"I'll remember that," Carmen said. "I'm sorry I can't do more."

"You're just being smart, getting out of a game with worn-out players and nothing left to score. There's not much left to do here except remember when we made history instead of being history." The officer squinted at the nearest wall panel showing an image of space outside. "I may go down and out, too. Why not? Hey," he told the sailors. "Come on. I'll buy you all a last round before the final crew of the *Bolivar* breaks up for good."

The sailors went off toward one of the bars while Carmen boarded her shuttle. She shifted the view on the entertainment panel in front of her seat until she spotted the long, lean shapes of three destroyers near the transfer station. Compared to the big, stout merchant ships around the station, the destroyers looked like the predators they were, three barracudas drifting amid schools of fat, slow fish.

When she tapped the images on her panel, the information that popped up identified all three as "inactive—surplus." No names left to them, nothing to mark what they had done in the service of Earth or the crews who had served on them. Just "inactive—surplus." In some ways, that felt like a metaphor for what Earth was becoming. Still there, but passive and no longer heeded by the children she had sent out to seed the stars.

Boarding the new ship *Mononoke* was a welcome relief from thoughts of decline and decay.

She dumped her luggage on the bunk of a stateroom barely large enough to hold her and the three other women who would share it with Carmen. The medium-sized carryall and her backpack didn't hold much, but Carmen had learned in the dog-eat-dog shantytowns of Mars that clinging to material possessions was foolish.

The displays on the walls, one by each bunk, were all showing the path the *Mononoke* would take down and out. Out beyond the previous bounds of human settlement, and down this spiral arm of the galaxy in the direction of the center of the Milky Way. Carmen zoomed in the display to see the details of the crooked path the ship would take as it jumped from star to star.

Another woman came in and claimed the other bottom bunk. "How far are you going?" she asked Carmen.

"All the way."

"Seriously? I'm just going back to Brahma." She stretched out on the bunk. "Old Colony is fine with me. Have you ever been in jump space?"

"No," Carmen admitted. "Is it as bad as they say?"

"Not at first. It gets worse with each day. It will only take six days to reach Brahma, which will just leave us feeling uncomfortable. The longest jump you're going to face after that is, um, about two weeks. Your skin will feel like it belongs to someone else by the time you end that jump."

Carmen sat down on her bunk, gazing at the route ahead. She knew why the ship had to jump from star to star, not skipping any. Partly it was because the jump drives didn't have enough range to go farther than the closest stars to whichever star they were jumping from. And partly it was because, as her new roommate said, jump space made people feel more and more uncomfortable the longer they were in it. There were already a lot of frightening rumors about what had happened to the people on ships that had spent too long in jump space. "Have you heard anything about piracy beyond the Old Colonies?"

"It's happening," her new roommate said. "That's about all I know. The more isolated the star, the worse your odds are. I've heard ships are getting waylaid more frequently the farther out you go. Enough ships that people are starting to talk about doing something. But it's all just talk. I doubt anything will actually be done."

"Aren't the Old Colonies worried that it might spread their way?"

"We've always been safe enough. It's not our responsibility to bail out a bunch of malcontents who headed down and out and ran into trouble."

That didn't leave much room for discussion, so Carmen changed the subject. "It'll take two weeks to get to the first jump point?"

"Yeah," her slightly-more-experienced-as-a-space-traveler roommate replied. "The *Mononoke* is faster than the average freighter, but not nearly as fast as a warship, so it'll be, uh, thirteen and a half standard days from Earth orbit for us to reach the jump point for Brahma. You know how the jump drives work, right?"

"Space gets stretched by the mass of stars," Carmen said. "That creates thin spots in the fabric of the universe that ships can use to enter and leave jump space. Jump points are the thin spots that give access to thin spots at other stars."

"Uh-huh. We can't just jump from anywhere."

"I've heard jump space is gray."

"Ha!" Her roommate's laugh startled Carmen. "It's the gray to end all grays, a gray so gray that you can't even imagine any color in it. It's the most boring kind of space imaginable. Except for the lights, whatever they are. Have you heard about them? They show up sometimes, then go away."

"What are the lights?" Carmen asked. "What causes them?"

"Um . . . no one knows what they are yet, but they'll find out soon, I'm sure," her roommate predicted confidently. "You're a lawyer, aren't you?"

"No," Carmen said.

"Sorry! Are you a physicist?"

"Me? No. My job's a lot more difficult than physics," Carmen said. "Conflict resolution."

"Conflict resolution? At least you'll have job security down and out," the woman from Brahma observed. "You're originally from Earth?"

No way was she going to admit the truth to this woman. "Yes."

"And you're going to the end of the line? That's . . . Kosatka?"

"Right," Carmen said.

"What's so special about Kosatka?"

"I'll find out when I get there."

"What's the problem?" Lochan Nakamura demanded.

"That's what I'm trying to find out." The young and hard-looking man who wore a doctor's patch on one shoulder pointed Lochan to a seat in the small infirmary that served the asteroid way station. "Shut the door, sit down, and shut up."

Lochan, his temper and patience both worn after a couple of weeks at the station, considered walking out. But he had learned to pick his fights, and there would be time later to turn this encounter into a face-off if he felt like it. He sat down on the indicated platform under a wall-mounted universal-scan.

The doctor paused to touch a couple of commands on his comm pad, then fixed Lochan with a flat stare. "I've got nothing against taking sheep like you for all the money you've got. But there are lines I don't cross."

"Which line is this?" Lochan asked, speaking calmly.

"Human trafficking." The doctor checked his pad again. "I've got a routine running that is spoofing the surveillance gear in here, but I don't want to run it any longer than I have to, so keep quiet and let me talk. In three more days, a freighter is going to show up, saying it's from Varaha. They'll agree to take you on to there."

"Why is that a problem?"

"I told you to keep quiet. That freighter will actually be from Apulu, where they need warm bodies to do unpleasant jobs. They'll take you to Apulu whether you like it or not, and all of you will vanish as far as the rest of the galaxy is concerned."

3

"We're going to be kidnapped?" Lochan said. "That doesn't make sense."

"Why? Because of all the technology available these days? I told you, there's a shortage of people in Apulu Star System to handle the sort of hard, backbreaking jobs that Apulu needs done and their own people don't want to do."

"Forced labor," Lochan said. "Why aren't they using machines for those jobs?"

"Because those machines may be commonplace in the Old Colonies, but they are scarce and expensive out here, and keeping them running is expensive. Importing stuff like that also costs a lot of money, but you guys have paid your own way out here." The doctor bared his teeth in a humorless smile. "People are adaptable and versatile, and relatively cheap, and if one breaks they are very easy to dispose of. You guys will disappear, no one will be able to track where that freighter actually came from, the records on this station will be clean, and we'll get a payoff from Apulu along channels that nobody can trace."

"What are we supposed to do?"

"I don't know. Not my problem. But I won't let you go into that without being warned. If you can come up with an answer, more power to you. Here's another warning. Don't try anything while you're still on this station. They're prepared for that. I don't want to have to put in all the work that might be required to fix you guys up after the riot suppression is finished."

Lochan eyed the hard young man. "What if I threaten to tell them that you warned me unless you help us?"

Another false smile came and went. "I'll say you're lying. And before you say they'll scan me to see if I'm lying, I'm the one who set up the parameters on the scans. I've already rigged them so they'll always say I'm being truthful, and no one else on this station has the skills to know differently." The doctor held up an injector. "I'm supposed to tell you that you've got a developing immune ailment that this shot will cure. It's actually a compliance drug. Knocks down your ability to think independently and resist instructions. You've become the leader of your group, and the people running this station don't want you leading. Lower doses of the same stuff will be fed the other refugees with you in your meals starting today. Just enough to keep them a little complacent until all of you are locked down on that freighter. After you leave this office, act a little confused, a little hesitant, like someone with a few too many drinks under their belt trying to play chess."

"Thanks," Lochan said.

The doctor nodded once, then tapped his pad again. "That shot should take care of it," he announced for the benefit of the surveillance systems, putting down the injector as if he had just used it.

"I feel a little dizzy," Lochan complained, playing along.

"That's normal. Don't worry about it."

"Um . . . okay," Lochan said.

He left the infirmary, noting just down the hall a couple of other crew members from the way station, looking very much like they were pretending not to be watching him. Lochan paused, looking up and down the corridor as if indecisive, started down the wrong way, then hesitated before turning and walking slowly past his audience.

A brief, low laugh sounded after he had passed. Lochan pretended not to have heard.

He spent the short walk back to the refugees' living area trying to figure out how to let Mele Darcy know without anyone else hearing. He wasn't sure how to get out of the mess they were in, but he was positive that telling Mele was the right first step.

"Still not interested," she told him when he suggested getting together in his bunk.

"But I really need you," Lochan said in a low voice. He lightly tapped the table in front of him. Three times fast, three times with a pause between them, then three times fast.

Mele tilted her head slightly, regarding him, only her eyes revealing that she had recognized the signal. "Oh, why the hell not? Your bunk? Tonight?"

A communal hall wasn't the most private place, so anyone wanting to engage in personal activities used blankets to offer a pretense of solitude. Mele lay on top of him, a couple of blankets covering both of them. Her murmur in his ear was soft but also full of warning. "This better be a real emergency."

"It is." Lochan kept his own voice as low as possible as he

whispered what the doctor had warned him of.

When he had finished, Mele stayed quiet for a few minutes as she thought. "That doctor is right," she finally murmured. "I've been checking things out. They can flood this room with gas, and they've got a good supply of antiriot gear. We wouldn't stand a chance if we tried something here."

"What about on the freighter? Marines do that stuff, right?"

Her breath gusted his ear in a very light laugh. "I'm one Marine. No gear. And they'll be ready to lock us down on the ship. No. We have to take over the shuttle that the freighter sends for us."

"Then what?" Lochan asked. "There's no place else to go in this star system, and a shuttle can't jump between stars."

"We wait for another ship. I looked at the schedules before I booked this trip. It shouldn't be more than a couple of days after we take the shuttle before another ship shows up."

She made it sound easy, but Lochan thought about everyone cramped onto a shuttle not designed for long-term life support and without much in the way of food and water. He didn't have any better ideas, though. "All right. What do we do?"

"They're watching you. You act compliant like they expect. Keep everyone else calm. I know a couple of people who can help us, and as long as the way station crew keep their attention focused on you, I should be able to set things up. I've been careful not to act too smart, so they think I'm just a dumb Marine. They won't watch me too closely as long as nothing tips them off."

"How are we going to go over the plan?" Lochan objected. "How are we going to decide things?"

"We can't hold planning meetings and debate options," Mele said. "You've given me a job to do. Can you trust me to do it?"

That was hard. That was really hard. His fate depended on whatever Mele did, and he had never been happy with surrendering control. Not in his business dealings, not in his political campaigns . . .

Not in his marriage.

And look how well that had all turned out.

Maybe it was time to stop micromanaging the rest of the world and just focus on doing his part of things. Besides, Mele was right. The more they talked about stuff, the greater the chance the way station crew would suspect something and maybe even learn something.

"All right," Lochan finally said. "You trusted me from the start. I'll trust you. I'll do everything I can to make them think we're all being nice, happy, dumb sheep so they won't be prepared for any trouble, and they'll tell whoever is on that shuttle that there's nothing to worry about."

"And I'll set things up to take the shuttle."

As much as Lochan had to admit that his knowledge of how to do things like hijack a shuttle was limited to what he had seen on action vids (and he had a strong suspicion that what action vids portrayed had very little to do with the reality of such things) it was still hard to accept. "What if you run into problems?"

"I'll let you know," Mele said. "If everything goes fine, we'll just talk openly like we have all along, but you'll act compliant. Wow. It's a good thing I don't have to try acting compliant. I'm not very good at that."

"I'm not surprised to hear that," Lochan said.

"When I make my move on the shuttle, you back me, do whatever you need to do to help me, and keep the other passengers from freaking out."

"Okay." A thought came to him. "Why are you sure I'll be able to back you up when you need it? That I'll be able to improvise whatever needs to be done?"

"Because you're pretty sharp," Mele said. "If I do need to tell you anything, I'll arrange another meeting like this. Otherwise, I'm off to do some thinking."

"You're leaving?" Lochan asked, not being very successful at hiding his disappointment.

She breathed a soft laugh in his ear. "Yeah. Sorry. You'll get over it."

"What if I don't?"

"I'll feel real bad about that," she said with another laugh.

Mele flipped the blankets off of them and slid away from him, leaving Lochan staring up into the darkness, frustrated and worried.

Three days later, one of the way station workers casually informed the refugees from the *Brian Smith* that a freighter from Varaha named the *Harcourt F. Modder* had arrived at Vestri and would be sending a shuttle to pick them up in a few more days.

Carmen stood in one of the passenger lounges on the *Mononoke*, gazing at an image of Brahma's primary world that floated in the center of the room. The image was incredibly detailed and updated constantly by observations of the planet. Her short-term roommate had left, to be replaced by someone else heading out from Brahma.

She felt . . . anger as she looked at the planet. The only craters visible were ancient, the result of old, natural impacts. The customs officials had been almost comically relaxed and sloppy. The only armed guard that Carmen had seen was on a vid feed from the loading dock for the shuttle, and the guard hadn't actually seemed the least bit worried about anything. Brahma was fat and happy and comfortable. It was one of the oldest of the Old Colonies, and had always been under the protection of Old Earth. The riches of the planet and the entire star system had barely been touched as yet by the growing population.

Carmen imagined for a moment dumping half the population of Mars here, suddenly flooding this island of contentment with the hungry and desperate and ruthless. Then she felt ashamed for wanting to inflict on anyone else what too many already endured. Dragging down Brahma wouldn't pull up anywhere else.

But if only they weren't so damned *smug* about everything. And so selfish in their smugness, thinking that because they faced no critical problems, no one else possibly could. Old Earth's struggles and sacrifices were history, and the futures of others were not Brahma's concern.

Whatever she tried to do in the down and out, it would have to depend on the resources available there, not on assistance from the Old Colonies.

Most of the refugees walking through Vestri's way station toward the dock displayed a mixture of weariness after their enforced stay in the Spartan accommodations combined with hope of eventually getting where they were going. Lochan walked near the head of the group, frowning slightly as he had since his visit with the doctor, as if unable to mentally focus.

He noticed Mele with a group near the middle. Mele appeared to be completely carefree and wasn't wearing her betraying earring, but a couple of those near her seemed visibly more tense than the other passengers. Hopefully, the way station workers would set that down to the final accounting payments that had just been wrung out of the visitors. Lochan, still playing the role of someone who couldn't help but comply, had nodded in dull acceptance of every charge presented to him personally. If universal wallets actually carried physical currency, his wallet would have been much lighter by now.

Any lingering doubt that Lochan had about the doctor's warning vanished as he saw the three crew members from the freighter who were waiting to herd everyone on the shuttle. Two men and a woman, all with the powerful builds, sharp eyes, and lazy smiles of people whose job was to keep other people in line. All three wore long jackets that mostly concealed the shockers holstered at their waists, revealing only slight bulges on one side that wouldn't have aroused concerns in anyone not already on the alert.

As he boarded the shuttle, Lochan heard Mele giggle behind him like a harmless young soul without a single worry.

The hatch was closing behind the last refugee when Mele tripped, stumbling toward two of the guards, who tensed then relaxed as she caught her balance and smiled sheepishly at them. "Get strapped in," the woman ordered as if speaking to a child, pointing to the rows of bare seats.

Mele half turned toward the seats, then erupted into sudden motion, her arms and hands blurs as they struck. The male guard nearest her slammed against the side of the shuttle, already unconscious, then the woman guard fell to her knees, both hands going to her throat as Mele followed up with a blow that knocked her out as well.

The third guard had barely begun to shout and reach for his shocker when a short refugee named Lukas sucker punched him, following up with a series of blows that laid that guard down as well.

Up front, a refugee named Cassie had already slapped a device onto the bulkhead next to the hatch leading onto the flight deck, and another next to the camera that allowed the pilots to monitor the passenger deck.

"Everybody stay quiet!" Lochan warned as the rest of the refugees stared in disbelief. "These guys were going to kidnap us. We've got everything under control, and we're going to get everyone out of this." He bent down next to one of the fallen guards, finding, as he expected, that the guard had rapid-apply wrist ties in his pockets. "You and you, help me bind these guys. Mele?"

She was by the hatch, accompanied by Lukas, both holding shockers taken from the guards. "Cassie rigged something to jam the camera in here and also a skeleton key to override the lock on this hatch," Mele explained. "As soon as it works we'll take the flight deck and lift out of here. Lochan, take the other shocker and get by the main hatch in case the way station workers figure out what's going on and try to force it."

Lochan took the shocker, holding the weapon cautiously. Could he use it against another person? He took another look at the heavies who had been their guards and gripped the weapon more firmly, taking up a position by the hatch.

The electronic skeleton key chirped softly as it broke the lock code, and the hatch leading forward swung open. Mele went through in a rush. Lochan heard the pop of a shocker going off.

The warning light at the main hatch blinked, indicating someone was trying to open it from the outside.

The shuttle lurched sideways, bobbed upward, then began climbing fast, the refugees falling and grasping at any available handhold.

"We're all right!" Lochan called. "We're going to be okay. Mele's a Marine. You all know that. She's got this."

"What the hell's going on?" one of the refugees demanded. "Why would they want to kidnap us?"

"Forced labor on Apulu," Lochan told him and the others. "Just stay calm, and we'll get through this. It's under control."

He had wondered whether he could enforce his will on the group this way, but either his voice, his outer confidence, or the mild compliance drugs that had been in their food worked. The others got into seats, strapping down, as Lochan made his way forward against the force of the shuttle still accelerating.

One of the pilots, knocked out by the shocker, was sprawled near the hatch. The other, sweat running down her face, was at the controls. Mele was in the seat next to the pilot, her shocker almost touching the pilot's temple. Lochan had a vague memory that a shocker going off that close to someone's brain could produce a fatal result, which explained the nervousness of the pilot.

Lukas nodded at Lochan, smiling. "No worries."

"Thanks. You took out that guy pretty quick."

Lukas's smile broadened. "When you're a small guy, you learn how to take down big guys."

"Where do you want us to go, boss?" Mele asked Lochan, keeping her eyes on the pilot.

He leaned forward enough to view the display before the pilot. The freighter from Apulu was easy enough to spot, only a light minute away. So were the symbols marking the jump points in Vestri. "Head for the jump point the *Brian Smith* arrived at," Lochan said, pointing. "Any other ships coming in should show up there."

"How much endurance do you think this thing has?" the pilot snarled, her face tense with fear. "With all those people aboard? Life support won't last more than a few hours."

"We can do better than that," Mele said. "Cassie is checking it over now."

"Cassie has some unexpected talents," Lochan remarked.

"She's an engineer," Mele said. "The sort of engineer who has trouble just following instructions and refuses to overspecialize."

"There are advantages to being part of a group of misfits," Lochan said. "Looks like you did everything that we needed."

Mele glanced at him for just a moment before returning her gaze to the pilot. "You thinking you didn't do much? You identified a big problem, figured out who to task with dealing with it, then let her do the job without trying to interfere or micromanage. You kept an eye on the big picture, and trusted me to do it right or let you know if there was a problem. And when everything went down, you backed me up. That's a pretty good boss from my point of view."

Despite the tightness riding his guts, Lochan couldn't help smiling at her. "You're saying I did something right?"

"Yeah. Sorry to ruin your perfect record of failure."

"We're not out of Vestri yet."

"I don't know what anybody told you," the pilot interrupted. "We're just regular merchants. We were just going to take you to . . . to . . . Vahala."

"Varaha?" Lochan said.

"Yeah."

"I've already searched your copilot. His ID is from Apulu."

"Where's your ID from?" Mele asked, tapping the pilot's forehead with the shocker. "Your copilot was carrying a military-grade pistol before I took it away. Lethal weaponry. What's that doing on a regular merchant?"

"If you want to get out of this without a prison sentence," Lochan said, "you'll cooperate with getting us another ride out of this star system."

"None of this was my idea," the pilot insisted.

"Then you'll be happy to help us, won't you?"

"They won't just let you walk away with their shuttle," the pilot said. "The ship is going to come after us."

"Do they have any weapons?" Mele asked.

"Yeah . . . a . . . pulse particle beam."

Lochan saw that the pilot had hesitated for just a moment before replying. "You know," he remarked, "I have some experience as a politician, so I know it takes a little longer to think up a lie than it does to give an honest answer. If that freighter wants to chase us, fine. He's got a lot more mass than we do, and not all that much thrust. He'll take a long time to catch us, and once he's close we can outmaneuver him."

"This shuttle is expensive!" the pilot said. "They won't let it go! They'll wait until life support on this bird is failing and you guys have to give up or die."

"We'll find another ride before then," Lochan said with a confidence he didn't really feel.

A day and a half later, Lochan Nakamura's ability to fake such assurance was being tested as never before.

"Toxic levels in the air are close to critical," Mele Darcy told him in a low voice.

Lochan glanced back at the other refugees, slumped in their

seats, all of them showing the effects of thirty-six hours with little water, no food, rising temperatures inside the living compartment, and steadily deteriorating air quality. "How long do we have?"

Cassie shrugged, looking like someone who had spent the last day digging ditches in the hot sun. "I've tweaked the gear as best I can. Maybe six more hours before people start passing out. About eight hours maximum before we start losing some of them."

He looked forward to where Lukas was keeping an eye on the pilot. The freighter had indeed lumbered into pursuit of the shuttle, not able to keep up but staying within several light minutes. The shuttle itself wasn't built for long-distance acceleration, and the pilot had been complaining with increasing urgency that fuel was getting low. "I figure we've got about four hours left before we'd have to give up. If we wait longer than that, some of these people will die before we could dock with the freighter."

Cassie nodded. "That's probably right. The question is, do we give up now or wait those four hours?"

"Wait the four hours," Mele said. "We're not beaten yet."

"I don't see how it makes much difference right now," Cassie said. "I'd hate to cut it too close. I think we should give it up to make certain we don't lose anyone."

Mele looked at Lochan. "Lukas already told me he doesn't want to have to decide life and death for people. So I guess your vote decides it."

Mele and Cassie watched him, waiting for a decision. If there had been someone else here to pass the buck to, he would have done it. The idea of someone dying because he made another mistake was unbearable. But so was the possibility that another ship could show up after they had surrendered.

Mele was in favor of waiting, though, and if he had to make a choice of whose judgment to trust, she would be very high on the list. "Let's keep heading for the jump point," Lochan said.

"For how long?" Cassie asked, looking resigned.

"You said it. If nobody has shown up in the next four hours, we'll have to give up."

"Live to fight another day," Mele corrected him, grinning as she wiped sweat from her face. "If it comes to that, Apulu is not going to be happy they caught me."

"Here, too," Cassie agreed.

Lochan looked away, knowing that someone with political skills like his might be able to work his way up even within the confines of a forced labor system.

If he was willing to abandon Mele and Cassie and Lukas. Maybe sell them out.

He was tired of that kind of thinking.

"Yeah," he said, nodding toward the others. "If it happens, we'll make Apulu regret catching us. Is the shuttle's distress beacon still on?"

"Yes, sir," Mele said. "It's on the emergency rescue setting."

"That won't help," Cassie said, "unless somebody shows up in time to respond to it."

"Truth," Mele admitted. "But it can't hurt. And if anyone shows up, they'll know right away that we need help."

Cassie shrugged, making it a gesture of surrender to Mele and Lochan, then pulled herself upright before walking with slow, careful steps back to check on some of the others.

Lochan watched her go, feeling morose. "How the hell did I end up here?" he said, not expecting a response from Mele.

But she gave him an arch look. "You tell me."

"Do you want the truth?"

"Usually."

Lochan couldn't help smiling slightly at that. "You know I'm a failure."

"No," Mele said, shaking her head at him. "I know you've said that you've failed at a lot of things. Not the same."

"All right," Lochan said. "If that's how you want to see it. I've admitted to trying to micromanage everything. But I haven't told you, or anyone, why."

It was Mele's turn to shrug. "Does the why of it matter?"

"Yeah. It does." Lochan paused, tasting something bitter that didn't come from the foul air he was breathing. "Micromanaging lets you pretend to control things without understanding them or caring about them. And that's what I've done. I've never cared enough about anything to really try to understand it. Even my marriage. She should have been everything to me. Instead, I let being in charge be everything to me."

Mele cocked a disapproving eyebrow at him. "You didn't love her?"

"I thought I did. I swear I thought I did. But what I loved was . . ."

"The thought of her being in love with you?"

Lochan stared at Mele. "Yeah. I guess so. So I gave up. That's the truth about me, Mele. I'm out here because I'm looking for something that will make me care enough to try enough to be something other than a serial failure."

Mele looked around the cabin of the shuttle. "It looks like you cared enough about not becoming slave labor to try."

"Yeah, but assuming we get out of this—"

"Was it just you?" Mele interrupted. "Or did you care about what happened to the rest of us?"

He took a moment to think, trying to sort out what would sound right and what he really felt. "Yeah. I cared about the rest of you."

"Say we get out of this. We're home free. How many other people have already been hauled to some place like Apulu? Can you care about them? What about other places? This can't be the only star system where someone is taking advantage of the lack of adult supervision."

"There must be others, yeah." Lochan shook his head. "But that would be too big for anyone to tackle. One person couldn't make a difference."

"Did one person hijack this shuttle?" Mele sounded exasperated with him. "You've been going through life solo, even in your marriage. Haven't you figured out teamwork yet? It's not that you don't care, it's that you don't want to share the credit for what goes right. Stop pretending it's anything else. If it's worth doing, it doesn't matter who gets credit. What matters is that it gets done."

Lochan sat silently for nearly a minute, trying to come up with arguments that would refute Mele Darcy's blunt statement. And failing. Trying to get angry. And failing. But, for once, those failures weren't a bad thing. "I'm going to think about what you said, Mele. Thanks."

She grinned. "You're welcome for the chewing out. And lucky you, we've got nothing much else to do for the next few hours but think."

The next three hours would have felt longer if not for the way the increasingly foul atmosphere inside the shuttle and Lochan's growing fatigue kept causing him to drift off for short periods of unconsciousness that didn't feel like sleep and gave him no sense of having rested. Fortunately, that same lassitude was keeping the other refugees from panicking or demanding immediate surrender.

As the final hour began ticking down he moved up to the flight deck again, where Mele had relieved Lukas and was once again watching the pilot.

"How much longer are you going to do this?" the pilot asked Lochan in a dull voice.

"A little while longer," he replied.

"The kids will die first, you know."

"I've heard that, yeah. How long do they live on Apulu? What do you make them do?"

"I'm not a player in that," the pilot denied. "But the pretty ones . . . I've heard it's ugly for them."

"How do you play at all with a system like that?" Mele asked, angry enough to twitch her finger toward the trigger of the shocker aimed at the pilot.

The pilot shook her head. "You go along with something, then something else, then a little more, and before you know it you're neck-deep and can't see any way out. I'm not proud of myself. I'm not like those three apes who were going to guard you. They like treating other people like cattle. I just got stuck in it before I knew what was happening."

"Maybe you can help us even if we give up," Lochan said. "Give us some aid after we've been captured."

The pilot shook her head, her expression dreary. "I'm no hero. I'm not brave. I'm nothing except a bird driver."

"But the kids—"

"I try not to think about it. I'm not going to stick my neck out."

Lochan glanced at Mele, who shook her head to indicate that arguing with the pilot was a waste of time.

Forty-five minutes left before he had to make a decision.

Something new appeared on the display.

The pilot looked up, her face reflecting surprise. "Another merchant ship. Mixed passenger and freight."

Lochan exhaled slowly, fighting down an urge to laugh out of fear that it would sound half-hysterical. "How long until we can reach them?"

The pilot extended her hand, sweeping it through the virtual display. "On our own? Four hours."

"Too long," Mele said.

"You have to give up."

"What if they come to meet us?" Lochan asked.

"We're still half a light hour from the jump point," the pilot complained.

"Give me communications with them," Lochan said, letting his voice go rough and threatening. "Don't mess up anything because we're going to meet up with that other ship in time or you're going to die along with us." Did he mean that? He wasn't sure.

The pilot seemed convinced, though. She hastily tapped controls, then nodded to Lochan.

"This is Lochan Nakamura aboard the shuttle signaling an emergency, calling the freighter that recently arrived in Vestri Star System. We are former passengers from the freighter *Brian Smith*, stranded here by pirates. The freighter pursuing us is from Apulu and is trying to take us from here by force. We urgently request that you alter course to meet us. Our life support is badly strained and won't hold out much longer."

He stopped speaking, staring at the display and wishing that he believed enough in his ancestors to pray for their help.

"You can't wait for a reply," the pilot said, sounding desperate.

"They're half a light hour away, which means half an hour for them to get your message, and another half an hour before we hear their reply. In another hour, it'll be too late to meet up with my ship before the air gets too bad to sustain life. We'll all die."

"Maybe they'll come to meet us," Lochan said.

"They'll think it's a trick! They'll think we're pirates who want to trick our way aboard their ship!" the pilot insisted. "They won't change course! Everybody on this bird will die because of you!"

He almost wavered then, thinking of the others in the passenger compartment, thinking of the kids.

Lochan looked at Mele. "What's your advice?"

"Me?" Mele grinned. "I say we go for it. I wasn't going to live forever, anyway."

"She's a Marine!" the pilot hissed at Lochan. "They're all crazy!"

"I guess it wore off on me," Lochan said. He knew what Cassie would vote, not out of fear for herself but worry about the others aboard, and Lukas was still making it clear he didn't want to have the burden of decisions laid on him. Which meant that he was deciding this one. No, not just him. He and Mele. A team. He had never been a team player, but as Lochan confronted what might be his last decision he finally realized the truth of what Mele had told him, that being a part of a team wasn't about diffusing responsibility as he had long thought, or letting others claim credit, but about fostering support for both decisions and individuals. Something he could not have decided on his own, he could do with Mele's support. "We're going for it. Adjust course to intercept that new ship as soon as we can."

"It won't be soon enough!"

"Do it," Mele said, something in her voice causing even Lochan to feel a thrill of fear.

Shaking her head, the pilot made the adjustments, then sat back in her seat, eyes closed, her lips moving in silent prayer, or maybe in silent curses aimed at Lochan and Mele.

The last minute left before they could have still surrendered to the freighter from Apulu came and went. Lochan watched the slow progress of the new ship, wondering if he had doomed everyone aboard the shuttle.

It sure seemed like he had.

4

"They're adjusting vector," Mele commented. "Isn't that what's happening?" she prodded the pilot.

The pilot opened her eyes, scanning her display with growing wonder. "Yeah. About twenty minutes ago they started coming over and down toward us. But they couldn't have gotten your message yet when they did that. Why would they do that?"

"The distress beacon," Lochan said. "It's been transmitting for hours, so they would have heard that as soon as they arrived at the jump point, right? They must have reacted to it."

The pilot's hand flew through her controls. "We might make it. If they keep coming over to close on us. We might make it."

"I'll tell Cassie to keep us alive until we meet up with that freighter," Lochan said. He stumbled back to the passenger deck, feeling weak from more than the foul air. "There's a ship on the way to pick us up!" he called. "A big, new, beautiful ship!"

Twenty minutes later, Lochan was back on the flight deck when a message came in from the new ship, one that must have been sent soon after the ship arrived at Vestri. "This is the *Mononoke*, Brahma Star System registry. We have received your distress signal and are altering vector to meet you."

Carmen Ochoa sat on one side of a small, square table. She had been asked to be in this meeting because the ship's files had revealed her past experience at conflict resolution. Seated opposite her was the *Mononoke*'s executive officer. To her right was the *Mononoke*'s security chief. To her left was a rumpled-looking man named Lochan Nakamura, who had been leading the refugees from the shuttle. He had a pained expression that occasionally transitioned to a wince.

"Are you all right?" the executive officer asked.

"Yes, sir," Lochan Nakamura replied. He raised one hand toward his head. "Your ship's doctor said the headache is because of the life support problems on the shuttle before you picked us up. It should go away soon."

"The freighter *Harcourt F. Modder* has demanded that we turn you over to them to face charges for hijacking their shuttle," the security chief told Lochan.

"We told you what happened and why we did it," Lochan replied.

"The available evidence, thin as it is, supports your account," the security chief said. "We have complaints and warnings on file about the way station at Vestri. And we downloaded enough from the shuttle's systems before letting it go to confirm that it and the freighter both came from Apulu as you say, and not from Varaha as they claimed. That's enough for me to recommend to my captain that we not surrender you. But none of that is enough to build any sort of case against either the way station or the freighter, even if there was somebody who would act on that evidence. My recommendation is that you all write this off as an expensive detour that could have been a lot worse."

"What about the piracy?" Lochan Nakamura asked.

"Technically," the executive officer said, "Earth law applies here and everywhere in human-occupied space. But, in practice, there's no one to enforce that law. Local regulations push for whatever they can get away with, and unincorporated star systems like Vestri can get away with a lot. If they actually attacked a ship from Brahma like ours, then Brahma would do something. But they're too smart for that."

"Brahma *might* do something," the security chief grumbled under his breath.

Carmen nodded. "You're right. Brahma would probably send a complaint back to Earth, and maybe a year later you'd be told to take care of it yourselves." She turned to Lochan. "But Earth law can help you somewhat. When the way station charged you those exorbitant prices for services, did they download all of the charges through the universal wallets you carried?"

"Yes," Lochan Nakamura said. "How else could they do it? We had all our savings on those wallets."

Carmen smiled. "Under Earth law, you have the right to cancel and dispute charges you believe are unjustified. Get out your wallet. Enter EULS 281236.17722."

The man pulled out his wallet, entered the string of characters and numbers, then stared at what it displayed. "It says I can cancel those downloads and get all my money back. How is that possible? I came from Franklin, and bought this wallet in that star system. The laws on Franklin allow me to dispute charges but not to cancel them."

"Earth Universal Legal System *does* permit it," Carmen said. "And, as noted by this ship's officer, Earth law still technically applies anywhere in space. That cancel and dispute charges capability is in all the universal wallet software. The initial versions written on Earth required it, and all subsequent versions everywhere else have retained it—because in most cases, they didn't even know it was in there. The corporation running the way station can respond to your dispute, filing a legal claim for you to pay up. But they'll have to file it in Earth courts to unlock the charges you downloaded at that way station."

The *Mononoke*'s executive officer laughed. "How long would a case like that take?"

"By the time everything was done and appealed and resolved and communicated across so many light years? At least ten years."

"I just enter this?" Lochan Nakamura asked, looking between his wallet and her, as if Carmen were a genie who had just appeared before him to grant a wish.

"Yes. At that point, the funds are back in your wallet. The ship can relay the cancel/dispute to the way station, where receipt of it will immediately lock the payments you made and prevent any use or transfer of them." Carmen smiled wryly. "Sometimes, knowledge of Earth law comes in handy."

"We can all do this?" Lochan asked. "Citizen Ochoa, this is going to make my fellow travelers very happy. Some of them were completely cleaned out by that way station's outrageous charges."

"I'm glad that I could actually help someone," Carmen replied, feeling better than she had in months.

"We'll be happy to relay the cancel and dispute notification to the way station," *Mononoke*'s executive officer said to Lochan.

"Make sure everyone has done that so we can send a single bulk message. That way the station can't block receipt of subsequent messages from us. We're obligated under Brahma's space law, as well as Earth law," he added with a nod toward Carmen, "to take you on to the first safe destination. We have sufficient room for that, but some of you will be crowded."

Carmen eyed Lochan Nakamura, waiting to see how he would react, but he simply nodded. "We are more than grateful for that. Since it seems we're going to have money in our wallets again, can any of us who want to do it buy passage farther onward?"

"Certainly. We're going as far down as Kosatka."

"I'll spread the word and get the wallet cancellations done by everyone," Lochan Nakamura said. "Citizen Ochoa, we owe you. I owe you. Let me know if there is ever anything I can do for you."

She smiled at Lochan Nakamura, sizing up the man and deciding that he did have potential as an ally. "There might be something. I'll look you up later."

Rob Geary stared at the new defense subcouncil for Glenlyon, consisting of Council Members Kim, Odom, and Camagan. "You want me to command the cutter we captured, but the council doesn't want to officially give me any rank?"

"The council," Odom said sternly, "believes it is best to retain you in unofficial, temporary status."

"That belief is not universal," Kim said, glaring at Odom.

"It was voted on," Odom said. "By all members of the council."

"You are authorized the temporary rank of lieutenant," Leigh Camagan told Rob. She had the resigned look of someone who knew they had to give out bad news that was the fault of others.

"Glenlyon is still trying to feel its way through an unanticipated crisis, and some members of the council need more time to consider options. There is nothing we three on the subcouncil can do to change that in the immediate future though I will be working on your behalf for the long term."

"You've all read that intelligence report, haven't you?" Rob asked. "The one based on the data that Ninja pulled out of the captured ship's data files and what Danielle Martel told us?"

"Why should we believe anything that Martel says?" Odom demanded. "She was one of the officers on that ship!"

"It was her first mission for Scatha, she didn't know what she was getting into, and her information was confirmed by what was in the ship's files," Rob said. "Scatha Star System has two other warships. Former Sword Class destroyers. And substantial ground forces, at least substantial compared to our nonexistent ground forces. Scatha isn't going to be happy that we captured that Buccaneer. And even if we hadn't dealt them a blow, Scatha already has a demonstrated policy of aggression toward nearby star systems. The documents on that ship showed that Scatha's leaders believe they have the right to dominate this region of space, justifying it by arguing that Scatha is attracting a superior kind of settler, appealing to people who think they've been mistreated on Old Earth or in the Old Colonies."

Odom shook his head. "Nearly everyone heading down and out has some grievance against their lives on Old Earth or the Old Colonies. We can't be suspicious of all others because of that. We dealt Scatha a strong rebuff when they threatened us. They will most likely turn their attentions to less risky ventures in the future and perhaps seek cooperation."

"That is how bullies act," Kim said, voicing rare agreement with Odom.

Rob paused before replying to try to ensure his voice remained calm. The last thing he needed was to have his arguments disregarded on the grounds that he was being *too emotional*. "With all due respect, Scatha is clearly organized for aggression. We are not organized for defense. Not with one minor warship that has a skeleton crew and problems with its power core."

Kim looked at Leigh Camagan. "Corbin Torres has been contracted to bring the power core controls up to safe standards, hasn't he?"

"Yes," she agreed.

"But Torres won't be along when that ship leaves orbit for a mission," Rob argued.

"He's training a volunteer," Kim said, as if specialized knowledge born of years of work was easily passed on to someone else in a matter of weeks.

Rob felt the old, familiar helplessness that he had in Alfar's fleet when someone with experience and expertise offered their opinion, only to have it dismissed because it was inconvenient. He had often been in the middle then, a junior officer trying to get more senior officers to listen to skilled enlisted specialists. "I'm not sure I can commit to the assignment that Glenlyon is offering," Rob said. "There do not seem to be sufficient resources dedicated to the task. That would put not only me, but everyone else who volunteers to serve on that ship, at unnecessary risk."

"What do you need?" Leigh Camagan asked before either Kim or Odom could reply.

"A permanent assignment would give me better leverage to get the resources I need," Rob said.

"We are reluctant to create a professional military class at this early stage in the colony's development," Odom said, his voice taking on a stern quality. "We prefer that our defenders be part of the society they are defending, not separate from it."

"I don't want to be separate," Rob protested. "I just want to know that my work is being treated seriously, especially since it involves personal risk of physical harm."

"Of course your work is treated seriously!" Kim said. "The government is not yet ready to take the necessary steps."

"We do not agree on what is necessary," Odom objected.

"I'm not happy about this, either," Kim continued, as if he hadn't been interrupted. "But you know how important this is. If you don't do this, we don't have a good alternative. We're asking you, for the good of everyone in Glenlyon, to dedicate yourself a little longer to the defense of the colony."

Did they know that the original job Rob had been lined up for, supervising construction work for one of the colony's companies, had been given to someone else when he had been "absent" to deal with the warship from Scatha? If he turned down this assignment, he would be stuck looking for new work in a colony where every job had been signed for prior to the colony ship leaving Alfar. Maybe the police force . . .

Hell. He wouldn't be happy doing anything else knowing that whoever the colony got to run that ship wouldn't have the background to do it. And what would happen to the volunteers for the crew if their captain didn't have any experience at all? "All right," Rob said. "But I will put on the official record what is needed and what we don't have. The council has to decide whether to hope Scatha does nothing else or to be at least a little prepared when Scatha does something else."

He saw the slightly smug reactions from Kim and Odom, who had both apparently known he wouldn't leave others hanging, and a slow nod from Leigh Camagan, who from the way she was looking at him had expected the same but wasn't happy that he had been pushed into the decision.

"Lieutenant Geary," Leigh Camagan said, "since you have accepted the assignment, and I thank you for that, I'll inform you that the council has decided to name the cutter the *Squall*."

"The *Squall*? You mean like the weather event?"

"Yes," she said. "In the past, small warships have occasionally been named for violent weather. Since the council couldn't agree on any other name honoring individuals or places, we chose something that no one could object to."

"It's a proud name," Kim objected. "There have been many ships carrying the name *Squall* in human history."

"Yes," Leigh Camagan repeated. "That is true. We trust you and the crew of the *Squall* will be sufficiently inspired by the heritage of its name."

He couldn't tell whether she was being sarcastic or not. "I'm sure we'll do our best." Rob made his farewells and walked out, heading for the shuttle landing area so he could get back up to the captured warship. The *Squall*. It wasn't a bad name. It was an honorable name. And as far as Rob was concerned at the moment, it was much better than naming the ship after some politician.

Ninja was waiting outside. "Have you got a job?" she asked, falling into step beside him.

"Officially, no, I think," Rob said. "But unofficially, yes."

"You should have told them no," she said.

"Yeah, but I couldn't."

She looked off to the side as they walked together. "So you're going back up into orbit?"

"Yeah," he said again, feeling torn inside. He liked talking to her, and seeing her waiting after the meeting had given him a definite lift. "I'm . . . sorry I won't be around."

"I've got plenty to do." She waved off his words.

"I know, but . . . Ninja . . ."

"What?"

"Um . . . I'll be thinking of you." He knew how lame that sounded.

She finally looked back at him. "Are you saying that I shouldn't get another contract where you might be considered to be my boss?"

"I can't tie your hands," Rob protested.

"I can't make decisions when you can't make up your mind," Ninja said. They had reached the shuttle pad. "Take care of yourself."

"You, too." He left her and went to the shuttle, angry with himself for words unsaid. But would he have truly meant those words? He was going to be stuck up on the ship again, for who knew how long. He doubted that Ninja would want to accept that sort of relationship, assuming that she really wanted a serious relationship.

As the shuttle lifted off, Rob contemplated the irony of finding it easier to deal with the countless challenges and stresses of commanding a warship than it was figuring out what he wanted with Ninja.

Seeking distraction, he thought about Scatha. Two destroyers. If even one of those destroyers showed up at Glenlyon, defended only by a single Bucket with a makeshift crew, his path of command might be a short one with a dead end. Ninja would be better off if he didn't get involved with her.

Damn. He was thinking about her again.

* * *

Carmen Ochoa sat back, rubbing her forehead, worn-out from researching the latest data available in the *Mononoke*'s files on the new colonies. Maybe part of what she felt was the discomfort created by being in jump space, but there was more to it than that.

She decided she needed a walk, and a drink, and somebody to talk to about all this. She just wasn't sure who. Carmen had not socialized much with other passengers from Old Earth for fear that some betraying word or action would reveal that she had been born and raised a Red.

Having lost track of ship's time, it turned out to be much later in the ship's day than she realized. Still, the lounge she stopped to look in had every table occupied because there wasn't much else to do in jump space. Carmen started to turn away, then paused and squinted at one table with only a single occupant, a man she recognized.

She had wanted someone to talk to.

"Hi," Carmen said as she stopped by the table.

Lochan Nakamura looked up, startled. "Oh. Hi. The Old Earth lawyer, right?"

Carmen laughed. "Old Earth, yes. Lawyer, no. I passed the ethics exam, so they booted me out of law school. Are you in the mood to talk?"

"What about? I mean, sure." Lochan Nakamura gestured to another seat at his table.

"I wanted to talk about what happened to you," Carmen said, "and what's happening everywhere down and out."

He gave her a rueful look. "You're the second person I know who has brought that up. I'm realizing that's a subject I know too little about. Maybe if I had known more, I wouldn't have ended up trapped at Vestri."

"I actually want to bounce some ideas off you, if that's okay," Carmen said as she sat down. "Your original ship got taken by pirates, then you got fleeced on the way station, and finally you were nearly shipped off for forced labor."

"Yeah. Except for that, it's been a great trip so far."

He had a sense of humor. She liked that. "What are you planning on doing now?"

"I was thinking about filing a complaint, maybe bring charges," Lochan admitted. "But who would I complain to? Who would actually do anything? Is there anybody?"

"No," Carmen said. "Which was why you had to risk your life escaping on that shuttle." She looked down at the table, trying to decide what to say, then back at Lochan. "Do you know what the ship's officers have said about you?"

Lochan shrugged. "Did the words 'stupid' and 'crazy' come up? They did, right?"

"No. They said you had a lot of courage to do what you did, and that without your leadership none of you would have gotten free of that ship from Apulu."

He laughed, shaking his head. "I didn't do that much. Without Mele Darcy we wouldn't have made it."

"Mele Darcy? She's . . . ?"

"The former Marine from Franklin." He paused, looking down at his drink. "For some reason, she thought I was worth something."

Carmen realized he must have been drinking for some time. "Excuse me?"

He laughed again, but the sound held an undercurrent of old

91

pain this time. "I haven't had a lot of success in life. Maybe I had something to do with us escaping on that shuttle, but if so it's a . . . what do you call that? An anomaly."

"Then why did that Marine trust you? The other refugees from the *Brian Smith* all said you were their leader."

He twisted his drink one way then another in his hands, not replying for several long moments. "Maybe. Do you think this new-start stuff is true? That in the down and out, we can find a way to start over again and maybe not repeat the same mistakes?"

Carmen shrugged slightly. "Do you mean we as individuals or we as a species?"

"Oh, hell, I've got enough to do with trying to start over my individual life. How could I make any difference to the species?" He frowned as if remembering an earlier event or conversation. "If other people were trying to do something . . ." Lochan added, his voice trailing off into uncertainty.

She leaned forward toward him, her elbows on the table. "There are other people who want to do something. I'm one of them. Maybe you could be, too, if you're the kind of leader who could help the others escape from Vestri."

"Two people still isn't much." He frowned again, this time argumentatively, but Lochan's words seemed to be aimed at himself rather than Carmen.

"No, it isn't," she agreed. "But maybe even just a few people with the right skills, doing the necessary things while everything is still in flux and everybody else is still making up their minds, could influence a lot about what is happening out here. That would be a new start worth making, wouldn't it?"

He looked at her again, skeptical. "A team effort? I have to admit that my sole success in life so far involved that. What things are you considering necessary?"

"I don't know exactly. The question is, Lochan . . . can I call you Lochan?"

"Sure."

"Can I be personal?" Carmen asked. "You've told me that you know what failure is, on a personal level. I've seen it on a planetary level. Experiencing failure is important."

"I'm glad to know it served a purpose," Lochan said, sounding half-amused and half-bitter.

"People who've never failed, never beaten their heads against something that won't be fixed, tend to think that their own success in whatever they've tried is due only to them," Carmen said. "They don't realize the external factors that mess with the best plans, and they don't realize how aspects of themselves can contribute to problems."

The frown was back, causing Carmen to wonder if she had pushed Lochan too far. "You haven't talked to Mele Darcy?"

"No. About what?"

"Never mind." Lochan smiled wryly. "Let's just say I see your point. I know how things can go wrong when everything you're doing should be right. But even two people who understand that wouldn't have much influence."

"Not back on Old Earth . . . or Mars. Or in the Old Colonies," Carmen agreed. "Once a system gets fixed in place, all settled, it doesn't want to move, it doesn't want to change. But if you can catch it while everything is still in motion and make a few small shoves, maybe you can change how it settles out."

He grinned. "A little like Newton's Laws of Motion applied to human organizations? That's a weird idea." Lochan Nakamura paused to think. "It might have a lot of truth to it, too. It can be that way with people, right? Nudge them in the right direction before they make up their minds. But what does that have to do with me?"

Carmen chose her words carefully. "You know how it was. Old Earth kept the law in space for the Old Colonies. What happened in Vestri couldn't have happened a few decades ago because without the jump drives places like Vestri that are just on the way to somewhere else wouldn't even have been visited, and because if anyone set up something like that Old Earth would send someone to deal with it. It wasn't an empire, more like a very loose association of star systems that let Old Earth do the heavy lifting when it came to keeping the peace."

"That's true of down," Lochan objected. "Up, they cut themselves off. They don't want anything to do with Old Earth or the other colonies."

"Right. So now humanity is expanding very quickly, all of it apparently down, and there's nothing keeping any law in those regions."

"I don't know enough about it," Lochan Nakamura admitted again.

Carmen sighed heavily. "I've been trying to find out more about it. There's so much information, so many new colonies springing up in new star systems. And the amount of information lag varies all over the place. Some of the data are only a month or two old, and other bits are several months old or older."

"Is there anything about Apulu?" Lochan asked.

"That's a good example," she said. "There's almost nothing

about Apulu in the files. They registered a colonization plan with the Old Earth authority that people are still registering with, I guess out of habit, and that's all there is. Apulu is keeping real quiet about itself. Then there's, um, Scatha. Scatha Star System reads like a perfect little utopia from what it has reported to other places. But then I find information about Scatha buying surplus warships and ground weapons from Old Colonies, and that doesn't sound quite so much like a utopia, does it?"

Carmen gestured widely. "And there have been some colonization expeditions that just disappeared, apparently going so far down and out that we've lost contact with them."

"Why would anybody go that far?" Lochan wondered.

"I don't know. A few of those ships were owned outright by business leaders who made no secret about being tired of what they called interference by governments. Maybe they wanted to be able to operate without laws and regulations that restricted their options." She nodded to herself as a memory came. "There used to be things on Old Earth and on Mars called company towns. A big corporation owned everything, the houses and the stores and the businesses, and everybody worked for the corporation in one way or another. Mars still has places like that though the owners could be considered more like gangs than corporations. Something like that setup could be what the people who went very far out wanted."

"A whole planet for their playground? I wonder what promises they gave their workers to get them to buy into that?"

"I don't know," Carmen said. "They went so far out that it will be a while before the expansion of new settlements encounters them and finds out what came of their experiment in corporate rule."

Lochan shook his head. "We all wanted some form of freedom

from what we're leaving. But we're also leaving behind laws and rules that protected people like us and the workers who took their families to those corporate colonies. What the hell is happening?"

"Things that are going to shake out for centuries," Carmen said.

A man at the next table got up and glared at her. "I couldn't help but overhear. You're trying to make a case for some great landlord to keep us all in line, aren't you? We've had enough of that, on Old Earth and on the Old Colonies. My people are finally going to have our own home, at a star we've already named Eire. And we'll thank you to keep your hands away from our home!"

Carmen, having dealt with gang enforcers as a little girl, gave the man a flat, unintimidated look in return. "And what if someone else breaks into your home? What will you do?"

"Tell them to leave off, or fight if we must!"

"Fight? With what? And how well did that work on Old Earth when it was just you by yourselves? Your home was never conquered?"

The man's glare held a moment longer, then he shook his head. "You know nothing of our history."

"I know more than you think," Carmen said, having identified where he had come from on Earth by his way of speaking. "Would you be a happier people with a happier history if you'd had strong friends to call on for help when invaders struck? And if others had known you had such friends, would they have ever invaded?"

He paused to think. "That depends on what price the friends demanded."

"A friend wouldn't ask for more than you'd be willing to give, right?" Carmen said. "I'm not interested in trying to force anyone into anything. But it wouldn't hurt for everyone to know who their friends are, just in case they need them. And to agree on any price before someone is in desperate need."

"I'll give you that," he said in a quieter tone. "Where are you from?"

"Albuquerque." If she told him the truth, he would probably walk away in disgust and check to make sure he still had his universal wallet.

"Oh?" If he suspected the answer was misleading, he gave no sign of it. "And where are you bound?"

"Kosatka."

"Kosatka? At least that's easier to spell." The man nodded to Carmen, then to Lochan, who had sat silently watching, before leaving the lounge.

Lochan gave her an appraising look. "You are one cool actor. I'd hate to play cards against you."

She shrugged. "I've learned how to deal with people. But my experience in other areas is limited. I can talk one-on-one, but when it comes to groups, I'm not as good." Carmen rested her chin in her hand as she gazed at him. "It would be nice to have someone working with me, someone I could count on if things get too hot, who could work with groups like I work with individuals."

He looked down again, grimacing. "I may not be the guy you think I am."

"Are you the guy you think you are?"

That brought her a smile from him. "You sound like Mele again."

"And that sounds like a compliment," Carmen said.

"It is."

"Are you two . . . ?"

"No." His smile shifted, becoming wry. "Just good enough friends to be honest with each other. You know, I learned one of the reasons politics is so ugly is because people aren't honest with themselves. They want things, but they often don't want to pay whatever price those things demand. So they elect people to do the unpleasant bargaining and trading and trade-offs and compromises for them. And then they look down on those doing the dirty work."

"You don't think that's fair?" Carmen asked.

"Not if you're one hundred percent honest as a politician," Lochan Nakamura said. "Not if you cut the best deals you can for the people you're representing. I know everyone thinks there are never enough politicians like that. And I can't claim I was perfect. I made a lot of mistakes. I deserved to lose that election. But my recent experience in Vestri showed me I did learn from that, even if it did take a Marine to pound the lesson home for me. Still, if you want a partner in this stuff, you should know who you're getting."

"You're being honest with me?" Carmen asked.

"Yeah, I'm—" He caught himself, grinning. "What kind of a politician am I?"

"The kind I need. The kind that the new colonies may need."

Lochan Nakamura took a drink, then paused in the manner of someone about to attempt something new. "What are you thinking we should do? How were you planning to do things?"

"We need to start with one of the growing colonies," Carmen said. "Get in on the ground floor and use what we can do there as . . . as a lever! That's why I'm going to Kosatka. It was settled about five years ago and already has a couple of cities and a scattering of towns, growing fast as new immigrants flood in and businesses serve the people and ships going farther down."

"Are they having trouble yet?" Lochan asked her.

"Some sort of domestic problems, at least as of the date of the information aboard this ship, and it's going to get worse. If we come in confident and authoritative, people looking for answers will listen."

"That sort of thing can be misused," Lochan observed. "I don't think you're the sort to do that. Why do you think I won't?"

"Because someone willing to manipulate others for their own benefit wouldn't have risked their own life helping everyone else escape from Vestri," Carmen said.

"How do you know what I was thinking?" Lochan insisted.

"I know everyone was on that shuttle," Carmen told him. "If you'd just been looking out for yourselves, you and the others could have hijacked the shuttle and left the rest of the passengers behind, instead of risking having the life support fail before *everyone* got rescued."

Lochan's frown was back. "It never even occurred to me to leave the others behind."

"Yes. That's the point. That tells me what I need to know about you." Carmen nodded in the general direction of *Mononoke*'s bridge. "The captain and I spoke earlier about what happened at Vestri, and she was candid with me. Her bosses at the shipping line are getting increasingly nervous about running ships down into new colony areas. The profits are great, but the chance of major losses just keeps going up. There is going to come a point when ships like this aren't going to be making runs anymore between the Old Colonies and new places in the down, and when that happens not only does the flood of new people into the newly established colonies like Kosatka get choked off, but so does all the trade."

He nodded, eyes hooded in thought. "All right. Sign me up to the, uh, team. Here's to Kosatka and saving the . . . galaxy?"

"This small part of it," Carmen agreed. Before she could say anything else, one of *Mononoke*'s security officers approached the table.

"Lochan Nakamura?" he asked.

"That's me," Lochan confirmed. "Is there a problem?"

"We have a passenger in confinement who gave your name as someone aboard who could vouch for her."

Lochan slapped his forehead. "Mele Darcy?"

"Yes," the officer said. "Could you come with me? The ship's executive officer would like to speak with you before you assume responsibility for Darcy, assuming you are willing to do so."

"I owe her that much," Lochan Nakamura said. "Citizen Ochoa—"

"Carmen."

"Carmen, I'm sorry, but I need to see to this."

She nodded, thinking that this was an opportunity to learn a bit more not only about Lochan Nakamura but also Mele Darcy. "Do you mind if I come along? To provide legal advice if necessary?"

"Would you? Thanks!"

About half an hour later, after a brief talk with *Mononoke*'s second-in-command, Lochan followed the security officer into the utilitarian part of the ship that a tiny private police force operated out of, still wondering exactly what Mele Darcy had done.

He had also wondered how Carmen Ochoa would handle being in an environment of confinement cells and security officers. Carmen, as best he could judge, was wary, alert, and cautiously polite. Her attitude around the private cops reminded him of someone he had once known who had grown up in a high-crime area on Franklin. Was Albuquerque like that? Lochan suspected that it wasn't, that Carmen, like his former acquaintance on

Franklin, avoided mentioning wherever she had actually acquired that guarded behavior around police officers.

It didn't bother him. He didn't want to be judged by his past, either. Wasn't the whole point of going down and out to get a new start, free from the mistakes of the past?

The officer they were following paused at one door, unlocked it, then gestured back the way they had come. "The paperwork is already processed. You can just walk out with her when you leave."

"Thank you," Carmen said for both of them.

Lochan tapped the control pad next to the door and watched it slide open. "What happened?" he called, as much to announce his presence as to ask the question.

Mele Darcy, seated on the small bunk against the far wall, her skin and clothing bearing the marks of fighting, grinned at him. "A bunch of bums in one of the bars were making fun of Marines. I asked them politely to stop."

"Politely?"

"Well, sort of politely. And then they got very insulting, and I had to defend the honor of my former comrades, right?"

Carmen had stayed back, out of the line of Mele's sight. Lochan leaned against the door frame, crossing his arms. "How many were there?"

"The bums? Ten." She paused, scrunching up her face in thought. "Maybe eleven."

"And you took them on by yourself?"

"Even though I'm a *former* Marine, that's still fairly even odds," Mele explained. "So we discussed the matter among ourselves, no bystanders injured, then ship security showed up and asked me what was going on and I asked if I could finish my beer and they said sure so I did, then they arrested me. Who you got with you?"

"Carmen Ochoa," she called from outside the cell. "Did security arrest the other eleven in the fight?"

"Maybe later they did," Mele called back. "You're that lawyer, right? Doesn't someone have to be conscious to be arrested?"

"I'm not a lawyer, but I think you're correct."

Lochan shook his head, desperately trying not to smile at Mele's story. "The ship's officers aren't happy. The next star system the *Mononoke* is going to visit is Taniwha. The executive officer told me he would really like to see you leave the ship there along with the passengers already planning to debark."

"Taniwha? Do you know anything about Taniwha?"

Carmen Ochoa answered. "First settled about six years ago. They have three cities on their primary world and a completed habitat and dockyard orbiting that planet. A lot of ship traffic heading down and coming back up goes through Taniwha."

"It's not a dead end, then?" Mele made a face as she thought, rubbing her jaw. "Okay."

"Okay?" Lochan questioned, surprised at the speed of her decision.

"I needed to get off somewhere. I probably won't stay at Taniwha, but it'll give me a chance to look at my options."

"All right, then," Lochan said, trying not to look disappointed. "Um . . . you've been released into my custody. I'm supposed to make sure you don't get into trouble again before Taniwha."

Mele's smile turned mischievous. "I could make life hard for you until then."

"But you won't," Lochan said.

"Nah. You're not so bad. How many days until Taniwha?"

Carmen Ochoa called out the answer. "Three more days in jump space, then three days heading in-system before a transfer shuttle is supposed to meet us."

"Almost a week?" Mele scratched her head. "Staying out of trouble that long is going to be difficult. Maybe you ought to tell them to leave me in here."

"Mele," Lochan said, unable to stop his smile this time. "I think if you wanted to stay out of trouble for a week, you'd manage it without breaking a sweat."

"You got me, boss." Mele stood, stretching. "And thanks, uh . . ."

"Carmen."

"I'll pay you guys back for having to handle this. Are the bars still open? It's on me."

"They're serving breakfast," Lochan said.

"No beer?" Mele asked.

"Do you ever drink coffee?"

"Do I ever drink coffee?" Mele grinned again as she walked out with Lochan. "Hi, Carmen. It's good to know I'm leaving Lochan in responsible hands." She waved good-bye to the security officers they passed. "No hard feelings."

"Just don't do it again," one replied.

"I'm good. I wouldn't do anything that would cause this guy trouble," Mele said, indicating Lochan. She kept talking as she, Lochan, and Carmen Ochoa headed to breakfast. "Where was I? Coffee. Let me tell you guys about the time I had to stay awake for a week, and there weren't any official go drugs available. I did it, too. No, really. This actually happened."

* * *

Six days later, Lochan escorted Mele Darcy to the loading dock where the shuttle would mate with the *Mononoke*.

Mele hoisted her bag as the passengers debarking at Taniwha started filing into the air lock. "Thanks for seeing me off, boss. How come you're so gloomy?"

"I was hoping you'd stay with us all the way to Kosatka," Lochan admitted. "You're the one who told me to start thinking about working with other people instead of trying to do it all myself or giving up."

"Guilty as charged, but no. Kosatka looks okay, but I've got a feeling I should go on a little farther into the dark. I'll know where I belong when I find it." She gave him a questioning look. "You and Carmen are both going to Kosatka?"

"Yeah," Lochan said.

"Personal reasons or mutual business, if you don't mind my asking?"

Lochan smiled. "Mutual business. Something I haven't failed at yet."

"Huh. Remember everything we talked about. It's not about running it all yourself, making every decision, and making sure you're the only one who gets credit. That's not what got us out of a one-way trip to Apulu. Give other people a chance to screw things up just as badly as you can."

Lochan nodded. "I'll need to see if other people are as good at screwing things up as I am. Being forced to let you handle things showed me that by insisting on controlling everything, I wasn't giving others a chance to show what they could do."

"So what have we learned?" Mele asked him.

He smiled ruefully at her. "That I'm not in this alone. To make the big decisions alone only when I have to, and ask for advice, and to choose people I trust to handle things?"

"And let them handle those things. There, you see? Not so hard. You might even succeed at a few things on Kosatka." Mele hugged him tightly, then stepped back again. "It was fun serving with you, Lochan Nakamura."

"Likewise, Mele Darcy. It's going to be pretty dull without you around. Take care of yourself, Marine."

Mele grinned. "I've got a feeling it might be more exciting than you think if you stick with that Carmen Ochoa. She's got the look of someone who's used to being in situations where she has to watch her back."

Lochan frowned. "You don't trust her?"

"That's not what I said. I think you *can* trust her to watch your back. You're going to need someone like that without me around." She gave him a casual salute. "See you later on a 'gator."

Not sure exactly what her farewell meant, but certain of its friendly intent, he watched Mele walk into the air lock and disappear from his sight. After waiting until the shuttle launched, Lochan headed back to the room he was sharing with some of the other refugees from the *Brian Smith*. He had a lot to think about.

After Taniwha, the next jump took them to a still-unnamed star that was only visited because it, like Vestri, was on the way to other places that people actually wanted to go. Another red dwarf, the planets orbiting it varied from way too close/way too hot to way too far/way too cold, varying mainly in the color differences between their surfaces of rock or ice.

Which made the presence of a new, small facility orbiting one of the frozen planets all the more surprising. "Another way station looking for suckers?" Lochan wondered out loud to some of the other refugees from the *Brian Smith* who were eating lunch with him. The *Mononoke* had arrived in the star system nearly seven hours ago and continued on her way through normal space toward the next jump point while passengers and crews speculated about the purpose and origin of the new facility.

"Maybe worse," Carmen Ochoa said.

Lochan turned to see that she had just walked up, looking unhappy. "What is it?"

"I just spoke with some of the ship's officers. *Mononoke* has received a message from that facility. It said that this star system has been claimed by Apulu and named Turan."

"They can't do that," Lochan said. "Can they? Just lay claim to a star system?"

"Under interstellar law as set forth by Old Earth, no. But who's going to stop them?" Carmen asked him. "Not Old Earth, I can tell you that."

"But why would Apulu bother claiming a star system like this? There's nothing here."

"Yes, there is." Carmen pointed outward, beyond the hull of the *Mononoke*. "There are jump points that ships need to use. The message from the facility said that ships passing through this star system will have to begin paying transit fees to Apulu."

"Can't ships go around? Use other stars?" one of the other refugees from the *Brian Smith* asked.

"Going around would mean a lot longer trip, a lot more time, and more money. If Apulu is smart, and they seem to be playing things pretty smart so far, their fees will be big enough to make this space grab profitable but small enough that ships will pay rather than try to go the long way around to stars like Kosatka."

Lochan finally understood what Carmen Ochoa was driving at. "Which means the ships will have to add that fee to the cost of heading to stars down from here, which means prices will go up on passenger fees and any cargo carried. Every star down from here is going to end up paying for Apulu's transit fees."

"And what's to stop other star systems from setting up the same toll deal at other unoccupied stars?" a bystander asked.

"Nothing," Carmen Ochoa said.

"This could choke trade all over the down regions of space," Lochan said. "The Old Colonies will have to—" He stopped as realization hit.

"Have to what?" Carmen Ochoa asked.

Lochan laughed, the sound low and bitter. "I've been a politician, and I've been in business. You know what's going to happen? Everyone is going to look at their bottom lines. How much would it cost to deal with this, and who is going to pay for it? More taxes? On who? The politicians aren't going to want to touch that for something so far away, not the way things are now. And the big businesses are going to look at short-term expenses and the costs of mounting a military effort to clean out places like this, and they'll balk."

"But in the long run—" someone started to argue.

"The long run?" Lochan demanded. "Do you know how hard it can be to get some major business owners to look past the next stockholders' meeting? This is something that would require just about everyone with a big voice in an Old Colony to be behind it, and too many of those voices won't want to. Don't look for help there."

"Where can we look for help then?"

"Out here," Lochan told the crowd listening to him. "This is our problem. We have to deal with it. And if we don't, why should we expect someone else to?"

An easy question to ask. How to get anyone in the fiercely independent new colonies to work together and invest limited resources in ways that benefited others would be a much harder question to answer.

5

"Lieutenant?"

Rob Geary woke at the call, blinking up at the pipes and ducts and conduits overhead, which weren't that far over his head. The grandly named captain's stateroom on the newly rechristened *Squall* was smaller than the cabin he had shared with another lieutenant aboard one of Alfar's destroyers. That didn't bother him nearly as much as the fact that the council's continuing failure to agree on an official status for him meant that technically he wasn't captain of the *Squall* despite being the ship's commander. "What's up?"

The watch-stander visible on the comm pad next to Rob's bunk had the look of someone suddenly jarred to alertness in the midst of what had been another uneventful watch in the middle of the ship's night. "We've spotted two ships that arrived at the same jump point as the Bucket, I mean, this ship, came in from."

"The jump point from Scatha? What are they?" Rob demanded, his pulse racing as he worried about Scatha's destroyers. It had been over a month since the *Squall* had been captured, which was time enough for Scatha to have heard and sent off a retaliatory attack.

"Freighters. They're broadcasting civilian identification, Scatha registry." The watch-stander paused, frowning. "They *were* broadcasting that, anyway. They both just went silent."

Rob shoved himself up from his bunk, trying to relax and wishing the report had led with that most important bit of information. "Can we see any weapons on them?" he asked, trying not to sound as impatient as he felt.

"Um . . . sensors can't identify any weapon modifications. Both freighters do have a couple of heavy-lift shuttles strapped to them, though."

"Shuttles? Also unarmed?"

"Yes, sir." The watch-stander peered at his display. "Looks like they steadied out on an intercept with this planet in its orbit."

Two freighters. Unarmed, but coming here. What was Scatha up to?

Rob called up his own display, waiting impatiently while the old systems flickered before steadying. The freighters were moving at merchant-ship velocity, substantially less than that of warships. At point zero two light speed, they would take nearly two weeks to reach the planet.

The *Wingate* had long since departed. There was one other ship still in the star system, heading outward toward the jump point for Jatayu, back up toward stars like Kosatka and Taniwha. That ship had left the orbit of this planet only two days ago after off-loading a new batch of equipment and a large new group of men and women and children eager to get a new start on a new world.

Rob straightened himself up, trying to look serious and

professional, then touched the comm control. He derived some small satisfaction in knowing that since the ship's day on the *Squall* was matched to the night and day hours at Glenlyon's still-only city, he would be waking up council members with his message. "This is Lieutenant Geary on the *Squall*. Two freighters showing registry from Scatha have arrived in this star system and are heading toward this world. As far as we can tell, the freighters are unarmed. They are projected to reach this planet in thirteen days at their current velocity. I request instructions for dealing with the ships. My recommendation is that the *Squall* be sent to intercept them and conduct searches to ensure this isn't another hostile act."

Council President Chisholm called back a quarter of an hour later. She looked half-worried and half-rumpled from being woken. "Why do you think this might be another attack, Lieutenant?"

"Because the last time Scatha sent a ship here, it was an attack," Rob explained. "And because these ships broadcast their identities once after arriving, then went silent. That's not normal. Maybe the *Squall* wasn't just going to extort money from us but would have also hung around this star system to provide escort for those two freighters."

"Why would the freighters need an escort? What can they do?"

"I don't know," Rob said. "That's why I recommended intercepting them and searching them."

Chisholm paused, thinking. "How long will it take you to intercept them?"

"About three days if we don't push it. That's after we get under way, which will probably take another day to get necessary people and supplies back aboard."

"Four days will be fine," Chisholm said. "Go intercept them, leaving as soon as you feel your ship is ready. While you're on the way there, the council will deliberate and decide on a course of action."

"We need to search them," Rob said.

"The council will decide on a course of action," Chisholm told him, her tone reassuring even though her words didn't actually promise much.

"May I make one more suggestion?" Rob asked, trying his best to sound diplomatic. "We can get Lyn Meltzer on contract again to check out the freighters for whatever she can find out. It's possible she could break into their systems enough to find out what they are doing."

"That's an excellent suggestion," Chisholm said. "The council will handle the contract, though."

"That's fine," Rob said, meaning it. Maybe the council thought it was ensuring that Ninja was answering to them and not Rob, but such an arrangement meant that he wouldn't once again be Ninja's boss. And he was increasingly feeling like he wanted to avoid that.

As soon as the call ended, Rob started double-checking the status of the ship. What needed to be done to leave orbit and head for an intercept with those freighters? The council had continued to make only short-term purchases of necessary supplies like food and water, so he only had about six days' worth of food on hand. He would have to get the council to cough up enough money for the ship to be out for weeks, though since most of what they were getting were emergency rations siphoned from disaster-readiness supplies, no one would be happy with the quality of the food. Rob double-checked to ensure that there was enough coffee on hand. Ships ran on fuel cells, but crews ran on coffee. At least in the matter of fuel, he could still make use of the supplies the *Squall* had carried when captured from Scatha. There were enough fuel cells aboard to handle power for more than a month of routine operations.

Danielle Martel had pretty much stayed on the *Squall* since the ship's and her own change of allegiance. She had confessed to feeling unwelcome on the planet, and Rob had to admit she had good cause for that. He felt guilty because that social isolation meant that Danielle, the only other trained sailor, was always available to help him handle matters on the ship. There were several members of the volunteer crew down on the planet who would have to be brought up, though, and one contractor who would have to be sent down if he wouldn't volunteer to help out. Rob didn't have a lot of hope on that account.

After getting a shuttle on the ground alerted to the need for a lift in the morning, sending the council a list of the supplies needed, and having word passed to the crew members who were being recalled, Rob went in search of the contractor.

It was still an hour before ship's dawn when Rob roused Corbin Torres from sleep. "We're going to be leaving orbit on orders from the council. I'd like to have you along, but I can't insist on it. It's up to you."

Torres scowled at him. "I did my time. I'm not going on any missions. When can I hop a shuttle?"

"One will be here in five hours, so you have time to wrap up what you were working on and pass on any more essential information. Are you confident that the people you trained can safely operate the power core?"

He got a shrug from Torres in reply.

"Are you comfortable knowing you're sending them out with what little you've been able to teach them so far?" Rob asked, letting his voice grow cold this time.

Torres glared at him. "I'm not the one giving the orders for this ship to go somewhere. Save your self-righteousness for the people in charge, which happens to include you! You're making the decision to send them out, not me!"

"Nothing is your responsibility, huh?" Rob said. "Just get off my ship." He turned to leave.

"Do you think they'll be grateful?" Torres yelled after him. "Do you think they'll really care about what happens to you? You're an idiot! A young, idealistic idiot who thinks sucking up to the people in charge will earn him rewards!"

Rob paused long enough to look back and shake his head at Torres. "I'm not doing anything for other people. I'm doing this for myself because I think these things need to be done. And, no, I don't expect any rewards. That doesn't matter."

He walked away, knowing that it really did matter even if he told himself otherwise. Lack of recognition did hurt. That was a big part of why he had left Alfar's fleet with its small, clubby officer corps and the exclusive set of men and women who knew all the right people, got all the right assignments, and got medals and promotions like clockwork regardless of how well or how little they had actually done. But it also really didn't matter since he would do what needed doing, anyway. That much was true, that he had to do what he thought was needed because he would have a hard time living with himself if he didn't. The last thing he wanted was to become as bitter and burnt-out as Corbin Torres. Avoiding that fate was, in the end, why he had left Alfar. And, for that matter, why he was in command of the *Squall* when anyone with common sense would have already told the council to pound sand.

Twelve hours later, his current "full" crew of fourteen men and women aboard, along with enough additional food, water, and coffee to keep everyone alive if not fulfilled, Rob took his seat on the bridge and studied the projected tracks on his display. The path of the two freighters from Scatha formed a broad arc of about four light hours' distance, which came to over four hundred billion kilometers. If things worked out, the freighters would never finish that journey, instead being forced to turn back, because Rob fully expected to find something on those spacecraft that Glenlyon wouldn't want in its star system.

Squall would leave her orbit about this planet, already being called Glenlyon after the new name of its star. Swooping along another arc that intersected that of the freighters, *Squall* would meet them nearly two light hours from the planet, more than four days before the freighters would reach Glenlyon. That would allow plenty of time to search the other ships and take whatever other steps the council would authorize.

The great majority of *Squall*'s crew were excited and worried. With only two exceptions, the crew had no experience with naval missions. For them, this was something new, thrilling, and daunting.

One of the exceptions was Rob, who wasn't feeling any thrill but plenty of daunt. The other exception was seated at the operations watch station.

Danielle Martel had occupied that same station for Scatha when the *Squall* had belonged to that star. Getting the council to agree to letting her be part of the crew, working for Glenlyon now, had been almost impossible, but Rob had stuck to it because she knew the ship better than anyone else, because she was apparently what she claimed to be, someone trapped into a contract with Scatha who was grateful to be working for Glenlyon now, and, just as importantly, because she was a former junior officer in Earth Fleet. But she had no rank, no official status, and Rob knew from personal experience how that must rankle. "Anything?" Rob asked her.

"No. I've gone through all the records again from when Scatha owned this ship," Danielle said. "Including all the things I wasn't allowed to see. There's nothing about any plan involving those two freighters."

"Do you think the former captain knew anything?"

"I doubt his bosses shared anything with Screamin' Pete that they didn't have to," Danielle said. "As far as I could learn when working for Scatha, everything is organized into stovepipes to keep anyone from finding out what anyone else is doing. Except for Central Security, which looks into every stovepipe. All I can do is guess, and my guess is that if Scatha sent those freighters here, it's to do something that Glenlyon won't like."

Drake Porter, one of the Glenlyon volunteers who had helped capture the *Squall* and stayed on to help crew her, shook his head from his post at the comm station. "Nobody's going to listen to you, though. Except us."

"I know," Danielle said with a sigh. "You'd think I was the first person to ever be tricked by a bogus recruiting pitch."

Drake nodded sympathetically. Rob had noticed that he liked Danielle Martel. Maybe more than liked, but so far, Danielle had just been friendly in response.

A soft tone brought Drake Porter's attention back to his display. "You've got a call, Lieutenant."

Rob checked his own display, seeing the link that Drake had already posted. He tapped the accept command and saw Ninja's face appear before him. "Good afternoon, or evening."

"Is it?" She grimaced at him. "You got me another job, huh?"

"Working for the council," Rob pointed out. "Not me."

"I noticed that. Which means?"

"Um, that no options are closed off."

"No options are closed off?" Ninja gave him an irritated look. "Don't take anything for granted. You're going out to meet those guys, aren't you?"

"That's what I've been told to do," Rob said. "They appear to be unarmed."

"Sure. Is Danielle Martel all calm and relaxed about that? I didn't think so. I'll find out what they're doing since that seems to be the only way I'll be able to keep you from flinging yourself into space to force entry on those freighters," Ninja said.

She ended the call, leaving him wondering what he'd done wrong.

"Let's go," Rob told the bridge crew. On a larger ship, or a ship with a full crew, he would give helm commands to a watch-stander, which would be repeated back and checked against the commands recommended by the maneuvering systems. But the *Squall* didn't have enough people aboard for that kind of redundancy to ensure that the right commands were entered. Instead, Rob took a final look at the commands, repeating them out loud to himself to ensure they matched what he wanted the ship to do. "Turn port zero six zero degrees, up zero three degrees, accelerate to point zero five light speed."

He felt an odd sense of history, looking around the bridge at everyone who was looking at him. "Here we go on the first operational mission for the *Squall*, the first operational warship of the Glenlyon Star System."

Rob tapped the execute command, and the automated maneuvering systems took care of the rest.

Squall would never be the nimblest warship in space, but Rob still felt himself smiling as she swung about smoothly under the push of her thrusters, the main drive lighting off to push her away from orbit about the planet and onto the vector needed to intercept the incoming freighters.

A small round of applause sounded on the bridge. "You should have given a speech," Drake Porter said.

Danielle Martel laughed for the first time since Rob had known her. "I'm part of something new! The first time for something! Do you have any idea how strange that is for someone from Earth?"

"I guess we should have brought along something to toast the event," Rob said, grinning.

"I could get some coffee," Drake Porter offered.

"That's probably the most appropriate beverage we could have," Rob agreed. As Drake left the bridge, Rob glanced at Danielle. "Do you know how long we've used that system for maneuvering in space? The whole port and starboard thing?"

She paused to think. "I learned that once in a navigation course. When was it? Mid-twenty-first century, I think. Maybe late in that century. We didn't need it until we had enough ships maneuvering independently between planets. Ships at sea had used port and starboard, and the one fixed reference in a star system is the star, so they decided to use starboard for turning toward the star and port for turning away from it. And then up and down based on the plane the planets orbit in."

"That's not a new something, then."

She laughed again. "Not even close."

* * *

There were so few crew aboard the *Squall* that Rob had to stand watches on the bridge along with the others he thought capable enough for the task. It made for a short night's sleep, but everyone else aboard was doing the same thing. He had just come off four hours on the bridge, which included the start of the next ship's day, when Rob finally heard from Ninja again. The time lag between *Squall* and the planet had grown to nearly half an hour, making a real conversation impossible.

Ninja looked frustrated and stubborn. "Bad news. Those two ships sent out a single transmission with their registry information when they arrived in this star system, then apparently shut down every transmitter and receiver. I can get in past locked doors. I can't get in if there aren't any doors! Before you ask, I'll tell you what I'm going to tell the council. The freighters aren't running any links between themselves. No active transmissions of any kind. No receivers active that I can tell. Scatha must have heard how we took the *Squall*, and since they couldn't trust their firewalls against me, they pretty much isolated those freighters from any signal traffic. Obviously, with how far away those freighters still are, I've only had time to bounce one set of signals off them, looking for ways in and getting the results back. But if they stay locked down like that, I won't be able to get into their systems no matter how weak their firewalls are. I'll keep trying, but don't hold your breath. Sorry."

Rob rubbed his lower face, worried. He had expected Ninja to work her usual magic, but Scatha had figured out a way around that.

He touched the reply command. "Thanks, Ninja. If you can't get in, nobody can. Is there any way we could plant some kind of physical tap on them when we get close enough, something stuck on their hulls that you could use to break into their systems from outside? It would have to be something we could improvise from components on this ship, which I imagine means the answer is no, but let me know if I'm wrong. Thanks again." Should he say anything else? This was an official transmission, after all. "Geary, out."

The excitement among the crew when they had started out had slowly subsided into the dull routine of traveling millions of kilometers through space lacking much in the way of variety. Rob and Danielle Martel had both experienced this sort of "adventure" drudgery, but the others in the crew were new to it. And people who were tired and bored, and not used to handling that, made for leadership challenges.

"Back off, both of you!" Rob ordered, glaring at the two volunteers who were about to come to blows. "Vlad, if you come within a meter of Teri again I will put you in a survival suit and duct-tape you to the outside of this ship."

Vlad turned a sullen glower on Rob. "I don't have to put up with this."

"Yes, you do. If you want to quit when we get back to Glenlyon, that's fine with me. But as long as you're on this ship, you will listen to orders and treat your shipmates with courtesy and respect!"

Rob waited until Vlad, grumbling under his breath, had left. "You okay?" he asked Teri.

"I'm okay," she said, face still hard with anger. "I could have taken him."

"That's not the point. You're not supposed to take him. That makes it personal. This is about discipline on the ship. If he violates discipline, then I take him."

"Yes, sir."

Rob turned to see Danielle Martel watching. She walked with Rob as he headed back toward his stateroom. "Nice command voice," Danielle remarked.

"I have a command voice?" Rob asked, giving her a skeptical look.

"Yeah. Your voice gets lower in pitch and a bit louder in volume."

"Huh," Rob said, surprised to realize that he had been doing that. "Is that how Earth Fleet would have handled that?"

"Why do you care how Earth Fleet would have done it?" Danielle Martel asked.

"Because they're the model," Rob said. "The oldest and the best."

She laughed though it carried a sharp edge that didn't sound like amusement. "If only Earth Fleet lived up to its rep! Yeah, that's what I would've done. You were a lieutenant for Alfar, right? What do you care about a former ensign's opinion?"

"You're a pro," Rob said. "Whether you realize it or not. That's why I care. I'm still learning this stuff."

"You'll never make admiral with that attitude," Danielle Martel said.

The *Squall* had traveled for almost a day and a half, to one and a half light hours from the planet, when the council's guidance finally came in, delivered by Council President Chisholm herself. Chisholm had sent the message from her new office, a room mostly devoid of decoration, the walls apparently left nearly bare in the expectation of many future plaques and pictures and displays in the centuries to come. "Your instructions, Lieutenant Geary, are to intercept the freighters from Scatha as previously directed. You are to insist on the right to inspect the freighters and ensure they are carefully examined by whoever you send over for that task. Do not send Danielle Martel."

Rob slapped his forehead at that last, grateful that the message wasn't anything like real-time and his reaction couldn't be seen.

"If the freighters refuse to allow inspection," Chisholm continued, "you are to instruct them to reverse course and leave this star system."

He breathed a sigh of relief, having feared that the council would balk at such a necessary step.

"It must be clearly understood," Chisholm said, "that you are not to fire upon the freighters under any circumstances. No weapons are to be employed, either aimed at the freighters or near them. They are civilian spacecraft, they are unarmed, and therefore cannot be attacked by warships under interstellar space law."

Rob's feeling of relief vanished.

"Keep the council apprised of your actions, and if you need to do anything not already covered by your instructions, ensure you request and receive approval before acting. Chisholm, out."

Rob played the message again, hoping that he had missed something.

He hadn't.

Needing somebody to vent to about the message, he called Danielle Martel into his stateroom. He doubted the council would approve of that, but they hadn't told him not to share his "instructions" with anyone else.

She watched it in silence, not reacting except for a wince when Chisholm mentioned her name. "Why did they think they needed to tell you not to send me?" Danielle asked when the message was over. "If you were that dumb, you shouldn't be commanding this ship."

"In all fairness," Rob said sarcastically, "they haven't made up their minds yet about my commanding this ship."

"Oh, yeah. It's sort of disappointing that they think *I'm* dumb enough to want to put myself back into the hands of Scatha. But you can't shoot. What if the freighters ignore your orders to go back to the jump point?"

"I guess I'm supposed to use harsh language," Rob said.

"Not without requesting and receiving clearance from the council," Danielle Martel admonished him. "Do you think they realize that by the time we intercept those freighters it will be a multihour process just in terms of the time for light to carry the messages back and forth?"

"What do you think the freighters will do?"

"It depends on their orders. They'll do whatever they were told," Danielle said. "When I was working for Scatha, I was given a very clear impression that it is a very bad idea to not follow orders. Central Security takes a great deal of interest in that sort of thing."

Rob shook his head, gazing at the spot over his desk where Chisholm's message had been visible. "Why did you leave Old Earth's fleet to come out here and deal with this kind of thing? We must look like idiots playing the amateur hour."

She smiled and shook her head. "No. In Earth Fleet, we'd have a checklist for every possible circumstance, a checklist that itself contained multiple subchecklists, and regulations required following those checklists and subchecklists and subsubchecklists to the letter. Earth Fleet has been doing this stuff far longer than anyone else, and every time anyone made a mistake, it got added to the checklists to make sure no one else did it."

"In Alfar's fleet, we looked up to Earth Fleet," Rob said, leaning back as he looked at her. "I've told you that. You guys are the old pros, the men and women who could outfight anyone and anything."

Danielle shook her head again, suddenly looking older. "If you want the truth, Earth Fleet is a zombie. It's already dead. It's been dead for a while. But it keeps going because it doesn't know it's dead yet. Tradition and denial are keeping the pieces moving and the ships cruising. But not much longer." She grew somber. "Earth is tired of war, Rob. You may not think humans could ever tire of their favorite destructive pastime, but Earth has seen too much and endured too much. They're getting out of the game."

"So it wasn't just wanting to do something new? You left because Earth Fleet is on its last legs?" He found the idea that Earth Fleet could someday be gone hard to grasp.

"Yes." Danielle Martel's eyes became haunted with memories. "Everyone followed procedures and carried out their patrols and pretended it wasn't all coming to an end, but it was. No one was even supposed to talk about everything winding down because that would signal a *negative attitude* and *adversely impact morale*. We were all on a death watch but supposed to smile and act like everything was fine. I couldn't handle that."

She sighed, then her gaze on him grew demanding. "I won't be the only remnant of Earth Fleet heading down. You're going to meet others. Let me tell you, Rob, when you encounter other Earth Fleet–trained officers, they will be fiends for following procedures and regulations. They'll be sharp and look sharp and know how to drive their ships, and they're likely to be brave and fight as well as they can, but in any emergency they'll look to the book for an answer, and if the answer isn't there, they'll be lost."

"They won't innovate?" Rob asked, skeptical.

"They can't innovate," Danielle said. "It's been trained out of them. It doesn't matter if they succeed in an assigned task. If they failed to follow every step on the checklist and every applicable rule for that task, they will be judged as having failed. The process is what matters, not the outcome."

"You're serious?" Rob demanded.

"Absolutely. Why do you think I was willing to believe that fairy tale the recruiter from Scatha spun? I couldn't wait to get out."

Rob nodded to her. "I'll remember that. Do you know if Scatha already has any other Earth Fleet vets?"

"Maybe," Danielle said. "But I don't know. One of the first things that tipped me off that Scatha was bad news was when I first reported and asked about that. I was told that who was in the crews of the other warships was none of my business."

"That's weird," Rob said, startled.

"More like paranoid. I wanted to work where I could make a difference, not where I had to watch every step I took."

"Good luck with that," Rob said.

"The people running Scatha are as bad as Reds," Danielle Martel said. "I bet a lot of them are Reds originally."

"Reds?"

"From Mars. Haven't you heard about it? The planet is a mess of little klepto-states run by gangs and dictators. Half of Earth Fleet's missions in the last century involved dealing with Red scams and predations. If you meet a Red, keep one hand on your wallet and use the other hand to call for backup."

"Everyone from Mars is like that?" Rob asked, skeptical.

"Everyone I ever heard of," Danielle assured him. "Why'd you leave Alfar?"

"Mostly because everything you did was supposed to be the way it had been done before. You couldn't breathe differently than they had twenty years ago because the way they breathed back then was the way it should be done. Plus, their fleet was small and getting smaller." He looked away, remembering how it had felt to know that the future held nothing but less and realizing in that he and Danielle Martel had experienced similar things. "Not dead or dying, but shrinking with no hope that it would ever grow again. Why do you suppose Old Earth and the Old Colonies started drawing inward when humanity started expanding outward?"

"Maybe it was easier," Danielle suggested. "Everybody actually looking forward to the future is heading out here. Like you."

"And you." Rob paused as a thought struck him. "And the people who colonized Scatha. You told me they're recruiting citizens by promising they won't let anyone push Scatha around. Are the old places exporting their troublemakers? Sending them off to mess with each other and leave the past to slumber undisturbed?"

"If so, you're in on the ground floor of a growing business," Danielle commented.

He laughed. "Yeah, nothing but opportunity. Look how far I've come! I have a temporary, conditional sort of command of a Buccaneer Class cutter, whose few weapons I am not allowed to employ, crewed mostly by inexperienced volunteers who are discovering that this stuff is a lot more fun when viewed on a vid, and under the orders of a council that wishes none of this was happening. And if anything goes wrong, it will be my fault."

"You didn't think *that* would change, did you?" She gave him a sharp look. "Why did you ask me to view that message?"

"I needed someone else's point of view," Rob said.

"That wasn't the only reason."

Rob grimaced. "No. I wanted to vent to someone."

"So you picked me. May I speak freely, Lieutenant Geary?"

Rob's expression changed to a frown as he looked at her, wondering why Danielle Martel had adopted such a formal demeanor. "Of course you can."

"You're the commander of this ship," Danielle said. "The senior officer in what military force Glenlyon has. Which means you can't vent like that. Not when it comes to civilian oversight. Your crew is listening. Maybe hearing you talk like that would make them respect you less as well as respecting the government less. Or, worse, maybe they'll continue to respect you but respect the government less. Where does that vector lead?"

Rob shook his head at her. "I would never threaten the government."

"What about those who come after you?" Danielle Martel asked. "Everything you say and do will play a role in what becomes the traditions of Glenlyon's military. You're laying the foundation for whatever military Glenlyon ends up with. What do you want that foundation to look like?"

He hadn't really considered that before. "I've just been trying to get by, doing what needs to be done. Do you really think what I say matters that much?"

"Do you really think it doesn't?"

Rob shook his head. "No. You're right. I guess I've spent too much time thinking about what I can't do. But I can do other things without even realizing I'm doing them. This is the first ship in Glenlyon's fleet, no matter how much larger that fleet someday gets or how small it stays. What we do here, what I do here, will influence what comes after, won't it? All right. I'll set a good example." As she got up to leave, he looked at her, feeling depressed. "Nobody will remember, will they?"

"What?" Danielle asked.

"What we did. Stuff like this. Maybe people will remember the traditions, but not us. That will be in the footnotes of history, buried in databases. No one will remember you and me."

She shrugged, looking down at him. "Is that why you do things? Because history?"

"No. Because of me or people or things I care about."

"So what's the problem?"

"I'd like to think it mattered what I did," Rob said.

Danielle shrugged again. "I thought we'd agreed it did matter. But its mattering and your being remembered are two different things."

"It really doesn't bother you?" Rob asked.

She smiled slightly. "Rob, I come from Earth. It's old. Countless men and women have come and gone there. They've left their marks. Old ruins and new ruins, changes to the landscape, species wiped out and species preserved, structures thousands of years old. It gives you perspective, I guess. A lot of their names aren't remembered, but what they did contributed to what Earth is. There's no sense complaining about it. That's how things work. If you want something different, you could try some of the reverence for ancestors movements that are spreading everywhere."

"I thought that was mostly on Alfar," Rob said. "Looking back to Old Earth, where we came from, and the people we came from."

"I've noticed it seems to be everywhere out here," Danielle said.

"There's always been that form of belief among some groups on Earth, but it's very popular in the new colonies. Reverence for the past, for the Earth, and for our ancestors, who hopefully care about us in places where everything else is unfamiliar. It might be a fad, but that doesn't mean it's *just* a fad. Is death a final ending or a new beginning? We still don't know. Maybe we never will."

He grinned, for some reason feeling better. "We'll all find out eventually. If they don't come up with the immortality fix that's been on the horizon for how many centuries now?"

She smiled back. "Do you know what a horizon is? It's an imaginary line that recedes as fast as you approach it."

"Thanks, Danielle. I really appreciate being able to discuss problems with a real pro."

"You're a real pro, too, Lieutenant," she replied, saluting him with a solemn expression. "Don't forget it."

Wary that the freighters from Scatha might be Trojan horses filled with well-armed troops that would try to board the *Squall* and retake the ship, Rob brought *Squall* to only within a light second of the other ships before matching vector with them. No matter how well trained or equipped they were, no soldiers were going to be jumping three hundred thousand kilometers through space.

Nervous as well about the potential for a Scatha hack aimed at *Squall*, Rob kept checking the firewalls that Ninja had installed to protect the systems on the warship.

"They're trying to get in," Danielle Martel reported. "But our firewalls are holding. That stuff Ninja patched in is solid."

"But the automated intrusion routines that Ninja sent still aren't finding any way into their systems," Rob said.

It felt odd to realize that on the surface, the three ships were racing through space, no sign of conflict or hostility between them, yet on a level outside of direct human observation, battles were being fought at light speed. The only immediate casualties in those invisible battles where codes and radiation strove against each other would be in damaged code or deflected intrusion attempts. But should one side triumph, the men and women on the losing side would suffer for it.

"This looks like a standoff," Drake Porter said, putting Rob's thoughts into words.

"Let's try some macro coercion," Rob said. He put on his best "I am in charge" attitude and tried not to be self-conscious about using the command voice that he hadn't been aware of having until Danielle pointed it out. "Ships from Scatha, this is Lieutenant Robert Geary of the Glenlyon fleet, aboard the cutter *Squall*. You are in space owned by and controlled by the government of Glenlyon. You are directed to immediately identify your intentions in this star system and to open your automated systems to examination by my ship. You are also to signal your willingness to be boarded by inspection parties to determine what you are carrying. If you fail to respond as ordered, you will be required to reverse vectors and return to Scatha."

Only a light second lay between the freighters and *Squall*. No noticeable delay should have held up the reply. But no reply came as the minutes went by.

"Now what?" Drake Porter asked.

Rob exchanged a glance with Danielle Martel, who spread her hands in the age-old gesture of helplessness.

He could repeat his demands, but that would just emphasize

his inability to get the freighters from Scatha to reply. He could increase the level of menace in the demands, but the only way to do that was to threaten to fire on the freighters, and if they continued to ignore him he wouldn't be able to make good on his threat. Aside from personally embarrassing him, that would create an impression with whoever was on the freighters that Glenlyon was all talk and no action, which might lead to further problems.

There was only one thing he could do. "Given my orders from the council," Rob told Drake Porter and the others on the bridge, "all I can do is request permission to threaten those freighters."

"How about powering up the pulse cannon and locking it on one of them?" Drake said.

Rob saw Danielle Martel shake her head so fractionally that it was barely noticeable. Her opinion was clear though she was diplomatic enough not to openly say it.

The idea was tempting, though. Technically, that wouldn't be a violation of what the council had told him.

But it would violate the spirit of those orders. He couldn't pretend otherwise.

"No," Rob told Drake. "My orders are clear. I'll request that the council permit us to take other action."

"If we did something, it'd be over long before the council even saw it," Drake argued.

"This isn't a matter of debate," Rob said, his resolve stiffening. "Drake, if we decide we can do whatever we want, even if the government has told us not to, then we're introducing a fatal illness into Glenlyon. The government gives us weapons *and* responsibility. We follow orders. That may sound dumb, but it's far preferable to what would happen if we established a tradition of the military ignoring orders from the government. None of us want to go where that would lead someday."

He waited, watching the others, and one by one they nodded. Danielle Martel smiled as she nodded as well.

All right, Rob consoled himself as he went to his stateroom to compose his message to the council. So he hadn't stopped the freighters yet. But he had stopped something that might have done a lot more damage in the long run.

"The freighters have refused to answer my transmissions. They are not responding to demands to allow us access to their systems and that we be allowed to inspect them, and are not responding to orders to return to the jump point and leave this star system. If I am not given more options for dealing with these ships, I will not be able to prevent them from reaching the planet. Given my current orders from the council, I have no means of discovering what the freighters are carrying or what their mission is or whether they are carrying anything that would be a threat to the population of Glenlyon. I recommend that I be given authorization to threaten firing on them to enforce our demands. If I am allowed to fire on them, the shots can be aimed to damage equipment such as the main propulsion unit with minimal risk to whoever is on the freighters. I must repeat that given my current orders, I cannot prevent the two ships from Scatha from reaching the planet and cannot determine who or what they are carrying before they reach the planet. I must also remind the council that according to our best information, Scatha has a significant number of ground forces at its disposal, while Glenlyon has no effective means of dealing with hostile soldiers if they are landed on our world. Geary, out."

He couldn't spell it out any more clearly than that.

This time the reply took nearly a full day, as the three ships continued on toward the planet at point zero two light speed, or twenty-one million kilometers per hour, and Rob as well as his crew continued to grow more worried and frustrated.

Rob was surprised to see that this answer came from Council Member Leigh Camagan. She didn't look happy, her expression as stern as her voice. "Lieutenant Geary, we understand your concerns and your recommendations and the reasoning behind them. However, you are not authorized to fire on the civilian vessels from Scatha. You are not authorized to threaten to use force against them. Glenlyon cannot be seen as the cause of any conflict or as having acted aggressively. The council does not trust Scatha and is worried about Scatha's intentions, but if Scatha intends expanding aggression against us, we cannot stand alone. If we are to gain any support from other star systems, it has to be clear that we were attacked and that we did nothing to provoke that attack. We will take the first punch if necessary, Lieutenant, so that when we strike back it will be clear that we had no choice. I know that we can count on you to ensure that the *Squall* remains ready for whatever tasks are required. Camagan, out."

Rob sat back, staring up at the overhead. "Great. Take the first punch." He wondered where and how that would land.

And realized what the council must surely know as well, that whatever Scatha attacked, it wouldn't be the *Squall* since the freighters lacked any apparent means to do so. Any blow might fall instead on the planet and on the council itself.

"*They're* going to take the first punch, aren't they?" he asked Danielle Martel after sharing the message with her.

"Yeah," she agreed, nodding and looking impressed. "Maybe it's because they can't agree on what to do until that happens, but still they have to know Scatha is aiming at the planet. There's no other explanation for those heavy-lift shuttles."

"Is that why Camagan looked so grim?"

"Maybe." Danielle shook her head at Rob. "But maybe she wanted you to know that she meant every word. If she had displayed any other behavior, there was a chance you could have taken it as a wink-wink, nudge-nudge that disobeying those orders would have been all right in the eyes of some members of the council."

"That's possible," Rob admitted. "Their experience with me is limited, so I can understand their not wanting to take chances. And Scatha is being very clever with this whole game. If they had responded to our capture of the *Squall* by immediately sending warships to attack us, then they would not be able to deny being the aggressor. Instead, they sent civilian ships, so if we fire on them we'll be seen as the ones who started a war." A thought occurred to him. "Do you think Scatha would have sent noncombatants on those freighters?"

"Civilians?" Danielle paused to think, frowning. "I wouldn't put it past them to have families on at least one of those ships."

"And there's no way for us to know." Rob sat for a moment, brooding, then looked up at Danielle Martel again. "If those freighters are carrying troops, and they land them on Glenlyon, they'll be able to take over the one city we've got easily. The police won't be able to stop them."

"Yes. And?"

"Council Member Camagan told me to ensure the *Squall* was ready for any mission that is required," Rob said. "If our city is attacked and taken, other colonies are almost certain to do something. But only if they hear about it before Scatha has dug in."

She nodded in understanding. "Your mission will be to carry the word to other star systems. Scatha must know that you'd do that, though."

Which meant that Scatha had something on those freighters designed to knock out *Squall*.

But what?

6

"The freighters appear to be loading their shuttles. We can't tell what's being loaded," Rob said. The blue and white and brown and green globe of Glenlyon slowly went by beneath as *Squall* continued to monitor the two freighters from Scatha. In order to do that while the freighters were in orbit, *Squall* had been forced to come much closer to the other ships, only about fifty kilometers away.

"Can you tell where the shuttles are going to land?" Council Member Leigh Camagan asked.

"I have no way of knowing at this time. A lot of the planet is accessible from this orbit. About all we can rule out is the north and south polar regions. When they launch, it will give us some ability to estimate the general area they are aiming to land at. But until they launch, we can't even guess."

"Ninja tells us she is still having no luck hacking into the freighters' systems," Leigh Camagan told Rob. "Are you prepared for anything?"

"As well as we can be," Rob said. "Our weapons are ready."

"Be advised that half of the council remains in the city. The rest of the members have been dispersed to three different locations outside the city. If the city is overrun by whoever comes out of the first shuttle drops, someone will be able to contact you to give you approval to destroy the shuttles when they rise back into orbit."

"What if Scatha jams your signals?" Rob said. "They could have gear to do that hidden on their freighters."

Leigh Camagan paused before replying. "Use your best judgment, Lieutenant. You have followed the spirit and letter of your instructions up to this point, so I feel confident that you will not act contrary to what you know the will of the council to be."

Apparently, there were times when good deeds were rewarded. Or at least acknowledged. "I understand," Rob said. "Glenlyon can count on all of us up here. We are still concerned about the freighters, whether they have some means available that will neutralize *Squall*. Because they will want to do that."

"Do you have any idea what that means could be?"

"No," Rob said. "Our best guess is that they may have intended to hack our systems just as we once did to this ship, but *Ninja's* firewalls have prevented that."

"Let's hope you're correct," Leigh Camagan said.

As Leigh Camagan's face vanished, Danielle Martel called out from her watch station. "The freighters are altering orbit again!"

Rob frowned at his display, seeing the ships from Scatha using their thrusters and main propulsion to nudge themselves higher in orbit and closer to the planetary equator. "That's the third time since they reached the planet. What are they doing?"

"No idea," Danielle said. "You can set the maneuvering systems to automatically maintain position on the freighters so we don't have to order maneuvers every time they shift."

"I know," Rob said. "Warships at Alfar had that capability." But he paused, frowning again, as he brought up the menu to set the maneuvering systems on auto. Scatha knew about that capability, too. So why were the freighters moving around like they were? They must be aware that *Squall* could almost effortlessly match their orbital alterations.

He looked at the options menu, feeling increasingly uneasy for reasons he couldn't have explained, and finally tabbed the "maintain relative position automatically but request permission" selection. It would slow things down, it would put an extra burden on him, but something made him feel like that was a good choice.

"You don't need that approval step," Danielle said as the change popped up on her own display. "Those systems are very reliable."

"I know," Rob said.

She gave him a puzzled look, then shrugged and turned back to her own display.

Fifteen minutes later, the freighters shifted orbit again, this time a little lower and up toward the pole. Rob glared at the automated solution that instantly popped up for his approval, annoyed by having to review it. The orbital change was simple enough, a curve swinging over and slightly down to maintain the same position relative to the freighters. Why did he need to bother with approving it?

But as he reached to change the option to full auto, Rob tapped the approve command instead.

Squall swung over and down.

Rob made a fist and softly pounded one arm of his command seat as *Squall* settled into her new orbit. "Why are they doing this?" he said out loud.

"They're messing with us," Drake Porter said.

"Yeah, but *why*? Why are they messing with us in a way that shouldn't be bothering us? They know we can have the ship automatically maintain station on them."

"It is bothering you," Drake pointed out.

"Yeah, and why is that?" Rob looked at Danielle. "I don't understand why they're doing this."

She shook her head. "Maybe they think making us follow them around will make us do something to justify whatever they're planning on. Or maybe they're enjoying making us follow them around. It kind of emphasizes our inability to stop them from doing what they want."

Rob sat back, glowering at his display.

Five minutes later, another alert sounded, and Rob saw the symbols for the shuttles falling away from the freighters.

"They've launched," Danielle Martel announced. "We don't have a vector yet. I'll get that to you as soon as . . . the freighters are shifting orbit again."

Rob closed his eyes, counting to five inside, determined not to let the annoying maneuvering by the freighters get to him, especially when he needed to focus his attention on the shuttles.

When he opened his eyes, the proposed automatic maneuvering solution for *Squall* was displayed. Rob reached to hit approve, angry.

And stopped himself.

There was something about the curve of that path through space to the next orbit. What was it?

"Lieutenant?" Danielle Martel asked.

"Hold on." What was bothering him? Rob stared at the proposed path through space, trying to understand. Was he simply losing his nerve? Freezing up when confronted with a difficult situation as the freighters and the shuttles both required his attention?

Rob tapped approve, fighting against his own worries.

He was in command, Rob thought as *Squall* began adjusting orbit. He couldn't just give in to fears when all he had to do was let *Squall* follow—

Danielle had said something earlier. *"They're making us follow them around."*

He stared at the curve of *Squall*'s projected path. Which this time ran directly through the orbital location where the freighters had been when they launched the shuttles.

Rob didn't realize he had reached for and punched the main propulsion command until he had done it. *Squall* leaped as the main propulsion cut in at full, jarring everyone on the ship.

"What the hell?" Danielle gasped, staring at her display, then at Rob in disbelief.

Out in space, hitting the main propulsion like that would have altered the vector of the ship, flattening the curve of her path. But in orbit, the rules were different. Adding velocity caused *Squall* to rise, jumping upward into higher orbit as well as flinging her forward faster. Her projected path, which would have run through the spot where the freighters from Scatha had been, swung upward instead, passing above that orbital location.

Still accelerating and rising in orbit, *Squall* leapt over her earlier path. As she tore past the orbital location the freighters had previously occupied, alarms blared.

"Something blew up!" Danielle Martel shouted. "Combat systems estimate we are just inside the danger zone!"

Squall rocked as fragments and a shock wave struck her shields aft and toward the bottom of the ship, then steadied out again.

Jerking himself back into action, Rob cut off the main propulsion, breathing heavily.

"What was that?" Drake Porter asked, sounding scared.

Danielle Martel answered, staring at Rob. "At least one mine. The freighters must have dropped off some stealth mines at the same time as they launched the shuttles, using the same loading docks. How did you know?" she asked Rob.

"I didn't," he said. "I just . . . they wanted us to follow them."

"And you figured out why. If we'd stayed on that vector, *Squall* would have been badly damaged or destroyed."

"We were far enough out, and going away from the blast, so the shields held," Drake said. "No damage to the ship."

Rob nodded, grateful that he had listened to his instincts. He only gradually became aware that everyone was staring at him with a mix of grins and wonder. And that the Scatha shuttles were still heading down toward the surface of the planet. "Back on task, people! Figure out where those shuttles are going and get us back close enough to those freighters to engage them if we get orders to!"

"Why can't we shoot them up?" Drake Porter demanded. "They attacked us! They tried to destroy this ship!"

"We don't have any proof that they did," Rob said. "And I don't have orders authorizing me to engage those freighters!" He touched the comm control, trying to get his breathing back to normal. "*Squall* was nearly lured into a minefield," he reported to the council. "It must have been laid by the freighters from Scatha when they launched the shuttles, but we have no proof of that as of yet. All we can tell about the shuttles so far is that they are headed for a landing site somewhere in the midlatitudes of the northern hemisphere."

He was waiting for a reply, *Squall* swinging cautiously onto a new vector to close once more on the freighters, when three more explosions erupted near the same location where Rob's display showed a bright red danger marker.

"They just destroyed the evidence," Danielle said. "They knew we wouldn't go back through there."

"What have they got as backup?" Rob asked her. "Scatha must have something as backup if the mines didn't work."

"No idea," Danielle said. "You seem to be a hell of a lot better at this than I am, Lieutenant."

Rob blinked, surprised to realize that he had impressed an Earth Fleet–trained officer. "Can we spot if they drop any other mines?"

"Yes. They'll have to open something like they did when launching the shuttles. The mines themselves are stealthy enough to fool our systems, but we should be able to spot when they could be deployed."

"Good."

"Message from the council!" Drake Porter called.

Rob brought it up, seeing Council President Chisholm's face this time. She was still in her office, one of those waiting in the city in the face of the possibility of an assault by Scatha. His opinion of Chisholm rose a few notches. "Lieutenant Geary, have you fired on the freighters?"

"No."

"What are they doing now?"

"They're holding orbit," Rob said. Why weren't the freighters making any attempt to run after their attack failed? Why weren't they at least splitting up to make it much harder for *Squall* to engage them? The reason why suddenly struck him. "They *want* me to fire on them."

"Yes," Chisholm said. "The provocative act. They still want us to start this. Scatha *will* commit the first aggressive act, Lieutenant Geary. We want no doubt of who began hostilities. And after Scatha does its worst, we will show them just how big a mistake they've made."

Before Rob could reply, Danielle called out. "We've got an estimated landing site for the shuttles!"

Rob saw the map image appear before him and tapped it to send the same image to the members of the council. "They're heading for the other northern continent."

"Get over the landing site!" Chisholm ordered. "We want the best possible overhead view to see what those shuttles drop off!"

"We're on our way," Rob said.

As *Squall* shifted orbit again, moving lower and away from the freighters, Ninja called.

She glared at him. "Still alive, huh?"

"Ninja, it's not a good time—"

"The shuttles and the freighters are staying silent. I still can't hack them. But I've been looking at the stuff they sent to try to hack you. It's really good."

Rob took his gaze from the path of *Squall* and the two shuttles on his display long enough to give her an alarmed look. "Are we in danger?"

"No!" Ninja said, sounding insulted. "The walls I set up can handle stuff a lot worse than that. But standard walls wouldn't have held, not even the stuff I saw being sold at Alfar just before we left. Scatha has spent the money to hire some decent code monkeys."

"So they expected their remote attack on our systems to work?" Rob asked.

"Yes." She narrowed her eyes at him in question. "And?"

"You must have heard that they tried to hit us with mines, which would have torn this ship apart. I've been trying to think what their backup attack would be," Rob explained. "But based on what you just said, I think the mines were the backup attack. Scatha wanted to recapture *Squall*, not destroy her. If that failed, they were ready to take us out the hard way."

"Huh. Yeah. That's likely right." Ninja rubbed her face with both hands. "They might have to start talking when the shuttles set down. Can you make sure I get a relay of any signals you pick up between the shuttles and the freighters?"

"Drake?" Rob called. "Can we link Ninja into any signals we intercept?"

"Ummm, yeah . . ." Drake Porter replied. "Give me a couple of minutes to figure this out."

"We're working on it," Rob assured Ninja. "I've got to get back to monitoring things."

The moment Ninja's face disappeared, it was replaced by orbital imagery. "I think I've localized the landing site the shuttles are headed for," Danielle announced. "Unless they make major adjustments in their paths, this is where they're headed."

Rob squinted at the imagery. "An open plain where a big river meets the sea. That looks awfully familiar, doesn't it?"

"It's a lot like where we set up our first city," Drake Porter said. He looked startled. "Hold on," Drake added, pulling out his personal pad and checking something on it. "Yeah. A whole lot like it. That's a spot marked for a future city site by the council."

"I'm getting a feeling that our plans have been overtaken by events," Rob said, feeling tired. "Heavy-lift shuttles. Freighters that can carry lots of equipment and people. And a landing site very suitable for a city location. What does that look like to you?"

"They can't do that!" Drake protested. "It's illegal!"

"They are doing it," Rob said. "Planting their own colony on our world."

Squall reached a good overhead location as the first shuttle landed. The images of the site were slightly hazed by the intervening atmosphere, so they weren't clear enough for perfect detail. But it was still possible to pick out men, women, and children moving out onto the scrub grass that covered the land there. "Families," Danielle said. "If we'd fired on the shuttles, we would have killed kids."

The second shuttle grounded and began disgorging building equipment much like that Glenlyon had landed, as well as more family groups.

"We can intervene now, right?" Drake Porter demanded. "We have to—" He paused, looking worried. "What can we do? The police . . . the people down there already outnumber our police force."

"Lieutenant," Danielle Martel said, "if the council hasn't already started looking for spies, they need to start. Scatha seems to have a really good picture of what Glenlyon has in the way of defenses."

"It's a pretty small picture," Rob said, but he had to agree. Every move Scatha had made had reflected inside knowledge of Glenlyon. "Whoever is feeding them info can't be too highly placed or too up-to-date because they didn't know enough about Ninja's work on our firewalls to know they wouldn't be able to get through them. But they certainly knew that we didn't have anything able to swoop in there and put a stop to that new colony work. They could have gotten that information from Alfar, though, just by knowing what our colony brought with it, and that would have only required combing through open-source contracts."

It only took another five minutes before the council called again. Council President Chisholm looked openly furious, and the shouting in the background made it clear her emotions were shared by many in the council. "Can you disable those shuttles when they lift again?" Chisholm demanded.

Rob glanced at Danielle, who shrugged, then shook his head at Chisholm. "Maybe. Our grapeshot couldn't be used. It's just a tight field of ball bearings that's not precise enough in the damage it does. Our pulse particle beam could, in theory, hit just the shuttles' main drives. But even these heavy-lift shuttles aren't that big compared to ships. Just about every spot on and inside them contains something important, and particle beams don't just stop, not until they hit something so dense they can't plow through or they lose enough energy. I can't promise that shots aimed at a shuttle wouldn't hit other critical components, or passengers."

"They won't have any passengers on the way up, will they?" Chisholm demanded.

"I don't know," Rob said. "Scatha has been really clever about this so far, and they are making no attempt at all to mask what they're doing on the surface. That might mean—"

"A few of the families are getting back on the shuttles," Danielle reported.

"That's what I thought they'd do," Rob said. "Yeah, they're getting ready to lift again. Scatha is making sure that those shuttles have civilians, including children, aboard both while landing and lifting."

Another outburst of shouting sounded behind Chisholm, who gritted her teeth at Rob's news. "As far as you know, would we be legally within our rights to fire on those shuttles?"

"If we warned them, and they didn't comply, yes," Rob said. "But if we then asked for help, we'd be arguing points of law, and Scatha—"

"Would be displaying the bodies of dead children," Chisholm said. "I understand. It appears that anything we do would be worse than doing nothing."

Rob did not want to agree with that. Wasn't the whole point of having a military unit like *Squall* to be able to act at times like this?

But he had to admit to the truth of it. *Squall* and her weapons were a hammer, but the problem they were facing was nothing so simple as a nail. "At this point, I believe that is correct, Council President."

"Continue to monitor what Scatha is doing and wait for instructions!" Chisholm ordered Rob before breaking off the call.

He sat back and looked around the bridge. "We're to stand by for instructions. I have a feeling this is going to take a while."

"It's going to be hard to stand by while we watch those Scatha shuttles taking more and more stuff down onto our planet," Drake Porter said.

"I know."

"Do we have anybody on the planet who knows how to handle stuff on the ground?"

Rob shook his head. "Not as far as I know. When I did my search for vets to put together a team to capture *Squall*, no one showed up as having any ground forces experience. That mixed passenger-freighter that left just before the ships from Scatha showed up dropped off several hundred new people. Maybe someone on it knows how to do ground operations. Did that ship come from any of the Old Colonies?"

"Not as far as I know," Drake said. "I think it originated at Taniwha."

Mele Darcy hadn't spent long at Taniwha. It hadn't felt right, for no reason she could have explained in any detail. She had swiftly hopped a ship heading farther down and ridden it to the end of the line.

She had reached what seemed to be the current outer edges of the human expansion, a colony barely established, where opportunities were both boundless in the long term and limited in the short term. Unfortunately, long-term opportunities wouldn't pay for short-term needs like food and shelter. The local police force was up to strength and not hiring, and Mele's work skills didn't seem to suit her for anything else available. She had sniffed around the beginnings of a naval force that the colony was putting together, but she had no experience with being part of a ship's crew or any real desire for that line of work. There didn't appear to be any local interest in standing up ground forces or Marines. She had actually been more interested in a job that involved exploring the surface of the new planet to augment the orbital surveys, but at the moment everyone's attention was focused on the area around where the first city was growing. Which left her highly qualified in doing things that weren't in demand.

Just to make it worse, she had arrived along with a bunch of other new colonists, many of whom were also looking for work. And there was a lot of talk about two more ships on the way to the planet that might be bringing even more competition for Mele's job search. There was something odd about those ships, a strange lack of information from the government about exactly what they were and where they had come from, but no one on the street seemed worried about them.

Mele was studying the online want ads, morosely trying to decide whether farmwork or construction would take her, when the blare of a news alert sounded through the brand-new coffee shop where she had been nursing a single espresso for the last hour.

What the news alert lacked in detail it made up for in drama. "Blatant and unprovoked aggression!" the announcer declared, looking outraged. "The two ships that entered our star system two weeks ago have been identified as having come from Scatha. While pretending to be conducting innocent trade, they reached orbit and began sending down people and material to establish another colony on *our world*." A map appeared, zooming in on a location thousands of kilometers away from the city where Mele was. She couldn't help nodding in understanding for why Scatha, whoever that was, had chosen that location. It was far enough from the existing city where she was to make any reaction difficult, and by its placement would block expansion by the original colony onto the continent the invaders had occupied. The site made sense tactically and strategically, regardless of whatever its other virtues were.

"We have it from reliable sources," the announcer continued, "that our own warship, the *Squall*, intercepted the ships from Scatha over a week ago but did nothing for reasons known only to the governing council. Our sources indicate the commander of the *Squall* requested permission to stop the freighters but was denied and told to merely escort them to our world! Even now, with an invasion under way, *Squall* has been told to do *nothing*."

Further outrage was interrupted by an official announcement that was accompanied by a dramatic musical intro. A woman seated in a large but mostly empty office spoke calmly enough but with an edge to her voice that she couldn't quite hide. "This is

Council President Chisholm, speaking on behalf of the council. We are as shocked as anyone by the wanton disregard of law and personal liberty displayed by the rulers of Scatha in attempting to establish their own colony on a world granted solely to us in a star system granted solely to us. We do not intend to let this provocation go unanswered, or our own freedoms be limited by the actions of another star system. But the severity of this threat, coming so soon after we have established our first city on this world, is such that the council wishes to have as much input from our citizens as possible before deciding on a course of action.

"There will be an emergency meeting of the citizens and council of Glenlyon at 1400 local time this afternoon. The meeting will be physically held in the new amphitheater on the south side of the city. All citizens are invited to attend, either in person or by virtual means. We will discuss what is known of Scatha's actions and our own options to deal with a blatant invasion of our world."

Mele took a sip of espresso that had grown cold, thinking that perhaps she might find another job opportunity opening up soon. There just might be some call for her skills after all.

She decided to attend the meeting in person.

The amphitheater was one of those construction projects that would once have been the work of thousands or hundreds of people for years. Automated machinery built light years away, using an architectural design originally developed on Old Earth, had dug away part of a hill on the southern side of the city, compressing and fusing the excavated dirt and rocks into the rising rows of seating. Most of the data-support network hadn't been built and installed yet, though, so the amphitheater still depended on ancient fallbacks like a speaker system and drones to home in on anyone who wanted to contribute to the discussion. Mele, dredging up memories of high school history, thought the public meetings in ancient places like Greece and China and New York must have been like this, with people having to physically walk to microphones to be heard.

Virtual 3D software and equipment was also either still missing or not yet calibrated, and that stuff still tended to have a lot of bugs in it, meaning that those attending the meeting from other locations had to be content with their presence being marked by a couple of large display screens that presented shifting tiled images. The technology felt a little medieval, but it worked.

Mele, not being tied to a job, had snagged a place not too far from the platform where the council would be seated for the meeting. Her military service having given her plenty of experience in waiting, she dozed lightly while the many other seats in the amphitheater were filled by later arrivals.

As 1400 approached, Mele yawned and came fully awake, listening to the talk around her. People were worried and angry, arguing among themselves about what to do about Scatha's latest aggression. Or rather, as was usually the case, arguing about what someone else should do about it. Many expressed anger at *Squall*'s lack of action, but opinion seemed split on whether to blame *Squall* or the government for that.

Twenty minutes after 1400, the council finally filed out onto the platform to a mix of applause and jeers from the audience. Once that was finally quieted, the council president stepped forward and repeated the same information that Mele had heard presented on the newscast a few hours earlier.

"They're still landing materials and equipment," Chisholm finished. "All the signs are that they are establishing their own colony on part of this planet."

A babble of shouts rang out.

"They can't do that!"

"They *are* doing it."

"What do we do?"

"Call the . . . Notify . . . Who do we tell about this?"

"Why didn't our ship stop them?" someone bellowed. "Aren't we paying to keep operating that ship?"

"Let's hear from our ship!" came from numerous throats.

Chisholm gestured and one of the display screens shifted to show a man who Mele could see was seated aboard some sort of military ship. "This is Acting Lieutenant Robert Geary," Chisholm said.

Geary looked out across the amphitheater. "I am on the *Squall*. We are maintaining orbit over the site being occupied by Scatha. We—"

"WHY AREN'T YOU DOING ANYTHING?"

Once the commotion subsided, Geary spoke in a flat voice. "I am following orders from the council. If you have questions regarding those orders, you need to speak to them. I cannot act contrary to what the council orders me to do, and my orders are to watch and not open fire."

Mele grinned as Geary tossed the problem right back to the council, where it belonged. Most of the council did an impressive job of looking at other council members as if expecting them to handle it.

"Did the council ask for your advice?" "What did you tell them?" other members of the audience demanded.

Robert Geary paused before answering. "The council did ask

for my advice. I gave it. I cannot disclose that advice without their permission."

A rumble of outrage rolled through the amphitheater.

One member of the council finally stood up. "For those who do not know me, I am Council Member Leigh Camagan. Lieutenant Geary told the council that he could not engage the shuttles from Scatha without running a serious risk of causing the death of civilians, including children. The council could not agree to take such action. Do any of you object to that? Scatha wanted us to attack ships and shuttles full of unarmed men, women, and children, so that we would be seen as aggressors. We will need assistance against Scatha. But if we were perceived as having attacked what Scatha would claim to be a peaceful mission, we would not be able to gain the help we need."

"Help from where?" the question came. "Who else is going to help us?"

"Earth!" hundreds of shouts responded. "Old Earth!"

"Earth will do nothing!" other shouts came in reply. "We're on our own!"

Mele saw police moving through the amphitheater, quieting the competing cries so that one person could pose a question to the council. "Who are we going to tell? Who will do anything about this?"

"We have to assume," Leigh Camagan said, her voice ringing through the amphitheater, "that we are the only ones who will act. We will seek help from neighboring star systems, and, yes, from Old Earth. But there are no guarantees aid will come."

"We shouldn't just react without thinking," another questioner insisted. "We need to do this in a lawful way. We need to give Old Earth a chance to deal with this."

Council President Chisholm finally spoke again. "It would take at least six months for a message from us to reach Earth and a reply to be received. That's if we use a fast ship, which we would have to hire, and Old Earth acts immediately, and there is no reason to think it will. Some of you came directly from there. What do you think? Will Old Earth send forces to help us?"

The silence that followed answered the question better than any words could have.

A man on the stage stood up. "I am Council Member Kim. We cannot afford to wait while Scatha continues to expand a settlement on the surface of a planet that belongs in its entirety to Glenlyon!"

"We can't attack a colony just because it's not our colony!" another council member protested.

This time the babble of argument erupted among both the council on the stage and the audience in the amphitheater.

The storm of debate was broken off by Lieutenant Geary, his voice booming out of the primitive loudspeakers. "We're seeing something different coming off the latest shuttles. About four hundred people who are clearly civilians have already landed, along with plenty of civil construction equipment. But these latest shuttle loads are not the same. We're still analyzing them."

His image was replaced by relayed orbital video. Mele watched the ranks of men and women exiting the shuttles, saw how they moved and interacted, and knew what they were before Lieutenant Geary said anything else. She also recognized the types of containers they were bringing out. Just as military personnel usually wore uniforms, there was a certain uniformity to the containers they employed as well.

"They're military," she called out. "Ground forces, most likely."

A few heads turned her way, staring at Mele, but most remained fixed on the images from orbit.

"How many are there?" Council President Chisholm asked of nobody in particular.

"It looks like about a hundred," Lieutenant Geary reported.

"One hundred soldiers mixed in with families!" Council Member Kim said with disgust. "Using their own civilians, their own children, as human shields!"

Council Member Leigh Camagan cut off the babble of talk that followed. "We can now be clear on one point. This is not simply an illegal colonization effort by Scatha. This is an actual invasion."

"Scatha will claim those soldiers are there for self-defense!" another member of the council protested.

Most people shifted their gaze to the stage and the once-again-arguing members of the council, everyone appearing stunned by what had happened. Mele kept her eyes on the orbital video and saw something she thought she recognized. "Hey, Lieutenant!" she called, hoping he was still listening to the audience as well as the council. "That thing coming out from a shuttle now. That's a heavy, isn't it?"

Lieutenant Geary's response came a moment later. "Yes. The ship's database identifies it as a major component for an antiorbital particle beam. When they get that set up, they'll be in a position to threaten any ship orbiting over or near them."

The sound from the crowd in the amphitheater more resembled a gasp of despair than a cry of anger.

"Is our ship in danger?" Council Member Odom demanded.

"No," Lieutenant Geary replied. "It will take them a while, at least a few weeks, to get it properly set up and emplaced. It'll also require their surface power plant to be functioning to provide the energy necessary for it. Once it's operational, it will only be able to engage targets in certain orbits. But . . . yes, if we kept this ship orbiting over Scatha's base, it would be endangered by that weapon. So would any other space traffic within the firing arc of that weapon."

"That means no satellite will be able stay up there," Leigh Camagan said. "We won't be able to use orbital surveillance to keep track of what they are doing at their invasion site."

"We can't just call it an invasion site," Council Member Odom complained. "There are families among them. We've seen children!"

"Human shields," Kim repeated. "To keep us from simply bombarding that site out of existence from orbit."

"You can't be seriously suggesting that as an option!"

"Exactly what do you think Scatha would do?" Kim demanded. "Lieutenant Geary! That ship you're on, that we captured from Scatha, has orbital bombardment capability, doesn't it?"

"No," Lieutenant Geary replied. "These cutters weren't designed for that sort of mission."

Mele saw Council Member Kim pause, frowning, before speaking again. "But the other warships Scatha has? Two destroyers? They have that capability?"

"Yes. Danielle Martel says she heard discussions about using the threat of orbital bombardment to force us to cough up the money that Scatha was demanding if we refused to give in to the threats from the cutter."

"How much can Martel be trusted?" another council member grumbled. "She was one of them! A mercenary for Scatha!"

"She's former Earth Fleet," Lieutenant Geary argued. "Like

others of us out here, she came down looking for a new start and was recruited by Scatha, using false assurances and promises. Danielle Martel has been screened, and all indications are that she is being honest and straightforward with us."

"Screenings are not foolproof," Council Member Odom objected. "Why didn't this Martel warn us that Scatha was planning something like this?"

Mele recognized the type of look on Lieutenant Geary's face and wondered if he would go there.

He did.

"With all due respect, sir," Lieutenant Geary said, "Danielle Martel did warn us that Scatha would not simply accept our defeat of their first attempt to coerce us. She warned that Scatha would make other attempts, and those warnings were conveyed to the council."

He had every right to point that out, Mele knew. But she also knew that superiors rarely accepted being reminded that they had failed to listen to timely warnings of looming problems. That lieutenant would probably pay a future price for his candor. But not until the government here didn't need him anymore.

Council Member Kim broke the resulting silence. "And those warnings were not taken seriously enough!" he cried, earning himself a glare not only from Odom but from several other members of the council. "We should have done something to prepare for this!"

Leigh Camagan interrupted what looked like the beginning of more major public bickering among the members of the council. "What we should have done, what we could have done, no longer matters. What we have to decide is what we should do now. Our options are limited because we lack resources to deal with an invasion. The capture of the *Squall*, which I will remind the council was the result of Lieutenant Geary's actions, gives us a limited defensive ability in space but cannot counter the problem we face on the surface of this planet."

"What about the police?" someone called from the crowd.

"Our police force is twenty officers strong, armed with nonlethal shockers. The entire force would have trouble handling five hundred uncooperative civilians. Sending them against one hundred soldiers would be suicide."

"We could ask for volunteers," Council Member Kim suggested. "Form a militia, get some military weaponry of our own constructed—"

"That'll take time," another council member said. "If you're talking about the latest military-grade weaponry, the designs are complex, and we'd have to get some of the necessary materials by mining since we didn't stock everything needed for such weapons."

"What about slug throwers?"

"Those would be easier, but, I understand, not as effective as modern weapons."

"Weapons and volunteers alone are not enough," Council President Chisholm said. "We need leadership and training. Lieutenant Geary, if you took on that job, how long do you think it would take to produce the sort of force we would need?"

Lieutenant Geary, looking startled, shook his head. "I couldn't take on that job. I don't know how ground forces do things. I could organize a military force, but I wouldn't know what training they needed, or their tactics, or how to plan their operations. You need someone with ground forces experience. Or a Marine. Who was that who first recognized the soldiers that Scatha landed?"

"Here she is!" the people around Mele called, pointing at her.

Mele stood up, wondering what her big mouth had gotten her into this time. "Yeah. That was me."

"Do you know anything about ground forces?" Chisholm asked. "Any experience at that sort of thing?"

"Yes," Mele said. "I'm a former Marine with Franklin's fleet."

She heard "Marine" being repeated all around. Those surrounding Mele stared at her as if she were an alien creature who had suddenly appeared among them.

"Who are you?" Council Member Odom demanded.

"I'm a recent arrival here. Mele Darcy."

"Why did you come to Glenlyon?"

Mele shrugged. "The same reason as most people here, I guess. Looking for a restart."

"Why did you leave the Marines at Franklin? Did you commit a crime?" Odom pressed her.

Straightening a little more and crossing her arms as she met his eyes, Mele shook her head. "Not that it's any of your business, but no. Did you?"

Odom's glower increased, but if he planned on saying anything else, he was cut off by Council Member Leigh Camagan. "What was your specialty as a Marine?"

"We were a pretty small organization," Mele said, forcing herself to relax, "so we didn't specialize much. I trained for ground and space assault, force reconnaissance, special missions, whatever was needed."

"I see. Then this situation falls within your training and experience? What would your advice to the council be?"

Mele looked around at the thousands present and the screens showing tile images of thousands more. "Um . . . my advice would be to offer my advice in a less public setting. No sense in tipping off those Scatha guys about what might happen."

She sat back down while everyone debated about that. Half of the people at the meeting seemed to think that she could single-handedly defeat the Scatha forces on the ground, and the other half seemed to believe that Mele intended a nefarious plot to subvert the government of Glenlyon. She wasn't sure whether to be annoyed or flattered at the widespread belief in her abilities, a belief that hadn't been shared all that much with the superiors writing her performance evaluations back in Franklin.

Why had she even gotten involved? Why not beg off and walk away? Glenlyon had one small warship and nothing in the way of ground forces to deal with another star system that was far better equipped and organized for fighting. This looked like a hopeless cause.

But Mele stayed in her seat, waiting.

She had always been sympathetic to hopeless causes and had always wondered whether she could win a hopeless fight. Maybe it was time to find out.

7

Eventually, the people and their representatives got tired of debating and discussing. Various council members gave heartfelt speeches promising to protect the colony no matter what sacrifices had to be demanded of someone else. Mele found herself being escorted by a couple of police officers through the crowds leaving the amphitheater and to a newly constructed office along with Council Members Chisholm, Kim, Odom, and Camagan.

Inside the office, a display on one wall showed that Lieutenant Geary was also part of the meeting. Mele eyed him warily, grateful for the chance to get more of a feel for what Geary was like. Her experiences with officers had not always been positive ones.

A frazzled-looking Council President Chisholm sat down at the big desk in the room, rubbing her temples. "That was interesting." She turned to Mele. "Now, we would like to hear your recommendations."

Mele nodded to her, then to the others, shifting to an attention posture without even realizing it before she spoke. "You've got three options, as I see it. One is to do nothing, to just accept that Scatha is going to take over that continent piece by piece, but I don't have the impression anyone here wants to do that.

"A second option is to improvise whatever weaponry you can and hit them with as many people as you can at once. You've got thousands of people in the colony, so if enough could be persuaded to join, you could overwhelm even a force of a hundred soldiers that way. That would solve the problem pretty fast, but it would likely be a really expensive option."

"By expensive," Odom said, his voice heavy, "you mean in terms of lives?"

"Yes, sir. At least a few hundred dead. I don't recommend doing that."

"I'm happy to hear it," Odom replied, sounding sarcastic.

"The third option," Mele said, "which is what I'd recommend, is to get together a smaller force of volunteers, take enough time to train them and manufacture at least a few military-grade weapons, then stage a raid to take out that antiorbital cannon and any other installations or equipment we could manage. After one raid they'd probably jack up their security, so after that it'd be a matter of wearing them down by picking off Scatha patrols or individual soldiers. If you put enough pressure on them, they could crack before reinforcements arrive."

"Reinforcements?" Chisholm demanded.

"Sure," Mele said. "No way Scatha will just leave that small a colony there. They'll grow it, add more defenses, get dug in."

"They're going to try to control that entire continent," Leigh Camagan said.

"If we plant another city to block their expansion—" Odom began.

"We can't," Chisholm broke in. "We don't have enough people or equipment to split off a new city already. Anything we put out there would be small, isolated, and in danger from those soldiers!"

"I agree with that," Mele said.

"You said you needed enough time," Kim said to Mele. "How long is that?"

"A few weeks, at least, depending on the quality and experience of the volunteers. It would still be risky, but if you knew what you were doing it would be the least risky defensive move. A few weeks isn't enough time for any help to arrive, if you send for it, but it could prepare the ground for when you have more capability."

"We are going to ask nearby star systems for help," Chisholm said. "Did you gain any knowledge of their military forces while coming here?"

"Not much, no," Mele admitted. "Most of them seemed like you." She didn't go into detail, not wanting to rub in their lack of resources against aggression.

"Kosatka," Kim said. "That's only two jumps away from us. And they've been established longer. If there is any star system nearby that could help, it would be Kosatka."

Mele saw the council members turn to look at the image of Lieutenant Geary.

"We would have to send you," Chisholm said. "You are our only space defense, but we have no other ship available. How long would a trip to Kosatka and back require?"

Lieutenant Geary looked toward something to one side of him. "At least three weeks," he said, "counting time spent traveling to and from jump points. More likely a full month given the problems we still have with the power core on the *Squall*. We

163

can't afford to push it hard the whole way."

"Why would Kosatka help us?" Odom asked.

"With Scatha being this aggressive against us," Leigh Camagan said, "they might have pushed at Kosatka as well."

"Yes," Kim said, nodding vigorously. "Even if they haven't been directly attacked by Scatha, they must know what's happening. If Scatha gets strong enough, someday it will threaten Kosatka, too. But we can't just let Scatha keep building here for the months required for us to get military equipment from Kosatka. Assuming Kosatka does help, which is not something we can be sure of. And does Kosatka even have any military equipment? We must go with the proposed option three!"

Leigh Camagan eyed Mele. "Perhaps we should pursue option three and send for help. Put together a small force to wear at Scatha's presence on our world, while we also send for more means to combat them. You're a former Marine. Would you be willing to train and lead such a force?"

"We know nothing about her!" Odom protested. "Except what she has told us!"

"It will be easy enough to test her knowledge and abilities," Kim said.

"But why should she be counted on to defend Glenlyon?"

They all looked at her, expecting an answer. Mele had to think about the question before she replied. Why did she care about Glenlyon? "You people seem to be like my kind of people. Not looking for a fight but willing to defend yourselves if someone else pushes you. Scatha seems to be the bully in the neighborhood. If I saw a bully giving people trouble, I'd help."

"What was your highest rank in the Marines?" Chisholm asked.

Mele shrugged slightly. "I was a sergeant for a few weeks."

"A few weeks? What happened?"

"I had a disagreement with an officer about faking data on a unit readiness report. She got busted afterward for ordering me to fake the data, and I got busted for using disrespectful language when I refused."

"I see." Chisholm looked at the others.

Leigh Camagan picked up the questioning. "Is that why you left Franklin's armed forces?"

Mele shook her head. "Not entirely. There were some other violations of good order and discipline. Just minor stuff. But because of them, when the force downsized, my name popped up as a good candidate."

"Why should we trust you with this job?" Odom asked in a sharp voice. "How can we be sure you'll be able to do it?"

"First of all," Mele said, "I haven't said I'll do it. I was just a grunt. Not an officer. I haven't led or organized anything like what you need."

Leigh Camagan gave Mele an arch look. "Are you saying that you, a Marine, are not capable of doing this? That it is beyond your ability?"

Mele grinned at her. "You're good."

"I know. What's your answer?"

"If you put it like that, I'm willing to give it a shot."

"You still haven't told us why you should be offered the job," Odom said.

"It's not like I volunteered for this," Mele said. "I said I'd offer you what advice I could, and I did that. You guys are pushing me to volunteer to do more. It wasn't my idea."

"She's all we've got," Kim said.

"That's a good reason," Mele agreed. "I'll tell you this. I don't screw up on important things. I never have and never will. When lives are on the line, I do things right."

"You feel a sense of responsibility?" Leigh Camagan asked.

"I don't let down people who are depending on me," Mele said.

"Why should we believe you?" Odom pressed.

Leigh Camagan gestured toward Mele as she answered him. "Because she refused an order to fake data on a report. Because she told us she was only a sergeant for a few weeks. Because she admitted to other minor indiscretions. She didn't try to paint a perfect picture of herself or withhold information that we wouldn't have been aware of if she hadn't told us. She's been honest, which I think is the most important quality we can ask for."

"She is our only trained and experienced option," Kim said.

"Lieutenant Geary," Leigh Camagan said, "what is your judgment regarding Mele Darcy?"

Mele didn't think Lieutenant Geary looked happy at being called on. "I don't know her any better than the rest of you. But in terms of her attitude, she strikes me as a professional. And the way she carries herself is a sign that she does know what she's doing."

"Do you trust her?" Odom asked.

Lieutenant Rob Geary looked Mele in the eyes. She met his gaze calmly.

He nodded. "Yes."

Council President Chisholm exhaled heavily. "Then that is decided. We will speak to the rest of the council and work out an appropriate loyalty oath and contract for you, Mele Darcy. I am sure the council will accept our recommendations regarding you."

"So, what am I going to be?" Mele asked.

Leigh Camagan smiled crookedly at her. "You will be the commander, and at the moment the entire force, of the consolidated Glenlyon Marines and Ground Forces. Consider yourself to be once again a sergeant until informed otherwise."

"How are we going to pay for this?" Council President Chisholm asked.

"We'll have to take money intended for other purposes," Leigh Camagan said. "And try to raise some more without harming the growth of the colony's economy."

"This does not need to be discussed in her presence," Odom said, gesturing toward Mele.

"Can you give us an estimate of what you'll need to train a force and deal with that antiorbital weapon?" Leigh Camagan asked Mele. "Just something rough, so we know what we'll be dealing with."

"How big a force am I going to be authorized to recruit?" Mele asked.

"How many do you need?" Kim asked her. "And what equipment?"

Three hundred, she wanted to say. But that would be ridiculous. How could she train that many people? Just organizing them would take weeks. "Fifty people. I'm assuming at least some of those won't work out. For equipment, I'll take whatever you can get me."

"Good," Leigh Camagan said. "Lieutenant Geary will be leaving orbit about this planet soon. Please coordinate with him before then on any matters that need . . . coordination."

"Yes, ma'am." The moment seemed to call for a salute, so even though Mele wasn't in uniform (uniforms—she'd need to do something about those, too) she raised her right hand in a firm salute to the council members. Pivoting smartly on one heel, she marched out of the office, wondering just what the hell she had gotten herself into this time.

Mele hoped that Lochan Nakamura was doing a better job of staying out of trouble than she was.

Even though there wasn't a spark of romance between them, Carmen Ochoa and Lochan Nakamura had fallen into the habit of eating most meals together. She wondered how long that little ritual would survive once they arrived at Kosatka and how much of the irritability she was feeling was attributable to having been in jump space for days as opposed to being nervous about what she needed to say. "Lochan, we're going to reach Kosatka tomorrow. There's something you need to know about me before then."

He raised an inquisitive eyebrow at her as he took a drink. "From that solemn voice and look, it's something bad, which I find hard to believe. Are you going to tell me you really are a lawyer?"

That made her smile briefly despite her mood. "There are worse things than lawyers. Lochan, I'm a Red."

"A what?"

"You really don't know? Back on Earth, in the entire solar system, anyone from Mars is called a Red."

Lochan frowned at her and put down his fork. "The way you said that made it sound like an insult."

"It is. You've really never heard the term?" She didn't know whether to feel relieved or upset at the need to explain. "How much do you know about Mars?" Carmen asked.

"Um . . . not much," he admitted. "First new world ever colonized by humans, right? And, uh, independent?"

"Independent to a fault," she told him. "Mars was cursed by being close enough to Earth and close enough to being like Earth. When long-range spaceflight within the solar system became practical and cheap enough for colonization of other worlds to be feasible, the human presence on Mars grew like crazy as lots of governments and private companies and private groups planted their own little colonies in attempts to lay claim to parts of the planet and its resources, or just to claim their own independence from everybody else. Dozens of colonies, from large settlements to small groups. As the little colonies grew into cities, they stayed independent of each other, distrusting and disliking everyone else. The only time they have ever come together to cooperate in a common cause was for MAWFI."

"Maw-fee?" Lochan Nakamura asked.

"Sorry. That's how Reds say Martian War For Independence."

"Oh. And you are . . . okay." Lochan looked puzzled. "Who were they getting independence from?"

Carmen sighed. "The truth is that MAWFI was all about getting rid of the off-planet sources of law and order. Earth gov peacekeepers, law-enforcement and customs authorities, and tax collectors where those still functioned. But the average Red, to the extent that there is an average Red, got fooled into thinking that getting rid of those kinds of people would solve all of their problems. In reality, all it did was give the strong-arm rulers total freedom to do whatever they wanted. A lot of the heroes of MAWFI died soon afterward because the bosses didn't want them causing problems."

Lochan Nakamura's gaze on her was troubled. "An idealist is a person who helps other people to be prosperous," he quoted. "Some rich guy said that centuries ago."

"I'm an idealist," Carmen told him. "I think we can make things better."

"Yeah, but I've talked to you enough to know your idealism is grounded in reality," Lochan objected. "Instead of rejecting reality because it produces problems for your idealism, you believe that there are realistic ways to fix things for the better. So Mars is full of lots of different places that don't get along. What does that have to do with your not wanting people to know you're a, uh, Red?"

"I told you," Carmen said. "There's no central government, not even any strong regional governments. And all of the places that got set up by idealists who were going to establish little utopias sooner or later got taken over by bosses who were brutal realists. There is no overriding law on Mars. Most of the city-states are effectively controlled by kleptocracies, oligarchies, plutocracies, or red-dust dictators. Everyone else just tries to survive. And everywhere else in the solar system, anyone who sees a Red worries that they are a thief, a murderer, a con artist, or a beggar looking for handouts."

This time Lochan Nakamura's frown reflected distress. "It's still like that? People call you Reds, but they don't try to help?"

Carmen almost laughed in scorn. "No. And I don't blame them. No one on Mars is powerful enough to change it, and no one outside Mars wants to get sucked into the tar pit that trying to pacify Mars would become." Carmen blinked as memories flooded her. "Lochan, most areas are controlled by what amount to gangs. They may officially be called militias or neighborhood watches or something else, but they're gangs. Mars took all of the idealism that Earth sent it and reforged it into cynicism and a survival-of-the-fittest mentality that forces everyone to do whatever they must."

"You're not like that," Lochan objected.

"I was until I got off the planet," Carmen said. "I had to survive, and get an education, and one way or another earn enough money to bribe the right people to get approved for immigration to Earth. I'm not proud of it, Lochan, but I left it behind. No, that's not true. It still stains me in the eyes of anyone from Earth. If they learn I grew up on Mars, they are going to see me as a Red. A criminal. Not to be trusted or believed."

"How did you get a job with Earth gov then?" Lochan demanded.

"By showing the right people that I might have grown up on Mars, but I was not a Red," Carmen said. "And once I could, I started telling people I was from Albuquerque. For some reason, most people think anyone from Albuquerque must be respectable."

Lochan Nakamura eyed her for several long moments before saying anything else, his thoughts hidden. "Why are you telling me all this?"

Carmen ran one hand through her hair, feeling sick inside. "Because I need you to trust me. And the only way I can be sure of that is if I confess to you why many other people wouldn't trust me. If I had kept it secret, and you had later learned of it, you would have had every right to wonder what else I was hiding."

He shook his head, one hand playing with his fork. "Carmen, what you *were* is a whole lot less important than what you *are*. Isn't that the whole point of people coming out here to get a new start?"

"They are bringing their pasts with them," Carmen said. "No one is forgetting who they were or what they learned or experienced."

"All right," Lochan Nakamura said, giving her a stubborn stare. "My past is I was a failure at everything I ever tried because I was so afraid of failing that I kept going it alone and trying to control everything, which just guaranteed that I'd fail again. You clawed your way out of a hellhole and have been trying to help people ever since then. Right? So which one of us is supposed to be an unworthy friend?"

"Lochan, I've seen enough of you to know that's not who you are."

"Not anymore. I was ready to change when I got to Vestri. The events and people there got me moving. And just as you said of me, I've seen enough of you to know what you aren't," Lochan Nakamura said. "All right, you told me. And I think more of you than I did before. Are you going to eat?"

She looked down at her untouched food, then back at him. "Seriously? You're okay with it? Lochan, I wish you were my type. You make a great friend, though."

He rolled his eyes. "I'm noticing an unpleasant trend down and out," Lochan said. "I keep attracting the company of younger women who are only interested in my mind."

Carmen smiled at him. "I'm sure you'll find a woman who wants the rest of you as well. Maybe there's one on Kosatka."

"If you're right, we may be too busy on Kosatka for me to worry about romance," Lochan Nakamura said.

Carmen felt an odd twinge of foreboding at his words.

Getting ready for another short-notice departure was not Rob Geary's idea of a good time, especially since it really was an emergency requiring him to get *Squall* moving as soon as he could. The freighters from Scatha, having worked at off-loading around the clock, had emptied out and were plodding back to the jump point. Rob had worried that they would leave one or both of the heavy-lift shuttles, which would have been able to operate with impunity once *Squall* was gone, but both shuttles had nested with the freighters again and were also departing. That problem, at least, was resolved.

But before *Squall* could leave, there was more food to take on, a volunteer crew member who couldn't be away from the planet for a month and had to be sent down to the surface, and a replacement to be found and brought up to orbit. Not to mention a long call to Ninja, who, of course, had already found out and instead of giving him a hard time offered her best encouragement.

And there was a Marine to talk to during some of his very limited free time.

"Mele Darcy?" Rob asked. He had chosen his stateroom for this conversation, wanting the privacy.

She nodded back to him. Mele Darcy looked professional but guarded. She was standing in a field just outside the current limits of the city, wind ruffling her short hair, sizing him up at the same time he was evaluating her. "Yes, sir. Thanks for calling before you left. Council Member Camagan recommended that we talk."

"What exactly are you? Did the council approve your appointment?"

Mele Darcy gave him a smile twisted by sardonic humor. "Not exactly. It's temporary and provisional. I have now seen and heard those words enough to satisfy me for life."

Rob nodded. "I understand. My assignment is also temporary and provisional. What did they put you in charge of?"

She grinned, a winning expression. "I am commander and sole member of Glenlyon's Marines and Ground Forces."

"What rank did they give you?"

"No rank. They rated me sergeant."

Rob shook his head. "At least they let me call myself a lieutenant."

"That's all right, sir," Mele Darcy assured him. "I won't hold it against you."

He couldn't help laughing. "You're a sergeant, sure enough." Rob rubbed his chin with one hand as he studied her. "I did a research paper once on Marine sergeants back on Old Earth. More than one Marine sergeant in the past ended up as a king or ruler of a small country."

She appeared to be both amused and puzzled by the statement. "That doesn't surprise me, but what does that have to do with me, sir?"

"You came in a fairly short time ago. No one has had time to develop any loyalty to Glenlyon," Rob said. "You less than the rest of us. All we really have loyalty to is our ideals and our friends. What's your game, Sergeant? What's your loyalty to?"

Mele Darcy nodded to him, her expression gone serious. "Like you said, Lieutenant. Loyalty to my friends and some ideals. I left Franklin looking for something else. I didn't know what. I rode a ship to the end of the line, which turned out to be Glenlyon. It's true I don't have much history with you guys, but from all I can see, you're decent people trying to do right by other people. And there's no doubt that Scatha is trying to strong-arm you. So I figure I ought to help."

She sounded open and forthcoming, but then someone with big plans would know how to do that. "No long-term goals?"

Mele returned his gaze. "Are you worried about me?"

"Yes."

"I tend to produce that reaction in officers," she said, flashing another smile. "Lieutenant, if I was going to take over some place, I'd choose one that already had the system in place to take over.

Like Scatha, maybe. I've got no experience with running planets or governments, and no interest in trying to learn. I'm a grunt. I hope I can put together a small force able to take down that base Scatha just set up. And I hope not to get killed in the process. Those are pretty much my long-term goals at the moment."

Rob nodded back to her, impressed despite his worries. "Did you hear anything on the way here about other star systems that were recruiting Old Colony vets?"

"Yes, sir." Mele Darcy grimaced and waved outward. "I came here via Taniwha, where there were recruiters in the bars looking for vets willing to sign on with places like Scatha and Apulu. Nice promises from Scatha, but I've learned the hard way not to believe every word a recruiter tells me. I already knew enough about Apulu not to want to go there voluntarily."

"Oh?"

"Yes, sir. A little matter of nearly being hijacked to Apulu as part of a forced-labor scheme," Mele Darcy explained in the casual tones of someone describing a minor event. "After escaping being a victim, I wasn't going to play any role in that as an enforcer. So I asked around about Scatha. I didn't like the word on the street, and I didn't particularly like the sort of people they had recruiting for them. I'm not a mercenary who'll fight for whoever pays me, and once I looked over the fine print, I didn't like the sort of contracts they were offering. So I hopped a ride farther down and out, hoping to find a better option."

Geary nodded to her. "Do you want to be a hero?" he prodded. "Save Glenlyon?"

"Oh, hell, no," Mele Darcy replied with a laugh. "I just want to do what I'm good at to help people who need it. From what I hear, *you're* the hero type. Captured that ship and all."

"No," Rob said, embarrassed and uncomfortable at the idea. "I'm not a hero, either. You know I'm going to take the *Squall* to Kosatka to ask for their help against Scatha. Before we leave, I'll plant some satellites in orbit where they can watch Scatha's new base, but there's not a lot else I can do for you until I get back. My greatest worry is that Scatha will send reinforcements before I return. Scatha has two destroyers."

Mele Darcy was clearly unhappy to hear that, looking upward. "Bombardment from orbit is not something I want to experience as a target. You hurry back, okay?"

"I'll do that," Rob told her. "I don't know what your plans are, and I don't know what resources the government will offer you. But I was able to capture this ship thanks to Lyn Meltzer. There are other hackers in the colony, but none of them are nearly as good as she is. If a good hacker can support you in any way, I highly recommend you ask her for help and insist that the council authorize a contract with her." He wondered if it was unethical to recommend a friend for a government job. But he had no doubt that Ninja would be the best help for Mele Darcy, and also that if Darcy did try anything against the government, that Ninja wouldn't play along.

"Lyn Meltzer," Mele Darcy repeated back. "Does she understand the sort of support I'll need?"

"She's former fleet from Alfar, just like me."

"Another lieutenant?"

"No," Rob said. "Enlisted."

"Thank you, sir," Mele Darcy said. "I do appreciate the advice. I know two people who were headed for Kosatka, so maybe I can return the favor. If they've established themselves there, they might be able to help you. Lochan Nakamura and Carmen Ochoa."

"You think they might already have some sway at Kosatka?"

"Yes, sir, I do. Lochan is a more talented politician than he knows, and Carmen Ochoa is straight from Old Earth. She worked in some sort of conflict resolution office."

"Conflict resolution is what we need," Rob said. "I appreciate the tip even though new people might not have much influence yet."

"I'm new here, and look where I am," Mele said. "Sir, we're on the same side. I hope we've established that. I'm going to do everything I can to handle this problem with Scatha and keep faith with people like you. Good luck on your mission."

"Thanks," Rob replied. He paused, wanting to say more to the only other person who might really understand. "Does it feel odd to you? Having this kind of responsibility? Because it does to me."

"Yeah," she said. "We've got us an opportunity to excel. How many people you got on that ship?"

"Fourteen. If I get another volunteer to make good on her promise to show up if needed. Far from a full crew."

"That beats me. So far I'm a one-person Marine Corps and Ground Forces." She grinned again, an expression Rob found simultaneously reassuring, slightly disturbing, and a bit beguiling. "I'll take care of the place while you're gone."

After the call had ended, Rob spent a few moments thinking. Mele Darcy, he decided, was either just what Glenlyon desperately needed as it floundered about in search of ways to deal with a foe who had clearly already decided on its own course of action, or she was the sort of hero on a white horse who could do as much damage to her own side as to that of the enemy.

Only time would tell. And he had to use some of that precious time right now to hopefully gain Kosatka's support for Glenlyon.

Rob called up the command displays to check on the status of resupply and whether or not Yulia Jones had made it up to the ship yet, muttering curses as the data froze and the "restart now?" prompt appeared. He was growing to hate that prompt, but Ninja had told him that HEJU code was prone to that sort of thing, so he'd have to live with it.

He really hoped that "restart now?" prompt wouldn't appear during battle if he ended up having to fight one of those destroyers from Scatha.

Six hours later, Rob Geary dragged himself back to the bridge, thinking that at least once they left orbit he might have a chance to rest again. "All departments report readiness for departure," he ordered as he took the command seat, gazing on the projected path on his display. It formed a long curve through Glenlyon's star system, ending at the jump point leading back to the unoccupied star system of Jatayu, then Kosatka.

As *Mononoke* left jump space, the endless, bland gray disappeared, replaced by a universe full of stars, where even the emptiness between worlds felt welcoming.

Lochan wasn't sure if he felt so good because the *Mononoke* had finally reached Kosatka or because it had finally left jump space. "I'm not sure if saving years of travel is worth having to experience jump space," he commented to Carmen Ochoa.

She gave him an amused glance. "Try centuries of travel. If even that would get you this far down and out at achievable sublight speeds."

"I'm still not sure," Lochan said, rubbing the skin on his arms. That skin had felt increasingly wrong the longer he had been in jump space each time, as if it no longer fit his body. The sensation had been disquieting enough that he had no desire to experience it again soon.

He looked around the crowded lounge they were in. "Everybody could have watched us leave jump from the displays in their own staterooms, but we all come to places like this to watch it together. I guess humans are still social animals."

"Most of them, anyway," Carmen agreed. Lochan thought she seemed preoccupied, as if worried. "But it's also midafternoon ship time," Carmen added. "I'll bet if we'd left jump a few hours after midnight, the crowds would have been a lot smaller."

"What's the matter?" Lochan asked her.

She made a face. "I picked Kosatka as a place to head for because of rumors that old friends of mine on Mars had heard. Jobs to be had."

"What's wrong with that? It's a fairly new colony. They'll have lots of jobs available as they build."

"What's wrong with it is the skill sets that were supposedly being sought," Carmen said. "The sort of skills that don't build things but destroy them. And it wasn't Kosatka's colony openly recruiting for those jobs, it was someone working under the table. Whoever was seeking gangers for jobs on Kosatka was planning to cause more trouble. Earth had already heard of a few incidents when I left, but it wasn't the sort of thing Earth wanted to worry about, not when it was so many light years away. I've been worried about what might be happening out here, so I won't relax until I see the worst hasn't happened. In a few moments, the ship will have picked up any news being transmitted through Kosatka Star System, and we'll get to see it even though it'll be hours time-delayed."

"This is Kosatka, not Vestri," Lochan protested. "I thought our biggest challenge was going to be convincing people of the need to act before bad things happen."

"I hope that's the case. I hope we're going to be trying to get people to see the potential problems rather than dealing with existing problems."

Lochan gazed at the crowd around them. "Existing problems might make things simpler. In my experience, people have to be able to see the problems they're being warned of. "

"My experience was on Mars," Carmen Ochoa said, her eyes still on the displays where the local news would appear once the *Mononoke* had processed the signals. "Where the problems were so big that everyone stopped believing that things could get better, so they refused to work together in ways that could have made things better."

"Which guaranteed that things wouldn't get better." Lochan shook his head. "I guess we have to hope for problems just bad enough to push people to want to do something and get them working together because they don't think they have a choice."

"Do you mean fear?" Carmen Ochoa asked, her voice growing harder. "Fear is a great motivator. I know all about that. That's why I won't play that game. Fear can't be leashed, Lochan. If you start using it, fear will run wild and cause things to happen that no one should want."

"I'm not hoping for something like that," Lochan protested, feeling defensive even though he understood Carmen's position. "I wasn't talking about something we'd do to fan the flames or scare people. But if you're right, somebody else is planning to do something. Somebody else is going to try to use fear because they'll want to employ it as a weapon. Am I right?"

She nodded, her eyes dark.

"Everybody out here wants to be free to live their own lives and be independent and make all their own decisions," Lochan continued. "Whatever we do has to take that into account, or we'll be treated like that one guy did, accusing us of wanting to take away some of their freedom. That's when people stop listening, when they think you're going to take stuff that's important to them."

"I hate to think something terrible will have to happen first," Carmen said. "I wonder why it's taking so long for the local news to be displayed?"

As if in answer to her words, the view of the outside vanished from all of the displays visible to Lochan. *Mononoke*'s captain looked out at the passengers, her expression somber. "We will begin showing the local news in a minute. Before you see and hear it, I wanted to assure all passengers that there is no threat to this ship or anyone aboard her. There is no present danger. Everyone is to remain calm. At the moment, the ship's officers know nothing more than the same information you will see. We have sent a message to the authorities in Kosatka asking for further details and any guidance they have, but it will be several hours before we can hear back from them. In the meantime, remain calm. I repeat, there is no threat to this ship."

The captain's image vanished, leaving blank displays and a rising roar of excited conversation.

"What the hell was that about?" Lochan asked Carmen, knowing she had no more idea of the answer than he did.

"Something terrible," Carmen said, her words sounding as if they had been forced through her throat.

The displays flickered once, then steadied into the images of two men and a woman who all had the look of people confronting the unthinkable. One of the men was in midsentence as the sound kicked in, the words carrying easily. Everyone on the *Mononoke* seemed to have fallen silent, listening in disbelief.

"—exact number of dead remains uncertain, but the ship from Lares says most of the city the colony had been constructing was destroyed along with almost all of their manufacturing and construction equipment. The orbital bombardment was begun without any warning or demands having been issued, so the reasons for the deadly surprise attack remain unknown."

"The House of the People's Representatives is meeting in emergency session," the woman picked up the report, her voice grave. "The Office of the First Minister of Kosatka has just issued an official statement."

The reader's image was replaced by that of another woman speaking in the slow and clear style of someone conveying bad news. "Our first priority is the safety of the people of Kosatka. Measures to be taken to ensure the defense of our people against a similar attack are already being debated and decided upon. Everyone should remain calm. We will work together to protect this star system and offer what aid we can to the survivors at Lares. Contrary to irresponsible rumors being broadcast on social media, there is absolutely no reason to believe that what happened at Lares was the initial assault by an undiscovered alien species. The images sent to us on the ship from Lares clearly show that a spacecraft of human origin was responsible for the bombardment."

The speaker's image blinked out, replaced by that of the news reader again. "As just confirmed by the official statement, images of the warship that attacked Lares have been sent to the government. Those images will be closely analyzed in an attempt to identify those behind the attack. Our sources caution that because the warships in frontier regions of space are all obsolete craft discarded by Old Earth and the Old Colonies, it may not be possible to discover exactly where the attacker came from without extensive research into possible origins."

"To recap for those who have just joined us, a warship jumped into Lares Star System a month ago and proceeded in-system without identifying itself. Once in orbit, it began launching bombardment projectiles that caused extensive damage. The governing body of Lares had fortunately evacuated many people from the city as a precaution, but loss of life is still expected to ultimately be very large. The survivors at Lares have requested any assistance that we can provide."

Lochan shook his head, feeling sick inside. Orbital bombardment was something you read about in history books, something that had happened to places in Earth's solar system. It wasn't supposed to happen now. It wasn't supposed to happen in places where new ideas and new cities were being established. "There's the fear," he whispered to Carmen.

"Orbital bombardment," she whispered back to him, her voice shaking. "How can we stop enemies willing to do that?"

"We'll have to figure out a way," Lochan said.

8

It took nearly two more weeks before the *Mononoke* reached the place where transfer shuttles waited to take off the people and cargo intended for Kosatka. The still-new orbital facility felt amazing to Carmen. Used to the ancient legacies of Earth, and the centuries-old, patchwork-repaired structures of Mars, she stared around like a tourist, amazed to see a place that literally had no age to it.

But the newest part of the facility was a security checkpoint that everyone faced as they left the shuttle. Security guards in new uniforms and carrying a mixed bag of weaponry stood awkwardly around the checkpoint as recent arrivals were checked through. This wasn't some old routine using long-established processes to screen people. It was, Carmen saw, history in the making. Someday, this would be marked as the start of something.

She let Lochan Nakamura go through first. He had no problems, of course. Franklin was on no one's list of stars that bred troublemakers, and Lochan himself had a sturdy, reliable aspect when he worked at it. And work it he did, clearing security without a pause.

But as Carmen walked through the screening arch, one of the security guards held up a hand, his expression puzzled. "What's that?" he asked a younger comrade.

The other guard squinted at the display. "Something on her right lower arm. Uh, tap that. Yeah. It says to use the hand scanner."

"Okay," the older guard said. "Right arm, please," he instructed Carmen, sweeping a palm-sized disc above the arm that Carmen extended.

She was far enough through the checkpoint by now to see the display from the side, and with a sinking sensation saw a glowing pattern emerge on the image of her lower right arm.

"Okay, now *what's that?*" the older demanded of his younger colleague.

"Let's try . . . yeah . . . menu . . . options . . ."

Lochan Nakamura stood just beyond the checkpoint, waiting.

Carmen, trying to maintain a calm, assured appearance, wondered what a real threat would be doing while the security guards tried to figure out how their equipment worked. In most places on Mars, the guards focusing on their display would likely already be dead.

"It was a tattoo," the younger guard announced. "See? It got removed. But the gear picked up traces and . . . she's a Red!" he cried, his tone shifting from unconcerned to almost panicky.

Carmen kept herself from reacting as the younger guard hauled out his weapon and pointed it at her.

"A Red?" the older guard asked. Carmen saw other guards focusing on her, coming closer, several more bringing their varied assortment of weapons up.

"From Mars! That tat she had removed is a Red gang mark!

She must be trying to sneak in to . . . to . . ."

"It's all right," Carmen began in her most reassuring of voices.

"Excuse me." Lochan Nakamura sounded both authoritative and soothing. "Is there a problem with Citizen Ochoa?"

The rising tension paused as the guards glanced at Lochan. "You know her?" the older guard asked.

"We're working together," Lochan Nakamura said. "Look at her papers. Look where she came from," he said.

Carmen watched as the guards kept their weapons and one eye aimed at her and devoted the rest of the attention to the first guard scanning the automated documents that were still called "papers." "She's from Earth," the older guard said. "Old Earth."

"But—" the younger guard began.

"Look at her last job," Lochan urged.

"Earth gov." The older guard sounded both surprised and impressed. "Directorate of . . . Conflict Resolution!"

Carmen, used to attitudes on Earth and Mars, was surprised to see anyone being favorably moved by discovering that someone else worked for Earth gov. But Lochan had obviously realized that out here it would mean something positive. Old Colony attitudes that had carried over to the new colonies even while fading in the Old Colonies. "That's right," she said, trying to sound completely sure of herself.

"She's a *Red*," the younger guard insisted, as if that was the most devastating accusation that could be leveled against someone. And, Carmen knew, in many places it was.

"She has experience working in a lot of different environments," Lochan replied. He stepped a little closer to the guards, lowering his voice slightly. "Officially, Old Earth can't do much. But, if someone with the right experience just happens to show up in the right place unofficially . . ." He let that trail off as if something of great import was being left unsaid.

"Unofficially? Oh!" the older guard said. "*Unofficially.* And she's . . . So you're . . . And you're here to . . ."

"Right," Carmen said. Whatever she had agreed to, it was better than being seen as a threat. But she should ensure that expectations went the way she wanted. "We're here to help in any way we can."

"We can't just let her pass," the younger guard said though he looked a lot less certain. The other guards had relaxed, lowering their weapons.

"No," the older guard agreed. "She needs to get to the right people. Maybe even the First Minister? Call the supervisor. These two will need an escort down. If you'll wait over here?" he asked Carmen, acting respectful rather than fearful.

"No problem," Carmen said, smiling reassuringly.

"I hope you understand why we needed to, uh . . ."

"Absolutely," Carmen said. "You're all just doing your jobs. And being very thorough and professional about it. I appreciate your concerns and am glad we were able to clear things up." One-on-one, she could work well with people, and mixing praise with empathy never hurt. The older guard smiled happily at her words and gestured to the younger guard to finally put away his weapon.

Carmen and Lochan Nakamura were ushered into a side room that was comfortably fitted out and plainly not a holding cell. As they waited, Carmen glanced at Lochan and looked around meaningfully, hoping he would take the hint that this room was probably bugged.

He nodded in reply. "I hope it was okay my jumping in there,"

Lochan said, obviously choosing his words carefully.

"I could have handled it," Carmen said, hoping that was true, "but it certainly helped to have two of us vouching for each other."

"Everybody is a little on edge," Lochan observed.

"Did you notice that the new security checkpoint we went through had to have been installed at least a few months ago?" Carmen asked.

He stared at her. "It wasn't in response to the orbital bombardment of Lares?"

"No." Carmen let that hang, not wanting to divulge something that might be overheard and cause the security people to question her status or her supposed mission. Security checkpoints wouldn't stop orbital bombardments. But they would stop people. The sort of people her contacts on Mars had warned were being sought out for unspecified "work" at Kosatka.

The supervisor who eventually showed up proved to be the head of security for the facility, accompanied by the chief operating officer. Carmen, unaccustomed to being treated as a VIP, did her best to play along with their perceptions that she had been sent by Old Earth to help Kosatka. The fact that she wasn't sure of the exact nature of the problems made it a bit harder.

"We honestly don't understand what their grievances are," the chief operating officer told Carmen, who nodded in feigned understanding.

"We just need to crack down harder," the security head insisted.

"The government wants to take the right steps," the operating officer said to Carmen and Lochan, "but can't figure out what steps would be right. But things are getting worse. We need to do something soon and can use whatever advice you can provide. Your arriving when you have is a real stroke of luck. Or good planning by Old Earth!"

"I'll have to take a look at the latest information before making any recommendations," Carmen said, keeping her responses vague.

She and Lochan Nakamura were eventually escorted to the next shuttle heading down, accompanied by a station executive to help them after they landed.

Once the rest of the passengers and cargo were loaded, the shuttle dropped away from the facility and headed down into atmosphere, sunrise appearing before them with startling suddenness as the craft tore eastward and fell toward the surface of Kosatka.

The flight status information on Carmen's entertainment display indicated the shuttle was at twenty thousand meters above the surface, slicing through thickening atmosphere, when the shuttle suddenly lurched as if it had been kicked by a giant. Carmen felt the shock moving through the shuttle and heard the dull boom and knew that a bomb had gone off somewhere inside the shuttle.

The craft slid sideways at an alarming rate, but Carmen took what comfort she could in the fact that it hadn't already started coming apart.

Shouts of alarm and panic were erupting from the passengers as the shuttle wobbled and tilted while the pilots fought for control.

Lochan Nakamura stared at Carmen. "What is it?"

"It felt like a bomb," Carmen said, raising her voice enough to be heard over the tumult in the passenger deck. "But the fact that the pilots are still able to try to control the shuttle means there's hope."

"We might make it down?"

Carmen felt the thrashing of the shuttle diminishing as the pilots slowly recovered stability. "Yes!"

Lochan turned and yelled. "We're going to be okay! Everyone take it easy! The pilots are regaining control of the shuttle!"

As the panic began to subside, Carmen checked her entertainment display. It was still operating, which was another good sign. The shuttle had dropped five thousand meters fast, but the rate of descent was slowing.

The voice of one of the flight crew filled the passenger deck, silencing the remnants of alarm. "We have suffered an in-flight emergency and regained sufficient control to reach our landing site. Everyone please remain calm and strapped into your seats. We will provide updates as necessary."

Lochan was watching his own entertainment display. "Aren't we still dropping too fast?" he muttered to Carmen.

She took a look at the data. "I'm no expert," she whispered back, "but it does feel that way."

"How hard can we hit and not come apart?"

"I suspect," Carmen said, "that the pilots are asking themselves that same question."

The orbital facility executive turned to Carmen. "Are . . . are we going to be okay?" he asked, sweat beading his brow.

"The most critical moments are the ones right after the blast," Carmen said. "If the pilots hadn't regained control then, we'd be in trouble. But they've got the shuttle under control. We've got a good chance."

"You have experience with this kind of thing?" the executive asked.

"A little," Carmen said. Growing up on Mars meant hearing about and experiencing the occasional bombing. She had been startled by the initial panic, then realized that the people around her had never been near a bombing before. To them, this was something unprecedented, something that they had no idea how to cope with. "We're still alive," she said in a louder voice, which carried through the passenger deck. "That means there's a very good chance that we'll be all right."

The shuttle was bobbing about erratically as it dropped, the pilots still striving to keep the craft on a steady path. Carmen felt the pressure of higher G forces and knew the pilots were trying to convert some of the downward momentum into forward motion, swinging the shuttle onto a long glide toward the landing field.

Ironically, now that there was a chance, and the others were calming, Carmen had to fight down her own panic, striving to control her breathing. Dim memories of her mother and father, who had died in an aerospace craft bombing on Mars when Carmen was young, threatened to overwhelm her. Had she fought her way off Mars and come all this way only to encounter the same fate?

Swallowing hard, Carmen tapped her entertainment display to bring up an external view. The planetary surface appeared, growing closer at a rate that did nothing to calm her.

The shuttle's nose tipped upward, its propulsion roaring to life to try to slow the descent.

The passengers were mostly silent now, watching and waiting with silent dread, except for some muttering or sobbing prayers.

Something broke with a lurch and a bang, and the propulsion cut off, the shuttle yawing down and to the right.

Carmen realized that she was straining to the left and up, trying to change the path of the shuttle with her own body. Everyone she could see was doing the same despite the utter futility of the move.

Another lurch, and the shuttle's right side swung up, the nose rising again but threatening to pitch over.

Lochan grasped her hand with his. "See you on the landing field."

"Same here," she said, impressed despite her fear that he had managed to think of another at a time like this.

On her display, the ground was racing past so fast it was hard to tell how high they still were. It still looked like open country, so at least they weren't coming down inside the city.

"Everyone brace for landing!" the announcement came in rapid, breathless tones. "Everyone—"

Still going too fast forward and dropping too quickly, the shuttle hit hard and bounced back into the air, yawing and pitching. Another hit, another bounce. Someone screamed. The entertainment display showed brief images of dirt and rock flying from the impact, then broke into shards of pixels.

The third time the shuttle hit it stayed down, sliding across the surface with a rattling shriek of protest. Shuttles were designed to land vertically though they could slide to a landing in a pinch. Nothing like this, though, this prolonged jolting ride against what now felt like concrete.

The shuttle began twisting sideways as it slid, raising the risk that it might flip and roll, but as the trailing side began rising, the shuttle finally began to slow.

The rising side slammed back to the surface, the shuttle spun about completely as it slid through a dizzying arc, then it finally stopped with a last lurch.

The passengers sat silently, no one moving, almost as if no one dared to breathe, until the emergency exit panels blew out on both sides.

Carmen, knowing what would come next, was already up and

facing back toward the other passengers when they began to burst into sudden, frenzied motion to escape. "Calmly!" she shouted.

Lochan stood up beside her. "One at a time! Take it easy! We are down, we are safe, we are all right!"

The incipient panic stilled, the passengers began exiting quickly but without losing control. Carmen stood waiting, knowing everyone else needed an example of steadiness, despite her own desire to get off the shuttle. A craft beat-up this badly might explode, after all. Where were the fuel supplies? Hopefully still protected enough from the damage the shuttle had endured.

Lochan Nakamura remained standing beside her. This close, she could spot him shaking slightly, but to anyone farther away, he would have looked as apparently calm as her.

The station executive leaned on his seat for support but stood with them as well.

Only when the others had left did Carmen and Lochan, accompanied by the executive, move to the nearest emergency exit and drop onto the slides to the ground.

Once out, she looked back at the battered shuttle. It appeared impossible that the pilots could have brought it down the way they did.

As the pilots and flight crew dropped out of their own emergency exit, moving with wobbly legs and holding on to each other, Carmen began applauding, leading the other passengers to join in.

Emergency sirens were screaming all around as crash vehicles and security raced toward the wrecked shuttle. The sky was blue, flecked with white clouds. The air felt slightly chilly, tinged with the scents of fluids and fuel. Carmen drew in deep breaths, amazed by how vivid everything seemed.

"We managed to dump most of the fuel before hitting," one of the flight crew was reporting to the station executive. "That . . . means an environmental impact report will have to filed, right?"

The station executive began laughing as if barely able to maintain self-control. "We'll get right on that!" Others joined in the laughter, the sounds tinged with relief and near hysteria.

In the gaps between the noise, Carmen could faintly hear parts of an automated message repeating inside the ruin of the shuttle.

"Welcome to Kosatka! We trust you had a pleasant journey! Welcome to Kosatka! We trust you had a pleasant journey! Welcome to Kosatka! . . ."

First Minister of Kosatka Hofer looked like someone who had aged a decade in the last month. But a few years seemed to fall from him as he greeted Carmen and Lochan Nakamura. "I asked my grandfather for guidance last night, and he told me to wait because help was coming!"

"Your grandfather immigrated to Kosatka, too?" Carmen asked politely.

"What? No, no, he died twenty years ago on Io. You should try speaking with your ancestors," he added earnestly.

"No one's ancestors have helped us so far," a tight-faced woman said. She wore a security uniform and had been introduced as Safety Coordinator Sarkozy.

The third member of Kosatka's government who was present was an amiable-appearing man with recent stress lines around his mouth. "Cleon Ottone, Leader of the House of the People's Representatives," he introduced himself. "I'll admit to being surprised that Earth gov did anything."

Lochan Nakamura laughed. "You came directly from Old

Earth?"

"Yes. A city called Nantes." He turned to Carmen. "What about you?"

Carmen smiled. "Albuquerque."

"We heard that you had some experience on Mars?" Safety Coordinator Sarkozy asked warily.

"Yes," Carmen said. "Unfortunately, Mars offers a lot of experience with conflicts on every scale."

"I've wondered what role Reds might be playing in all of our troubles," House Leader Ottone confessed. "A lot of them have gone down and out, haven't they?"

"If you've ever been to Mars, you know why they left," Carmen said. She felt defensive even though she knew the man's concerns were partly justified. "And Earth itself hasn't been free of conflict during its history. Not to mention the colonies on the moons of Jupiter."

"What is Old Earth exporting to us?" First Minister Hofer grumbled. "I've heard that some places are emptying out their prisons by dumping the occupants on crowded ships and sending them to places like Kosatka!"

"There have been a few cases of that," Carmen admitted. "Transport of the unwanted to the down and out is an echo of an old practice on Earth. But the criminals involved are more likely to be political dissidents than violent offenders."

"Political dissidents are our problem!" Hofer turned to look out a large, real window set into one wall. Below, the new city spread out, wide streets forming a nearly perfect grid joined by traffic circles. "At least, that was our problem before this awful news from Lares. Please, everyone, take a seat."

Carmen and Lochan sat together on a short couch while the representatives of Kosatka sat down in individual chairs that emphasized their differing roles. "What's the latest information on the dissidents?" Carmen asked as if she were requesting an update rather than her first data on the situation.

"It's not much different than the older information," Safety Coordinator Sarkozy grumbled. "You know the very latest. That bomb on the shuttle. It was set among the cargo, but whoever loaded it put it next to the skin of the shuttle so the other cargo around it blocked much internal damage and most of the force vented through the outer hull. That's what saved you."

Lochan Nakamura nodded. "Have the, uh, dissidents clarified their demands?" he asked.

"Autonomy for Drava," First Minister Hofer said. "We only have two cities and a smattering of towns outside them, and they say they want autonomy for the second city! How absurd is that? We're not a totalitarian state. We're a constitutional representative democracy. The people living in Drava have the same vote as the people here in Kosatka."

"I don't have information on recent developments," Carmen said, probing carefully for more information. "Or on what led to the escalation from protests to violence."

"Your guess is as good as ours," House Leader Ottone replied. "We had no signs of trouble except the usual political disputes, then, out of nowhere, bombs start going off and manifestos are being issued calling for independence for Drava!"

"We thought we were getting a handle on it," Safety Coordinator Sarkozy said. "But then we got a new rash of bombings, and with this event at Lares we have to worry about diverting resources to protect ourselves against a new threat."

"I still think the Reds coming in are behind this whole thing," Safety Coordinator Sarkozy insisted. She gave Carmen a quick, estimating look from the corner of her eye.

Realizing that, of course, Sarkozy had been told of the tattoo found at the security checkpoint almost threw Carmen's thoughts off track. But she had known the issue would have to be confronted sooner or later. Carmen looked steadily at the others as if unfazed by the Safety Coordinator's words. "Your dissident problem exploded, if you'll pardon the term, out of nowhere. There was minor grumbling before that, right? Then suddenly bombs going off. And, you say, there are quieter periods, then a sudden outbreak of more violence. Just as if there are external factors influencing the bombings."

"Reds," Sarkozy repeated.

"Some Reds may be involved," Carmen said, trying to speak calmly. She had been through this kind of conversation many times. Too many times. "Most Reds who get off Mars are grateful for a chance at a new life and not a threat. But I am aware of information that someone was recruiting gang soldiers on Mars for some sort of work in this star system."

"Someone?" First Minister Hofer asked.

"I don't know who. It would mean that some third party is cultivating the separatists at Drava, using money and supplies and sending in people to create problems for Kosatka."

A long moment of silence followed. "Why?" Safety Coordinator Sarkozy finally asked. She sounded less skeptical than genuinely desiring to know more. "Why not just bombard us as they did Lares?"

"I don't know," Carmen said. "It's not necessarily the same people behind it. And they probably have limited resources, like everyone else out here. Kosatka already has enough means of its own that you could have reacted to an unknown warship approaching your world, right? You could have thrown something together and stopped a bombardment attempt."

"I wouldn't have wanted to be in the position of trying to do that," House Leader Ottone admitted. "But we could have tried."

"So," Carmen continued, "we can be certain your foe has limited assets, and Kosatka is growing strong enough that it could be a problem for a star system set on taking over other star systems. But not if Kosatka is tied up dealing with its own problems, internally divided and apparently at war with itself."

That set them back. "We're bystanders in this?" First Minister Hofer finally said. "We happen to be in the way, so we get bombs going off?"

"Worse things have happened," Carmen said, trying to sound both sympathetic and commanding. "Do you want my recommendations?"

"Yes!" the leaders of Kosatka chorused, though the Safety Coordinator seemed less enthusiastic than the others.

"You need to take the legs out from under the separatists," Carmen suggested. "Get rid of any grounds that might lend support to external attempts to stir up trouble. Legitimate grievances must be addressed. Are there any?"

"They want more local autonomy," House Leader Ottone said. "It doesn't make sense. They elect representatives just like everyone else."

"Local?" Lochan Nakamura asked. "What does Drava have? A mayor? A city council?"

They all shook their heads. "The government is in charge," First Minister Hofer explained.

"What?" Lochan said, looking surprised. "There isn't any mayor? What about this city? No?"

"We're not that big," House Leader Ottone explained. "The planetary government is perfectly capable of running both cities, and running both cities and the towns around them and the orbital facility is pretty much the same as running the entire star system at this point. It's well within our ability."

Lochan Nakamura looked to Carmen, and she gestured to encourage him to continue. "It's not about capability," he told the leaders of Kosatka. "It's about your being the people who run the star system. That puts you on a high level in the perception of your people. Look, I dealt with this kind of thing on Franklin. People want to talk to someone who cares about and deals with them. Not someone who deals with a whole star system. Both of these cities should have mayors and councils who deal with local issues and report to you."

"That's unnecessary redundancy," the First Minister objected.

"Yeah! I know! But the cities are going to keep getting bigger, and there are going to be more of them, and how long are the same people going to be running the entire star system and this planet and every city and town?" Lochan gestured dramatically outward. "While you guys worry about interstellar trade agreements and planetary economic trends, who do the people in each city and town go to when they need a new road or the neighbors start smelting lead in their backyard hobby barn?"

"Handling those issues is still well within our capability," House Leader Ottone said. "The people just need to enter them in the needs category of the gov net, and it gets routed to the appropriate people to take appropriate action."

"How long will that be the case?" Lochan Nakamura asked. "And if the system is working fine, why did you tell us some people are unhappy, especially in Drava? What happens when you found a third city, on another continent? Start distributing political power now, give your citizens a chance to vote for and interact directly, face-to-face, with the people who control their city, and when you reach the point where the central government would be getting overwhelmed or just too huge because it's trying to do everything, you'll already be in good shape."

"That's how things worked on Old Earth," House Leader Ottone admitted. "But we didn't want all those *different* governments like on Earth, which Drava seems to want, and we're so much smaller, we didn't think . . . yes. We've been reacting, not thinking. I think we should consider this," he told the First Minister. "Cut off the justification the separatists are using."

"Even if we do," Safety Coordinator Sarkozy said, her voice harsh, "we still need to deal with the bombers. And if what you tell us is true," she said to Carmen, "then those bombers are agents of another star system. We need to hit them hard, clamp down as tightly as necessary, get the bad elements neutralized."

"No," Carmen said. "You cannot go down that path! That's where Mars went, and that's what your enemies want: convince the security forces to start acting like occupation troops rather than defenders of the people they protect, and convince the people that the forces of law and order are brutal occupiers. If those narratives are not broken, you reach a point where the security forces *are* occupiers holding down a hostile populace, and it is only a matter of time before the occupiers either become what they once fought against, or the people kick them out and place themselves at the mercy of those for whom there is no law."

"The Martian War For Independence?" Lochan said.

"Exactly. The well-intentioned were used. The only winners were the ones who wanted war and the freedom to do anything they wanted to do."

"You seem very familiar with the history of Mars," Safety Coordinator Sarkozy commented to Carmen.

"Yes," she said, ignoring the implication. "Which is why I want to help you avoid the mistakes made there."

"Are you saying there are no Reds involved in the violence we're experiencing?"

"No," Carmen said. "Anyone wanting to cause trouble might well recruit from among gangs on Mars. That does not mean everyone from Mars is a danger."

"If they are pushing for changes to the government, we have to assume that they are doing so to cause trouble for us," Safety Coordinator Sarkozy insisted.

"You can't criminalize dissent," Lochan Nakamura objected. "Not everyone who has a complaint about the way things are done is your enemy. But if you treat them all like enemies, they'll all start to become enemies. Franklin has strong laws protecting dissent. I hope that Kosatka does as well."

"It does," First Minister Hofer said. His expression as he looked at the Safety Coordinator told Carmen that this was a matter that had already been argued more than once. "Let's consider the other part of the problem. Lares. We don't have much to spare, but we will help. What else do you recommend we do?"

Carmen paused to think, fighting off a feeling of nausea as she thought of the victims of the bombardment. It was odd that she had come through the near disaster on the shuttle without gut-clenching fear but felt sick now when contemplating the destruction at Lares. "Earth has seen this sort of thing many times, in many forms," she began. "Most recently during the Solar Wars. There are two courses of action that you need to avoid. One is to freeze in hopes the aggressors either don't notice you or decide you're not worth similar treatment. That too easily becomes an argument for not preparing defenses that might 'provoke' the aggressor. You need defenses."

"We are in agreement on that," Safety Coordinator Sarkozy said.

"The other action to avoid is panic," Carmen said. "Taking hasty steps that don't really address your problem and may make the problem worse. You want your people united behind you, and that will only happen if the steps you take have popular support."

House Leader Ottone shook his head. "We're already under a lot of pressure to 'take steps' and 'protect Kosatka.' We have to do something, or the people might recall us and put in some demagogue who promises them anything they want at no cost."

"We need alternatives," First Minister Hofer said, his chin resting on his fist as he gazed at Carmen and Lochan. "Just as with the dissidents. Show them that we are addressing their concerns. What would Earth gov do?"

Carmen spread her hands. "Ask the member governments for authority to do something, then wait while the member governments debated allowing any action. You, fortunately, do not face that problem. If you want to know what Earth gov would *suggest* doing, it would involve taking steps to prevent a repetition of the events."

"You already said it," Safety Coordinator Sarkozy said. She seemed unable to decide whether Carmen was giving good suggestions or Red-tainted advice. "Get some weapons up on some ships, so that anyone arriving in this star system with aggressive intent can be countered. I've already checked. We can shift some of the assembly processes to get some heavy particle beam cannon put together, mount one on the *Pulaski* when it gets back, and use the *Pulaski* as a warship until we can get something better."

"We only have two freighters," House Leader Ottone objected. "Taking one out of trade service would leave us with only the *Copernicus*. If we're dependent on foreign shipping for trade, that would cost us a lot more than simply the expense of adding a few weapons to the *Pulaski*."

The First Minister held up a hand to stop the debate, his brow furrowed in thought. "Costs. We need to debate this but decide quickly. The expenses caused by converting the *Pulaski* and in forgone trade can be calculated. The potential cost of Kosatka's enduring what happened to Lares would be incalculable."

"What about sending the *Copernicus* to Earth?" Carmen said. "The conversion of the *Pulaski* can be a temporary step. Earth has surplus decommissioned warships just drifting in space and former crews from Earth Fleet who are looking for work."

"Earth is a long ways," First Minister Hofer said. "How much would Earth charge for one of those ships?"

"I don't know the exact prices," Carmen admitted. "I do know it will be far less than the cost of constructing a new warship. I talked to Earth Fleet sailors who said the only reason Earth gov hadn't sold the warships for scrap was that it was cheaper to leave them in a fixed orbital point."

"Do you have names of ships?" House Leader Ottone asked.

"Yes," Carmen said, blessing the fate that had led her to speak with the sailors. "Three destroyers I know of. The . . . *George Washington* . . . the *Simon Bolivar*, and . . . the *Joan of Arc*."

"Destroyers." Safety Coordinator Sarkozy was tapping her comm pad rapidly. "Founders Class. Those are newer and better than the old destroyer that attacked Lares! This data is old, but it says they were expected to remain in service for another three decades!"

A smile slowly formed on the face of First Minister Hofer. "How about that? We get the work started to outfit the *Pulaski* and tell everyone we're going to acquire at least one modern warship directly from Earth Fleet. Get something done fast to fill the gap, *defend* this planet, *and* pursue a long-term solution."

"Our citizens will be vastly reassured," House Leader Ottone said. "And this course of action will probably be a lot less expensive than any of the alternatives we've been discussing. You're certain, Citizen Ochoa, that we can get one, or maybe two, of those ships cheaply? Along with trained sailors ready to handle them?"

"Absolutely," Carmen said. "I can help you get your request for the sale phrased properly and addressed properly so that it will clear the bureaucracy quickly."

It looked like her apparently futile years working for Earth gov might have given her the experience to do some real good out here.

Kosatka's oldest city (founded eight years before) boasted its newest hotel, an optimistically luxurious resort anticipating more and more visitors in years to come. Carmen found herself put up in a suite far nicer than any place she had ever lived.

"Did I understand right that you and I are going to Drava to help cool things off?" Lochan Nakamura asked her. He had the suite across the hall from Carmen's and seemed just as bemused as she was to be living in such grand quarters.

"Along with the leaders of the government, yes," Carmen said. "But it'll take a little while to set up the visit."

"I'm not sure what I'm contributing to this process," Lochan said, sounding perplexed rather than angry.

"You're doing a lot," she assured him. "You're really helping me understand how Old Colony and new colony people approach things. The way I think was formed back in the original solar system. We did some good work today, Lochan."

"And we survived the day!" Lochan Nakamura laughed. "I'm going to have nightmares about that shuttle crash someday, but today I'm still just amazed to be alive! And to think I was worrying about Mele before that bomb went off."

"Mele? The Marine from Franklin?"

"Yeah. Mele Darcy. She was good people."

"She struck me that way," Carmen agreed. "But she also struck me as someone who could take care of herself no matter what."

Lochan wandered over to the window and looked up at the stars. "Yeah, but also the sort who could find trouble in paradise. Or make trouble if paradise felt too boring to her! I wonder where she ended up? I hope she hasn't gotten herself into anything too hazardous."

9

"Darcy, you do stupid better than any other smart person I ever met."

The words of her old drill instructor came back to Mele as she tried to figure out how one Marine was going to defeat Scatha's base and why she had agreed to volunteer for the job.

Fortunately for Mele's attempts to plan operations against the invasion, Lieutenant Geary had made good on his promise to drop satellites in stationary orbits over Scatha's new base, so Mele had been able to accumulate a lot of information pretty quickly.

She wasn't sure what to make of Rob Geary's helpfulness. In her experience, fleet support to Marines usually came only grudgingly and after all proper channels had given all proper approvals. But maybe Alfar's fleet was different from that of Franklin. Or maybe the lieutenant hadn't been in Alfar's fleet long enough to learn all the ways to not be helpful in a timely fashion.

Unfortunately, all of the information she was picking up revealed that her task would be even harder than expected. The soldiers that Scatha had landed were conducting patrols in full battle armor around the outside of the base and appeared to have a decent number of military energy pulse or slug thrower rifles. From the numbers seen on the patrols and in other locations, there did indeed appear to be about a hundred soldiers. Four barracks had been placed separate from each other, each in the middle of what was clearly housing for the civilian families, so that taking out a barracks would almost certainly cause civilian deaths. Machinery had quickly excavated entrenchments around the perimeter that would make any attack on the base even more difficult. One of those entrenchments was a big bunker that clearly served as a command post. Warning sensors were planted a ways out from Scatha's base to provide notice of anyone or anything approaching it. And a few days after the *Squall* had departed, Mele saw the manta shape of an aerospace craft rise from the base and swoop around on a test flight. Eventually, a second aerospace craft appeared as well.

Granted, the equipment appeared to be older and secondhand. But that still left her facing a hundred soldiers with battle armor and military weaponry, dug in and protected by sensor fields, with two aerospace craft providing air support.

And all she had to counter them were some volunteers, whatever weapons could be scrounged up, and whatever equipment the colony already had that could be used to also support the sort of raid Mele would need to carry out to destroy that antiorbital weapon Scatha's people were working on.

But she also had the skills she had learned as a Marine for Franklin. And her experience dealing with the sort of soldiers that Scatha had probably sent.

She would need more, though. Fortunately, from all Mele had been able to find out from asking around, Lieutenant Geary's advice to seek out a certain hacker was on point. Mele had left the open field just outside of the city where a rudimentary training ground was being thrown together by machinery and workers diverted from other tasks, and now paused outside a newly constructed office in a newly constructed building. NINJA IT CONSULTING had been traced in silvery letters on the office door. Mele knocked, then tried the door and, finding it unlocked, went inside.

A slightly disheveled young woman seated before an array of displays and panels looked over at her. "Yeah?"

"Lieutenant Geary sent me," Mele offered, figuring that would make the best opening.

"He did?" The woman frowned at Mele. "Oh. You're the grunt. Hi, General."

Mele shook her head at the other woman. "Sergeant. I work for a living. You're Lyn Meltzer?"

"Uh-huh. My friends call me Ninja."

"What do I call you?"

"I haven't decided yet. The lieutenant told me you'd be stopping by." She looked Mele up and down. "You were a grunt for Franklin? I only met a few grunts before I got kicked out. They were kind of difficult to deal with."

"I met plenty of sailors before I got kicked out," Mele said. "They were also difficult to deal with. Knew their jobs, though."

"Yeah. So did the grunts. Why'd you leave Franklin?"

"Too many offenses against good order and discipline," Mele admitted, having come up with a personal appraisal of Lyn Meltzer.

"You got caught, huh?"

"Only when I wanted to be," Mele said. "Or when I had to take the heat for my red shirts."

"Your buddies in your unit?" Ninja smiled. "You got booted for the right reasons. Call me Ninja, sister."

"Thanks." Mele sat down on the packing container that constituted the other chair in the office. "I got stupid and volunteered to help handle the Scatha mess on the ground here. Lieutenant Geary told me that if anyone can provide me good backup, it's you."

"Maybe. What do you need?"

"Anything you can give me. The endgame is to get inside their perimeter and cause a lot of damage. I've got basic situational data from overhead collection, but I'm going to need more than that to get the job done right."

Ninja nodded, her mouth twisted as she thought. "The freighters and shuttles that dropped off Scatha's people maintained total silence, so I couldn't get into their systems. What about these guys on the ground? What have they got in the way of protection?"

"An alarmed perimeter. Sensors planted out about twenty kilometers beyond the boundaries of their camp. Foot patrols along the perimeter day and night. A couple of warbirds that fly out a little farther on regular sweeps."

"Foot patrols? Battle armor?"

"Yeah."

Ninja gave another nod, grinning. "Outstanding. Most of their security comms will be ground lines to prevent intrusion or detection. But if they're using foot patrols in battle armor they have to have a wireless net for command and control, and that gives me something to break into. And when I do get in, I should be able to figure out how to get at just about anything in that base. When I dug through the files on the Bucket that the lieutenant captured, I found out that Scatha is big-time into surveillance and monitoring.

If you can get access to their secure landline network with a physical tap, I'll be able to give you the tools to do a whole lot of messing around. Scatha's secure surveillance network will have a finger in every important system in that encampment of theirs."

"I like the way you work, Ninja. So you think by monitoring Scatha's net you'll be able to help me get in close enough to take out sentries?" Mele asked.

"Think so," Ninja said. "I'll give you what I can get after you've planted some taps to intercept their net, and you'll have to decide if it's enough."

"That's a deal," Mele said. "Can you help me get the taps we need with the right parameters? I'll see to getting them planted."

"Good," Ninja said, grinning again. "Because I am not the crawling through the underbrush commando type. I do my damage online."

"That's what I need," Mele said. "The council must have given you a really good contract."

Ninja waved a dismissive hand. "It's okay. The important thing is that Rob Geary asked me to look out for you."

"He talked a good game."

"He doesn't just talk," Ninja said. "He's the best in the business."

Mele heard something in Ninja's voice and raised her eyebrows at the other woman. "Are you two a thing?"

She smiled again. "Yeah. He hasn't quite figured it all out yet, though. Do you know who to lean on to get construction of those pickups we need prioritized? No? I do. Leave that to me. Someone owes me a favor. I'll bill the council for it."

"Are you sure you're a sailor?" Mele asked. "You're acting way too nice to this Marine. Oh, I've been talking to some people about getting a few drones built that should be stealthy enough to be able to drop the pickups close enough to listen in on Scatha's net. I think that's going fine because the drones are cool toys, so the engineers want to get them built and play with them. Do you think you'll be able to break whatever encryption Scatha is using?"

"Piece of cake," Ninja said with another dismissive wave. "I got access to Scatha's encryption tools when we captured their Bucket. They'll be using different encryption here, but following the same protocols, so breaking it shouldn't be too hard."

"Won't they have changed the protocols, too?"

"Uh-uh." Ninja spread her hands. "We're dealing with a bureaucracy. You know how those work. Change takes a lot of thought and evaluations and getting past the people who like the existing system and the people who run the existing system and hey it's an emergency so maybe in a few years? And these are ground apes, so whoever they work for will blame Scatha's space squids for the loss of the Bucket. Not the systems themselves. Blaming other people is a lot easier than trying to replace critical systems. What's my timeline?"

"Scatha has landed an antiorbital system. They're getting it set up, but it'll probably be a few weeks yet because of the construction challenge of emplacing the weapon and getting their main power reactor online."

"So you want this stuff before then? You want to hit them before they get the antiorbital big gun working?"

"Nope." Mele flashed her grin at Ninja. "I want to be ready to roll the day they finish getting that antiorbital system operational."

The field that Glenlyon's governing council had given Mele lay just outside the current boundaries of the rapidly rising city. It wasn't much in the way of a training facility, but the field was split by a small creek with steep sides that offered a natural site for obstacle work and a couple of small buildings had been hastily thrown up to offer offices and inside instruction spaces.

She had hoped for fifty volunteers, but only forty men and women had responded to the discreet request for volunteers floated through the colony's social media. A few of them Mele had been able to dismiss right away because they were too old, too young, or in too bad shape to handle the rigors of training and action. A few others tripped off warning signs during the routine psych screening and were also let go with plausible excuses for why they weren't needed.

To Mele's surprise, there had been two ground forces veterans among the volunteers, both former enlisted, both having come from Taniwha like her. One, a man named Grant, had been with the ground forces at Amaterasu, and the other, a man named Spurlick, with the ground forces at Brahma.

Others of the volunteers were techs who might not make great ground soldiers or Marines but whose skills might be critical to carrying out the sort of attack that Mele was envisioning. More importantly, they were willing to volunteer and to work.

She divided her remaining thirty-some volunteers into two groups and started running them through basic conditioning exercises and drills, rotating different men and women through responsibility for leading their group and watching to see who appeared to be a natural leader and anyone who did particularly poorly.

"Why are we bothering with this?" Spurlick demanded of her midway through the second day. "You've got me and Grant, so you know who should be your squad leaders."

"I like to see how people perform," Mele said, not happy with

Spurlick's tone but keeping her own voice level. She hadn't been impressed by what she had seen of him so far but didn't want to rush to judgment.

"I'd be happy to show how I can perform," Spurlick said with a knowing grin.

"Not interested, even if you weren't working for me." Mele thought it didn't say much for Spurlick's professionalism, or his brains, that he'd hit on his boss.

"Oh?" Spurlick didn't hide his unhappiness at the rebuff. "Look, you need me. You just don't know it. What are you planning, some typical Marine charge at the fortifications head-on and take heavy casualties in a glorious battle? That won't work."

"My plans are still being developed," Mele said, her temper rising. "Where did you get your impression of Marines?"

"Everybody knows about them! Marines all think alike and act alike. I'll tell you what you should be doing—"

"If I need advice," Mele broke in, putting force into her voice, "I'll ask for it." Without even realizing she had done it, she had straightened as she spoke, taking on an aggressive stance.

Spurlick frowned, changed that to a glower, then stomped off to rejoin his group.

The day was almost over, the two teams running through their last set of drills, when Mele noticed the second team had come to a halt amid arguing loud enough to carry across the field.

It didn't take a genius to spot the problem. Spurlick was standing by himself, his expression a mix of defiance and smirk. The others in his group were huddled together, either looking angry or trying not to look angry. "What's going on?" Mele asked a volunteer named Riley as she walked up.

Riley jerked his head toward Spurlick. "He won't do what anyone else suggests and refuses to suggest anything himself."

Mele shifted her gaze to Spurlick, keeping her expression unrevealing. "What's your story?"

Spurlick shrugged. "I'm just trying to do things right." He didn't outright say, *What are you going to do about it?* But his tone and attitude made that extra part clear enough anyway.

"Have you ever heard the old saying 'Lead, follow, or get out of the way'?" Mele asked, wanting to give him one last chance.

This time he did put it into words. "So?"

"So I'm leading, and you're in the way." This latest incident was enough to crystallize her earlier misgivings about Spurlick. "Thank you for volunteering," Mele recited without putting any feeling into the words. "Your service won't be required."

"What?"

"You're dismissed. Go."

"Dismissed?" Spurlick glared at her. "I'm the only one here who knows what he's doing!"

"No," Mele said. "I think, of the three veterans here, you're the only one who was kicked out of the service for the right reasons. Now get out of here."

"The hell I will! You don't have any power over me!"

Mele had already sized up Spurlick and had no doubt she could take him down, but this was supposed to be a military organization she was building, and in her experience officers didn't enforce their authority with physical blows. On the other hand, her new recruits weren't ready for the challenge of dealing with Spurlick if she ordered it.

She pulled out her comm. "Police."

The response came almost immediately. "Assistant Chief Tanaka here. What's the problem?"

"I need someone arrested," Mele said, while Spurlick stared at her. "Inciting riot, failure to comply with lawful authority, and trespassing on official property."

"Someone will be there within a few minutes."

Mele pocketed her comm, keeping the corner of her eye on Spurlick, so that when he suddenly rushed her she was prepared. Spurlick's reaching hand closed on air, and his fist swung at nothing. As Mele dodged and pivoted, she tripped Spurlick with one leg while her stiffened hand landed a blow that left him unconscious before he hit the ground.

Mele shook her hand lightly to relax it after the hit, noticing that the volunteers were all staring at her in gape-mouthed admiration that made her uncomfortable. "Never give your opponent an even break," she told them. "We're not practicing for a game here."

One of the virtues to living in what was still a small city in what was still a small colony was that when called the police were able to arrive quickly. Val Tanaka herself climbed out of the ground vehicle, eyeing Spurlick's prone body.

"He attacked her!" Riley called. "It was self-defense!"

Tanaka looked at Mele and shook her head. "He attacked you? He's that stupid?"

"Yeah, he's that stupid," Mele said. "I'm not interested in pressing any charges. I don't have time for that. I just want him off the training area with a clear understanding that he better not show his face here again."

"Are you sure that's all you want?" Tanaka asked. "He knows you're working on something to do to with that Scatha camp. If we let him go, he might decide to go to them and sell whatever he knows."

Mele paused, wondering if she should insist on Spurlick's being arrested. What if he did go to Scatha with what he knew?

What if he did? She stepped closer to the officer and lowered her voice. "No. I want him free to go. Did you ever hear that the things you don't know can be dangerous, but the things you think you do know that are actually wrong are a lot more dangerous? If he goes to that Scatha camp, he might do something worthwhile for us."

Tanaka raised both eyebrows at her. "How is that?"

"He has no idea what my plans are, but he's made it clear he thinks I'm incompetent and incapable. He'll tell Scatha that, and that I'm planning on hitting them head-on like some dumb grunt. And he believes it, and thinks he couldn't possibly be wrong, so if they scan him, he'll look truthful. I'd love for Scatha to think all that is true and base their own plans on it."

"Good thinking." Tanaka nodded toward Spurlick, who was beginning to stir. "We'll read him the riot act, let him go, and if he disappears from the colony, I'll let you know."

"Thanks." Mele watched as Val Tanaka cheerfully cuffed Spurlick and hauled him to his feet before shoving him toward her vehicle.

Mele turned back to the others, hoping she had handled Spurlick in the right way to reinforce her authority. "Now let's do this right."

Grant Duncan came by as she left that team to their drills. "Permission to speak?"

She snorted at the formal request. "What do you got?"

"I think you handled that guy right. Just in case you were wondering."

"I was," Mele said, grateful for the reassurance.

"Are they going to hold him?"

"No. Just make it clear he'd better behave."

"That kind of guy could make trouble," Grant warned, his expression serious.

"I know. The cops are going to keep an eye on him. If I make you first squad leader, who would you recommend for second squad?"

"Ummm . . ." Grant hesitated as he thought. "I'm not sure. Riley shows promise, but he's totally new at this sort of thing and shows it. Obi is looking really sharp even though she only knows this stuff from gaming. I'd say one of them."

"Train both so we'd have one as a backup if something happens to you?" Mele suggested.

"Or use both as we expand to three squads. We're going to have to expand, you know. Thirty ground apes, some of them tech types, aren't nearly enough to defend a colony this size. Scatha's base has a lot fewer people in it and covers a lot less acreage, but they've got a full company of ground forces."

"About a company, yeah." Mele nodded, as much to herself as in acknowledgment that what Grant said was true. She stood looking out across the field to where mountains loomed. The wind coming down from the heights carried scents of something like pine but with a sharper edge, and a chill snap from snow-laden peaks. She had thought about becoming an explorer or scout, being the first to walk places like that and augment orbital surveys. The colony hadn't been able to focus on that kind of surveying yet, but hopefully that option would exist once she'd finished helping out with this problem. "Yeah, this place will have to get a lot more serious about defending themselves. But I'm only in charge right now because I'm all they've got. I'm figuring they'll bring in some officers sooner rather than later to run this outfit, and I'll probably be out on my ear again. Until then, we can build a decent basis for a bigger outfit."

"And then those officers will take credit for it," Grant said.

"Yeah," Mele agreed with a laugh.

The next morning, Mele took a break from leading training when a police vehicle pulled up at the edge of the field. Worrying that Spurlick had done something superstupid, she jogged over to it.

"Hey, Marine. No problems this morning. I've just got a load for you," Val Tanaka said, stepping out of her vehicle. "This is what the colony has been able to collect for you."

Mele reached the vehicle as Val began pulling out a variety of weapons. Mele hefted one of the hunting rifles, putting it to her shoulder and turning to sight along it across the open land beyond the city. "Not bad."

"One of the best we got," Val said. "Four hunting rifles, two target pistols, and a half dozen shockers. That's the rest of it."

Twelve weapons for thirty volunteers including Mele. And only four of those able to deliver lethal blows. The in-theory-easy-to-reprogram construction bays were having problems with the available designs of military-grade weapons, so this was all they'd have for the near future. Mele shook her head. "It'll have to do."

"Can it?" Val Tanaka asked. "Seriously. I've got no idea, but I heard you say those Scatha soldiers have battle armor. I've seen that stuff. It's bad news."

"It is," Mele agreed. She gestured toward the rifle she still held in one hand, the barrel pointed at the ground. "But if I can get close enough, this can handle that armor. I know that gear. It's the same stuff Brahma imported from Old Earth, so at Franklin we drilled on how to combat it. I wouldn't be surprised if Brahma resold it to Scatha."

"It's got weak points?"

"Everything has got weak points." Mele set the rifle down carefully, then grinned at Val. "Armor. Weapons. People."

"You're the expert." Tanaka looked down at the small arsenal, then back at Mele. "I was thinking."

"That can get you into trouble," Mele said.

"I know," Val agreed. She pointed at one of the shockers. "I've spent a good chunk of my life working with these. Weapons designed to disable, not to harm. Oh, they can be misused. Anything can. But basically, the idea is not to kill with them."

Mele nodded, letting her own expression grow serious. "Whereas I'm in the business of killing and need weapons that do that."

"Does it bother you?"

"Sure it does. But I don't do it because someone ordered it or because I want something," Mele said. "I do it because if I don't, people like you would get killed by apes like those guys from Scatha."

"Yeah," Val agreed. "I just found myself wondering where it all might lead. I know a little bit of history from Old Earth, the sort of junk that happened there." She looked up at the sky as if the already-legendary globe of Earth would be visible above them. "And I thought, what if we ever get to the point where it happens here? Wars like they had back on Old Earth, where nobody uses shockers, and it's just about killing. What if our descendants forget that once upon a time we thought not killing was important?"

"I don't see how it could ever get that bad," Mele said. "Glenlyon is not happy to be doing this. I can feel it. They're only getting into military options because that's all there are with Scatha playing hardball."

"I hope you're right," Val Tanaka said. "But look at what's happening now. How many times back at Franklin did you use your training in earnest?"

"You mean actual combat?" Mele shrugged. "Once. A hostage-rescue operation. The hostage takers were some paramilitary bunch, though, not a real professional outfit."

"But here you are facing a bunch of soldiers, and we've already dealt with a warship threatening us." Val shook her head. "This isn't like the Old Colonies. Everything has gone off the rails. Who knows where we might end up?"

"All I can promise," Mele said, "is that as long as I'm calling the shots, we're not going to end up anywhere you'd be unhappy with."

"How long will you be calling the shots?"

"Probably only until they can replace me." Mele slapped Val on the shoulder. "But until then, I *am* going to lead this outfit in the right ways. Hey, I need to get over to the mining offices. Can you give me a lift?"

Getting to Scatha's base without getting shot to pieces meant coming in on the ground was out. Coming in by air, using one of the available shuttles, would just have been a more complicated form of suicide than a ground approach.

Which, Mele knew, left one available option. And that led her to the tech offices of the newly named Glenlyon Mining Corporation.

Not so long a time ago on a planet far, far away, Gunnery Sergeant Chopra had explained to a younger Mele how to get things done even if whatever it was apparently couldn't be done.

"You don't go to the boss," Chopra had advised. "And you don't go to the admin people who approve stuff. You go direct to the techs. The engineers. But you don't go in and say, 'The equipment can't do what I need. Can you make it do that?' Because if you do, the engineers will say, 'No, it can't do that,' because people tell them to do crazy stuff all the time, and they'll be tired of that. What you do is go in to them and say, 'I just want to confirm this gear can do this,' and the engineers say, 'Yeah, it can do that.' Then you say, 'What I really need is this other thing, but the scientists I talked to said it can't be done.' And they'll look real annoyed and say, 'Scientists? You mean theory guys? What is it you need done?' And then the engineers look at the specs and start talking to each other, and figuring out how to do it, because there's nothing an engineer loves more than doing something that a scientist says can't be done. Nine times out of ten, they'll figure out a way to do it, or a way that ought to do it. And they'll build it."

Gunnery Sergeant Chopra had paused to give Mele a warning look. "What you got to look out for then is that whatever the engineers built might not meet everyday rules for safety and common sense. It if looks like that to you, make sure you're outside any potential blast radius before they try it out the first time."

That was why Mele was walking into the tech offices, where two men and a woman looked up at her with open suspicion.

"Hi," Mele said. "I'm Sergeant Darcy, working on dealing with that base that Scatha set up. I figure I need to approach it belowground, so I came to you guys to make sure one of your mine snakes can handle it."

"A tunnel dig? Where at?" one of the engineers asked, still eyeing Mele with mistrust.

"Do you have data on the area around where Scatha landed?" She knew they did but waited for them to look it up. A layered display revealed the surface geography as plotted by orbital mapping. "I need to keep Scatha's people from seeing it, so I figured we could come in on the far side of these hills and start digging down about here, going to about here," Mele said, indicating a point short of Scatha's sensor field.

"Yeah, that's easy," the female engineer commented. "A two-meter snake can handle that without any problem. Why are you stopping the dig so far out?"

"It's this sensor field," Mele explained, sweeping her hand across the image. "It'll pick up vibrations from the digging if I get too close."

The third engineer shook his head. "There's a big river running right through there. All that water is going to be putting a lot of vibrations into the environment. And the coast is, what, twenty kilometers to the west? What are the waves like?"

"Fairly strong," Mele said. "It's potentially a good harbor, but until a breakwater is built up along this row of submerged rocks, the waves can roll right in off the ocean."

"So you've got good wave action hitting the area, too. What's the subsurface like?"

The woman engineer answered as she called up the data. "We've got satellite scans showing an average of four meters of topsoil. That's a floodplain, isn't it? Under that is several layers of sedimentary rock."

"Sandstone?" the third engineer asked.

"Overhead scans saw a mix of siltstone farther inland and limestone closer to the coast."

"That'll conduct vibrations from the wave action and the river pretty well," the first engineer remarked.

Mele feigned surprise. "Do you think there's a way to get the dig closer without its being detected? The approval office told me that was impossible."

"Approval office?" the third engineer said with disgust. "How close do you really want to get?"

"In my dreams? Here," Mele said, pointing to a spot inside the sensor field.

"How good are the sensors?"

"Here are the specs on them as best we know."

The three engineers huddled, calling up diagrams and schematics and soil-characteristic data. "That's doable," the first engineer finally said. "We bring the snake in along that line. Not the one you thought of. This will make better use of the geology. The snake sends out worms ahead to monitor the vibrations in the environment and send that data back to the snake so it can adjust digging speed to keep the noise low enough. You're going through topsoil, so it won't require eating rock."

"Rock eating can get noisy," the female engineer told Mele. "The snake seals the tunnel sides as it goes using instacrete, so you won't have to worry about tunnel integrity."

"We ought to modify these parts to reduce the operating noise," the third engineer suggested.

"Yeah, good idea since it's only going through soil. Add that in and . . . How soon do you need this dig started?" the woman engineer asked.

"Yesterday," Mele said. "I've got to hit Scatha before they get more stuff landed. You guys can really do this?"

"Sure we can," the first engineer assured her. "It's an interesting challenge. But it'll take a day or two to get this ready, and you'll need someone to tell the front office the council will pay for it."

"You guys are lifesavers!" Mele said, not having to fake her relief. "Oh, I've got to tell you, this needs to be kept really quiet. If Scatha finds out I'm planning to go in this way, they'd be waiting for me and . . ."

"Yeah," the third engineer said, nodding. "So this is real top secret stuff, huh?"

"It really is," Mele said. "Once we've hit Scatha, they'll search for and find the dig, so you can talk about it then. You said the tunnel will be two meters in diameter? That'll be a little tight, but we can run."

"No," the woman engineer said. "Use a tunnelpede."

"Tunnelpede?"

"Long, low, lots of little soft wheels. Designed to go into tight places where you might not want a lot of vibrations, you know? Like checking on cave-ins or unstable areas. Just get a tunnelpede long enough for everyone in your group to ride. How are you planning on getting the snake there? One of the WinGs?"

"Yeah," Mele said. "Can one of the smaller ones handle the snake?"

"Sure can," the first engineer advised. "Don't talk to Don. He's supposed to be in charge of scheduling the WinGs, but Bettine is the one who really handles that. She'll set you up."

As Mele walked out of the building, she looked up at the sky in what she hoped was the general direction of Franklin. "Thanks, Gunny!"

The WinG park had been set up down near the coast. All three Wing-in-Ground vehicles were there when Mele arrived. The WinGs only flew a few meters above the surface of the water, but the ground-effect cushion that lofted them allowed WinGs to transport waterborne ship-sized cargos at aerospace craft speeds, and the WinGs could land on water or on beaches or other unimproved sites, making them perfect for new colonies on new worlds.

The big WinG loomed over the others, roughly cylindrical, thirty meters wide and over a hundred fifty meters long, with broad, stubby wings mounted low and propulsion mounted high, and large aerospace craft maneuvering surfaces aft. The two smaller WinGs were each about forty meters long and ten meters wide, shaped similarly to their larger sister.

None of them carried any armament, but because they flew so low, one of the smaller WinGs could easily come in from the right direction to remain hidden from the Scatha base behind the low hills as it delivered the mining snake. As far as improvised combat-delivery vehicles went, the WinGs were as good as it got.

Mele went into the small office attached to a maintenance hangar, looking for Bettine.

Two days later, a visit from Val Tanaka interrupted another training session. "Your boy Spurlick is officially missing."

"Any clues?" Mele asked.

"Pretty big clues, actually. He volunteered to assist a team recovering an automated weather station along the coast about fifty kilometers south of where Scatha set up shop. When it came time to leave, he was nowhere to be found. I'd tipped off the team leader that might happen, so they didn't panic, and after a decent search to make sure he really had run, they reported it and came on back."

"Thanks, Val. You keep bringing me good news." Mele grinned. "You know, it's getting so I'm actually looking forward to seeing a police officer coming to talk to me."

Val Tanaka shook her head at Mele. "I know an act when I see one, Sergeant Darcy. You're not a bad girl. You just like testing limits. And right now, you've got a job that is testing your own limits in a good way. Let's keep it like that."

"I'll think about it," Mele said. "By the way, if you need to pass on anything else in the next twelve hours or so, just get ahold of Grant Duncan. I'm going to be busy."

Val raised her eyebrows at Mele. "Out of town?"

"Way out."

"Be careful. Do you need a ride to the WinG station?"

Mele nodded. "In about half an hour."

"It's a quiet day. I can wait. You're less likely to be noticed if you're scrunched down in my ride."

Unlike the hard but smoother grass of the area around the city, the scrub underneath Mele had sharp, small needles on tiny, stubby branches. Mele breathed a silent curse as she acquired cuts on exposed flesh while she wormed her way high enough to see over the rise. The plants gave off a slightly spicy, slightly musky scent that threatened to make her sneeze. Overhead, stars shone in patterns that still felt unfamiliar. The silence of the night around her was broken by occasional clicks and cheeps from unseen insects. Glenlyon didn't seem to have evolved anything like snakes, but there were a variety of small weasel-like creatures that could be trouble if their nests were disturbed, so Mele kept a careful watch as she crawled forward.

Scatha liked lights, it seemed. The base was brightly lit, with floods shining both inward and outward along the edges. Mele narrowed her eyelids to keep from losing all of her night vision, then eased back down and hauled out the drone a team of engineers had modified to be as stealthy as could be managed. The engineers had had so much fun with it that Mele had found it hard to "borrow" for the time needed to get her task done.

Loading passive signal collectors each the size of her thumb onto the drone, Mele breathed a short prayer before cautiously activating the drone and letting it rise less than a meter above the scrub. The signal collectors, at first pale against the darker drone, quickly shaded to match their surroundings, becoming very hard to see.

If the drone had sent out signals, or if Mele had transmitted commands to it, Scatha's sensors would have picked them up and alerted the defenders. Instead, a nearly invisible and very hard to break fiber-optic cord connected to Mele's controller unspooled from the drone as it slid toward Scatha's base. Each signal collector was linked to the cord as well, so that together they formed a network that could transmit whatever they overheard back along the cord to a relay transmitter out of sight of Scatha's sensors.

Mele had to estimate where to drop each sensor so that the long pin on the bottom would plunge into the topsoil and hold the sensor upright in place. One, two, three . . .

A spotlight mounted on a sensor pole came to life, playing over the sensor field in the general area where the drone was. Something must have spotted the movement of the drone. Mele dropped the last two pickups, then made the drone zig and zag wildly a couple of times before ordering it back up the slope at a fast clip, then dropping it low and slow. A sensor tech wanting to impress her had told Mele about that trick, which would lead anything detecting that movement to conclude a small animal had tripped the sensors.

She waited, tense, as the light flicked back and forth, but it never settled on the drone.

She got the drone back, carefully deactivated it, then slid down the back slope, out of sight of the base. Planting the relay unit didn't take long. Mele plugged in the fiber-optic link to the pickups, touched the link commands, and within a minute got the confirmation signals from the satellite overhead and the signal collection pickups. The relay would compress everything the signal collectors picked up and send it in second-long bursts up to the satellite, which would send the material on to Ninja.

Mele took the risk of crawling up the rise again to study what could be seen of Scatha's base. After several minutes of lying unmoving, she spotted what she had been looking for, the distant shapes of two soldiers patrolling the inner edge of the sensor field. She watched them intently, getting a personal feel for how those soldiers were moving and acting. As far as she could tell, Scatha's soldiers weren't looking around as they trudged along their patrol route, instead depending on their armors' sensors to alert them to any dangers that they clearly did not think threatened. They had probably heard that Glenlyon lacked any ground forces or military equipment, and nothing had happened since they arrived to cause them to think that Glenlyon would do anything but complain about their presence.

Mele wondered whether Spurlick had already made it to Scatha's base. Probably not. Spurlick hadn't looked like he could cover that much ground that fast. Still, she was glad that her best route to plant the pickups had been on the north side of Scatha's camp while Spurlick would be coming in from the south. There wasn't any chance of his stumbling across her.

Finally, Mele slid back down the rise and, keeping low, ran along the back side of the terrain until she reached the place where WinG Bravo rested behind a higher slope. She paused long enough to let the people inside the WinG identify her, then gratefully climbed into the personnel hatch that opened on the side.

"How was it?" one of the pilots asked, as the other gently brought the WinG up and around.

"Piece of cake," Mele said, gratefully drinking from the water bulb offered by the pilot.

"How come you're sweating so much, then?"

"Gland condition," Mele said.

The pilot laughed as WinG Bravo accelerated along the ground, over the beach in a flash, and swung south to avoid being spotted by Scatha's base.

10

"How's it look?" Mele asked, leaning to gaze at some of the displays wrapped in front of Ninja's desk.

"Very nice," Ninja said, her eyes on the displays as her hands and fingers moved around controls and inputs. "You didn't plant the listening array perfectly, but pretty close."

"It wasn't under ideal conditions," Mele said dryly.

"You got to crawl around in the mud and get dirt in your teeth, Marine," Ninja said. "I bet you loved it. Sorry there aren't any snakes to eat on this planet."

"Yeah, it's that far short of paradise," Mele agreed.

"Ah, lookee here," Ninja said. "I recognize that. And hit with this and . . . yeah. I'll be able to get in. What exactly are you going to need me to do?"

Mele pondered the question for a moment, thinking back to Gunny Chopra again. "Are you a scientist or an engineer?"

Ninja grinned. "I am a sorcerer. High priestess of the Temple of Lovelace. Practitioner of the High Code and Breaker of

Firewalls. And also Grand Deceiver of the SysAdmins."

"In that case," Mele said, laughing, "I need to be able to be invisible to Scatha's sensors, including their battle armor internals."

"Uh-huh. What else?"

Mele's laughter faded as she looked incredulously at Ninja. "I need their full security layout, patrol schedules, entry codes, and lock overrides."

"Yeah, of course." Ninja nodded and sat back, smiling at Mele. "When do you need it, Marine?"

"Whenever you can get it, Sorcerer. You know what my timeline is."

"Yeah," Ninja repeated. "So you also need their planned date for finishing work on the antiorbital system and activating it, and updates on whether they are keeping to schedule, right?"

"Right." Mele leaned against the wall, crossing her arms and grinning at Ninja. "Where have you been all my life?"

Ninja looked upward and sighed. "Trying to figure out how to hack the heart of Lieutenant Rob Geary. The rest of this stuff is easy by comparison."

"Maybe I can help nudge him your way," Mele said. "Something subtle like a kick in the butt. That usually gets a guy's attention."

"Thanks for the Marine romance tip, but I'd rather you focused on not getting killed. Even if I give you everything you want and need, this is still going to be dangerous as hell, right?"

Mele weighed possible responses, finally deciding on the simplest one. "Right."

She had been called on the carpet enough during her time in Franklin's Marines that Mele wasn't too intimidated to be standing before the three council members who made up Glenlyon's Defense Subcouncil. Not that she liked the experience.

It helped that Leigh Camagan was the chair of the subcouncil. Mele had quickly sized up Camagan as someone you played straight with because if you did, she would return the favor. Council Member Kim was a usually reliable ally except that he had exaggerated ideas of his own ability to understand real-world military operations. Council Member Odom, on the other hand, had been put on the subcouncil to represent the dovish sentiments in the colony, which meant he spent most of his time trying to second-guess, undermine, and block Mele. Not that that was entirely a bad thing. She had learned the importance of having oversight that made her question her own assumptions.

"When do you intend doing something about Scatha's intrusion on this planet?" Kim demanded. "They've almost finished work on setting up their antiorbital defense system! What are you waiting for?"

Mele spoke with calm certainty. "Aside from the need to get in as much training as possible and make the necessary preparations, I'm planning on hitting them the night *after* they make that system operational. That's what I'm waiting for."

Kim stared in wordless amazement. Odom gave Mele a suspicious look. Leigh Camagan rested her chin on the palm of one hand. "Why?" she asked.

Trust Camagan to ask for an explanation before making up her mind. Mele gestured in the general direction of Scatha's encampment. "Three reasons. First, I don't want to alert them that we're a danger. They've been sitting on this planet for a few weeks, and we haven't done anything except mouth at them."

"We have attempted to negotiate their departure and expressed our intentions to not accept their illegal actions," Odom corrected in a severe tone.

"Yes, sir," Mele said. "The point is, right now, those ground apes from Scatha are thinking we're all talk and no trouble. They've relaxed their guard. I was able to check them out from ground level when planting our surveillance pickups, and those apes are not staying sharp.

"Second, when they get that antiorbital cannon online, they're going to relax even more because they're going to feel really safe with that big gun working. They'll celebrate, they'll feel protected by the big gun, and they'll take it a little easier. That'll be the best time to strike."

Mele smiled, but this time it was a hard smile, with little humor to it. "And, third, because after feeling so safe and relaxed, having that system destroyed right under their noses is going to hit them all the harder. They're going to go from overconfident to extra-spooked, and once we have them scared, we can keep pushing with smaller moves that will wear away their morale and set them up to fold without a tough fight. If we have enough time for that. It's just like in a one-on-one fight. If you get the other guy scared, off-balance, then you can keep them that way, and they'll be that much easier to beat."

"I see." Leigh Camagan nodded toward each of her fellow members. "That sounds like excellent reasoning."

"Where did an enlisted Marine pick up that kind of thinking?" Odom demanded.

Mele smiled at him even though she wanted to make a very rude gesture in reply. Alas, part of being in command meant that she couldn't give in to that kind of temptation anymore. "Listening to my officers talk tactics and strategy. And reading. There's this guy named Sun Tzu. Real old Old Earth. Part of what he talks about is beating the enemy before you start fighting by laying the right groundwork."

"That's good," Kim said. Having seen Odom's hostility, he was throwing himself fully into support of Mele. "That's very good."

"She's working from theory," Odom said.

"She is trying to achieve victory by causing as few deaths among the enemy as possible," Leigh Camagan said. "That is your intention, is it not?" she asked Mele.

"Yes, it is," Mele confirmed. "In particular, to avoid any casualties at all among the civilians Scatha brought."

"That is surely what we want, isn't it?" Leigh Camagan asked Odom.

Odom hesitated, then nodded with a sour expression. "Yes."

"Then, having heard Major Darcy's explanation of her strategy, I move that we endorse it."

Mele ran the last sentence through her head again, wondering if she had heard right. No. She must have misheard part of it.

"I'm still concerned," Odom said. "We've seen the data our pickups are gathering. You say that Scatha's soldiers are complacent," he told Mele, "yet our pickups are detecting usually two or three weapon discharges a night by sentries."

Mele nodded. "That's one of the reasons I know they're slacking off," she explained. "Sentries and patrols get bored if nothing happens, and when they get bored, there's a real strong temptation to let off a shot just for fun. Usually, you claim that you saw something move and thought it might be danger. Back on Franklin, we called popping off a shot like that for fun *huntin' wabbits*."

"I've heard the expression," Kim said. "But that was from a former soldier from Brahma, who also emphasized it was not *rabbit* but *wabbit*. What is a wabbit?"

"I don't know," Mele said. "Maybe the saying originated on Earth, and they have wabbits there, so that's why everybody uses it. The thing is, a tight outfit, one that's well disciplined, doesn't tolerate that. Any sentry who shoots at wabbits gets hammered." She didn't bother adding that she knew that from personal experience. "So it doesn't happen very often. The fact that Scatha's grunts are popping off shots two or three times a night every night means they're not being hauled up short for it, which means their leadership is sloppy, which is good for us."

"Are you worried about being mistaken for a wabbit by those sentries?" Leigh Camagan asked.

"Ninja is working on our being able to break into their net and substitute our own data for whatever the sensors really see," Mele said. "She's confident she can do that, and when that happens, we can look like whatever we want to look like to the sensors, or we'll be invisible to anyone who doesn't actually see us with unaided eyes."

"Won't they do that?" Odom asked, frowning. "Look around with their own eyes?"

"No, sir. The sloppier an outfit is, the more they depend exclusively on their sensors. And these guys are sloppy. I'm betting my life on it. Not figuratively. Literally."

Odom grimaced. "I don't want to minimize that. You are running serious risks. I'd prefer that we also don't suffer any losses."

He meant it, Mele realized. She nodded respectfully to him. "Thank you, sir. I assure you that I am highly motivated to come back from this mission alive and in one piece."

"She's clearly thought this out," Kim said. "I move that we endorse Major Darcy's actions and plans."

There it was again. No doubt this time.

After a few seconds, Odom reluctantly nodded in agreement.

After the other two had left, Mele stopped Leigh Camagan. "*Major* Darcy? Two of you called me major."

"Yes. You've been promoted," Leigh Camagan said matter-of-factly.

"When did that happen?"

"This morning."

"Thank you for informing me of that," Mele said. "I've heard of sergeant-majors, but I never heard of anyone being promoted direct from sergeant to major," Mele said.

"These are exceptional circumstances. Don't you think you can handle it?"

"One of these days, you're going to ask me that, and I'm going to say no, I can't," Mele threatened.

"I don't think so," Leigh Camagan said, smiling slightly. "I make a habit of finding out what people are really like, so I know how to deal with them, and I try to be certain of my own motives and thoughts as well. 'Know your enemy and know yourself; in a hundred battles you will never be in peril.'"

It was Mele's turn to stare in surprise. "You've read Sun Tzu?"

"Of course. War is an extension of politics, as Clausewitz said."

"I haven't read that Clausewitz. Should I?"

"When you have the time," Leigh Camagan said. "To be honest, you seem to already know a lot of what he says. You were bored a lot as an enlisted Marine for Franklin, weren't you? That's why you got in trouble from time to time."

"There's truth to that," Mele admitted.

"I have good news for you. You won't have to worry about getting into trouble anymore because you are not going to have any opportunities in the future to be bored, Major Darcy." Leigh Camagan smiled at her, then left.

Mele stared after her, wondering what her last outfit would think if they heard that she was now a major. There had been one sergeant that she would absolutely love to see right now. And that snooty lieutenant.

And another sergeant who would shake her head, and tell Mele, "Darcy, you stupid boot, I always told you to stop screwing around and you'd make rank in a flash. It's about time you listened."

As she stepped outside on her way back to the grandly named Glenlyon Ground Forces Training Camp, Mele paused to look up. People did that a lot these days, she realized. Looking up to where they had come from or where they were going or where people they knew were. Had Lochan Nakamura gone on to Kosatka? Was he still with that Carmen, who had seemed to have had her share of hidden secrets? Mele wished he could know she had made major. But since that was unlikely to happen, she hoped Lochan was all right. Kosatka was supposed to be a quiet place, after all.

Someone had gone to the trouble of making Kosatka's second city, Drava, different in architectural style from the original city. Not hugely different, but with enough distinctive features to give it a feel of individuality. Lochan liked that. The people running Kosatka might have made some missteps, but they clearly were trying to do things right. Even more than the first city, Drava felt only half-occupied, having been overbuilt to accommodate the new immigrants coming in with every ship that arrived.

He took another look at Carmen as their vehicle rolled through streets with light traffic. She had been up and down all day, one moment seemingly elated by the progress they had made and the next moment gloomy and looking around as if expecting some sort of trouble. During the brief moments when he had felt safe to speak candidly with her and asked whether she was worried about anything, Carmen had only shaken her head, muttered "ghosts," and left it at that.

The meeting with representatives from Drava was to take place in a newly completed building. "No negative historical associations possible," First Minister Hofer had commented wryly to Lochan and Carmen. "As short as our history has been, places are already acquiring good and bad connotations. But this is completely neutral ground."

Entry was through broad doors into an expansive and mostly empty reception area. The new lift tubes were being balky, so the small group walked up two flights of stairs to the second story. Besides Lochan, there was Carmen Ochoa, First Minister Hofer, House Leader Ottone, Safety Coordinator Sarkozy, and a single guard. Lochan noticed that as they walked, the Safety Coordinator always positioned herself in the group so that she could keep an eye on Carmen.

After a short walk down a hallway with finished but bare walls, Lochan brought up the rear as the small group entered a suite on the second floor. "We need to discuss a few internal matters while waiting for the representatives from Drava," First Minister Hofer told Lochan and Carmen. "I hope you won't mind waiting in the outer room."

"No problem," Lochan assured him.

The First Minister, House Leader Ottone, and Safety Coordinator Sarkozy entered the inner room. As the door closed behind them, Lochan could hear the Safety Coordinator beginning to speak forcefully, but he didn't catch any words.

The guard with them took up position outside the inner door, ostentatiously blocking access but giving Lochan and Carmen a slightly apologetic look. Lochan suspected he was following orders from Safety Coordinator Sarkozy.

Lochan looked around the outer room, a rectangle maybe seven meters long and about half that wide, the doorway to the hall set in the center of one long wall and the door to the inner room set directly opposite it. One of the shorter walls had a big window set in it, but curtains veiled any view of the outside. Like the hallway, the outer room lacked any pictures or displays. If he hadn't known he was on Kosatka, Lochan thought, he could be back on Franklin, or even on Earth.

"It's funny," he commented to Carmen. "We go so far from Old Earth, we build something totally new on a totally new world, and from the inside, it looks like it could have been built anywhere at any time in the last few centuries."

She started to reply, stopped with a worried/puzzled expression, turned toward the outer doorway, then leapt toward Lochan.

He staggered back as she shoved him, catching a glimpse of someone in the doorway, a weapon aimed in at them.

"Alert!" the guard at the inner door shouted, clawing at the shocker holstered under his coat. "Lock the——"

The guard jerked three times and fell back against the door he had been guarding, his eyes open in a final stare at the man who

239

had killed him. The sound of the shots had been muffled but was still clear in the otherwise quiet building.

That man was already inside the room and spinning to target Lochan and Carmen. Frozen in surprise, Lochan got only a blurred glimpse of a wiry build, a balding head, and the muzzle of the weapon coming around to aim.

In the vids, this was where the bad guy would stop to give a speech, then watch without reacting as the good guys jumped into action.

But the killer's only hesitation came as he took a moment to decide which of them to kill first.

Lochan would have died in the seconds he needed to figure out how to react. But Carmen had launched herself into the assassin the instant she finished pushing Lochan aside, taking advantage of the killer's brief instant of indecision.

Lochan had seen Mele fight, seen the sure, practiced blows with which she disabled a threat. Carmen didn't fight that way.

Carmen fought dirty.

Lochan didn't catch everything she did as Carmen hit their attacker, but he saw a thumb driven into an eye and a knee go into a groin. Carmen and the killer fell to the floor, her teeth closing on the wrist holding a weapon. The killer rolled free, shouting in pain, his weapon now in Carmen's hand.

In the vids, this was where the good guy would stop and tell the bad guy to surrender.

The moment Carmen lined up the pistol, she fired, hitting the attacker. Taking only a second to aim better, she fired again, knocking him down for good.

Lochan was still grappling with what had happened when Carmen bent down, retrieved the shocker the guard had been trying to draw, and tossed it to Lochan. "I heard at least one more out there," she told him. "Get over on that side of the door. Can you use that?"

He looked down at the weapon, his head and guts swirling with adrenaline and emotion, then back at Carmen Ochoa. "I've never fired a weapon," Lochan said as he picked it up.

"You're a fast learner, aren't you?" Carmen had closed in on herself, no feelings visible in her expression. The only sign of distress in her was the tightness with which she was gripping the weapon taken from the attacker.

"What do they want?" Lochan asked as he knelt by the opposite side of the door from Carmen, his own weapon held awkwardly. It only now occurred to him that he had been standing between the doorway and the guard. If Carmen had not shoved him out of the way, the killer's bullets would have hit Lochan first.

"They want to kill any chance of peaceful resolution," Carmen said, her voice a monotone. "Commit another atrocity and cause a bigger crackdown. Feed a spiral of violence with innocent victims. It's an old, old strategy."

A voice called from the other side of the inner door. "Who's out there?"

"Ochoa and Nakamura," she replied. "Your guard is dead. There's at least one more attacker in the hall. We're holding the outer door. Keep yours closed in case they get past us."

After a long pause, the voice came again. Lochan recognized it as that of Safety Coordinator Sarkozy. "I owe you an apology, Citizen Ochoa."

"I'll accept it when we have the chance," Carmen replied.

She swung her gaze across Lochan for a moment, then focused once more on the doorway.

Lochan shivered at what he had seen in her eyes. Growing up on Mars. That was what it had meant. That's what being a Red meant. He finally understood that when Carmen had spoken of fighting for survival, of fighting her way off Mars, she hadn't been speaking metaphorically.

"Hey," another woman's voice called from the hallway. "You in there. You kill Graf?"

"Yeah," Carmen replied, her voice taking on a different accent. "He dead."

"You pretty good. Graf was bloody Red. You Hellas gang?"

"Shandakar. No gang," Carmen answered, her weapon aimed steadily at the doorway.

"Shanda? Ha! Graf be really mad if he knew a wimp Shanda kill him."

Carmen looked about quickly, then gestured urgently to Lochan to continue covering the doorway with his weapon. She faded back, moving as silently as possible, until she was against the outer wall in the corner next to the window.

"Hey, wimp Shanda," the woman in the hallway outside called. "You run, we let you go. Bonus life. Deal?"

Lochan looked at Carmen, who didn't answer this time. Instead, she shook her head angrily and indicated he should keep his attention focused on the doorway.

"Still there, Shanda? Deal offer expire real soon."

The window shattered, curtains blowing inward as a man broke through, rolling up to aim at the inside of the doorway. Before he could fire, Carmen fired two shots into him from her position behind him next to the wall. The man twisted partway, staggered, and fell, his weapon dropping from his limp hand.

Distracted by the activity at the window, Lochan nearly missed the woman dodging through the doorway. He fired without aiming, the pop of the shocker startling him.

More by luck than design, the shocker's charge grazed the spine of the woman. She fell, twitching, her lips drawn back as she tried to bring up her weapon.

Lochan extended his arm, aimed as the shocker recharged, and fired a second time. That shot hit her full on.

Carmen took long enough to check on the man she had just shot, then raced back to Lochan and looked over his victim. For a moment, he wondered if she would shoot the unconscious attacker, but Carmen shuddered and passed one hand across her eyes before returning attention to the doorway.

"Citizen Ochoa," Safety Coordinator Sarkozy called from the inner room. "Our response team is entering the building."

"Understand," Carmen called back. "I need an announcement when they get close. I don't know if there are any more killers out there."

"They're coming up to the second floor now. The officer in charge is Sergeant Dominic Desjani."

Lochan heard faint noises in the hallway and tensed again.

"In the room," a clear voice called, "this is Sergeant Desjani, Public Safety Rapid Response Team. Identify yourselves."

"Carmen Ochoa," she called back.

"Lochan Nakamura," he called as well, reassured that Carmen trusted whoever was out there this time.

"Place any weapons you have on the ground," Sergeant Desjani's voice ordered. "Then stand up, your open hands clearly visible. Is there anyone else inside?"

Lochan put his shocker down and got to his feet as Carmen answered.

"Four," Carmen said. "All down. Two dead, one maybe, one unconscious."

"Understand." A small flying drone swung into sight and entered the room, panning around to view everything within. "Remain standing. Don't move. We are coming in now."

Lochan's feelings of relief were replaced by renewed fear as figures wearing protective gear and carrying weapons swept into the room, some of the weapons pausing to stay directed at him. Most were nonlethal shockers, but Lochan thought one or two of the weapons might be something more dangerous.

After a few seconds of knife-edged tension, the man who must be Sergeant Desjani edged toward the inner door. "Commander? The outer room is secure."

"Good." The Safety Coordinator opened the door, looking relieved. Behind her, Lochan caught glimpses of the drawn faces of First Minister Hofer and House Leader Ottone.

Sergeant Desjani called out another command as he removed a protective face mask. "Stand down. Casualty status?"

"She was right," one of the other officers reported. "Officer Yeltzin is dead. That one is also dead. Multiple slugs. This one is almost dead. Same cause. I've called the EMTs up here for him. The third subject is out, shocker burns visible."

Lochan saw the sergeant look from the slug thrower at Carmen's feet to the shocker at his, then raise his eyes to study both of them. "These two are okay?" he asked Safety Coordinator Sarkozy.

"More than okay," Sarkozy replied, coming into the outer room and looking down morosely at the fallen guard.

"He was shot with this," Carmen said, toeing the weapon at her feet. "The same weapon that killed his killer. He died defending you."

"His memory will be honored. I'm sure you might have died as well," Safety Coordinator Sarkozy said. "I overheard a little of the conversation out here. You know where they came from?"

Carmen sighed. "I don't know who sent them here, but I know where they came from originally. Mars. All three are Reds. You can question the woman when she comes to, and she might be open to a deal to tell you what she knows. She sounded like a Vall-Mar. Tough. Threaten her, and she won't say a word, but Vall-Mars are usually willing to negotiate."

Safety Coordinator Sarkozy eyed Carmen, nodding in confirmation of earlier suspicions. "You know more about Mars than you let on. I thought so, but I also thought wrong. Kosatka owes you a lot." She extended her hand. "I have your back from this day on. Sergeant, Citizen Ochoa and Citizen Nakamura are to be given every trust and courtesy."

After Carmen Ochoa had shaken hands with Sarkozy, she walked over to where Lochan stood and gazed at him, worry in her eyes.

He knew what she was worried about. "It's okay."

"Is it? You just saw me. Really saw me."

"I saw part of you," Lochan said. "How did you know that guy would come through the window?"

"It's an old trick," Carmen said, her head lowered, looking depressed. "The one in the hallway talking to me to keep my attention focused on her and to cover any sound the other guy made getting into position. Lochan—"

"I said it's okay." He gave her his best sympathetic look. "It must be hard to live with sometimes."

"There are a lot of memories that are hard to live with," Carmen agreed. "I just picked up a couple more."

"I'm a lot more impressed with you now," Lochan said, meaning every word of it. "To come out of that and be who you are. That's amazing."

She finally looked at him again, skeptical. "You're impressed?"

"I'd be dead if not for you," he pointed out.

"I guess."

"I just realized something else," Lochan added. "Ever since I headed down, I'm attracting the attention of young women who not only aren't interested in me physically, they also keep putting weapons in my hand and telling me to use them."

"You must be making bad choices," Carmen said, smiling slightly.

"I think when it comes to people who are good to have around when things go bad, I'm making really good choices," Lochan said. He studied her, concerned. "You're not all right, are you?"

She shook her head.

"What can I do?"

"I may get seriously drunk tonight. If I do, I could use someone to keep an eye on me and get me back to my room."

"Deal," Lochan said.

"Most of those from Mars are like me," Carmen said in a rush. "Just trying to be decent people and leave the ugliness behind. But others look at us and see only Reds like those killers. And there are always enough Reds like that to feed the fears and the rumors and the anger."

Lochan was trying to come up with an answer when the sergeant joined them.

"Citizens," he said, looking them over again, "do you require any assistance?"

"We're fine," Lochan said.

"No injuries?"

Lochan looked to Carmen, who shrugged as she answered. "Just a few scratches and bruises. I'll be all right."

"You should let one of the EMTs check you," the sergeant suggested. "You took that guy down by yourself?"

"Yes," Carmen said, sounding reluctant to admit it.

"We're in your debt. If you need anything, please let us know. You can call me personally," the sergeant said, passing both Carmen and Lochan his contact information but looking at Carmen as he said it.

"It looks like you have another admirer," Lochan said to Carmen as the sergeant rejoined the other safety officers.

"That would be funny, wouldn't it?" she replied, gazing after the sergeant. "A Red and a cop. Not too likely, though."

To no one's surprise, the meeting with the representatives from Drava was postponed until the next day. But First Minister Hofer took pains to emphasize in a public statement that the meeting would go forward. "The three who killed a brave public safety officer and would have killed more except for the valiant actions of two individuals from Old Earth were not from Drava," he announced. "They were agents of an outside power, planning to place the blame for their actions on the people of Drava. We all know that attempt could not have succeeded because we are all one on Kosatka. I want to reassure the people of Drava that we will work to address any concerns they have, and that I personally still feel myself as safe here as I do back in my own home."

That night, Lochan sat with her while Carmen drank. She had decided to have a bottle sent up rather than be in a public place like a bar. After a while and after enough drinks, Carmen started talking in a low voice, sharing memories and events in the manner of someone unearthing things they had once hoped to keep buried forever. Lochan listened, saying nothing but an occasional vague sound to let her know he was listening. These weren't things meant for him to comment on, he knew, and he didn't feel qualified to judge or talk about such matters anyway. Carmen needed to talk, needed to share some of the burden she carried inside, and so he listened and took on a little of that.

He wondered what had changed, that she was willing to share such things. Perhaps it was that they had faced this last situation as a team. He had become, in a small way, someone who had shared an ugly situation. Someone who might understand choices driven by necessity.

Eventually, the bottle nearly empty, Carmen's voice drifted off to a murmur, and she laid her head on the table. Lochan got her up and into bed, making sure she was safe before going to his own room.

Once there, tired as he was, Lochan sat for a long time gazing at nothing. He had plenty of memories from his earlier life as well, not all of them pleasant, but nothing as bad as what Carmen Ochoa had endured. It had never before occurred to him how lucky he had been to be born and raised on Franklin. Not that Franklin was perfect. Like any other home of humanity, it had its better parts and its worse parts. But nowhere in Franklin's star system was there anything like the hellhole that Mars had become.

But that could happen out here, he realized. Even as apparently tranquil a place as Kosatka could be warped by internal and external pressures and mistakes, heading down that long road paved with good intentions that too often led to the same place where Mars was stuck. Stars like Apulu were already seeing what they could get away with, someone's warship had bombarded Lares for no apparent reason, and Lochan couldn't shake the memory of those corporate colonies that had gone far, far out to stars distant from anyone who could interfere with them. What sort of places would they become, especially if they joined together? Carmen Ochoa had good cause for her worries.

"I've been looking for somewhere," Lochan said out loud, speaking either to himself or to the planet as a whole or maybe to something bigger than that. He wasn't sure which. "Why not here? And if I'm going to fail again, why not fail trying to do something big? Something important? More important than me, anyway. Something that might prevent more kids from having to grow up like Carmen did, or like those three killers did. Something that might save lives."

Lochan sighed, looking down at the hand that had held the shocker. "I'm not a warrior who can carry weapons. Both times I've held one, it's felt . . . alien. Wrong for me. But people can fight in other ways, using other weapons. I'm going to fight for Kosatka. And maybe help Kosatka fight for others."

There was no one in the room to answer, at least no one he could see or any answer he could hear. But he finally went to bed, feeling more at peace than at any time he could remember.

Everything that Rob Geary had ever heard about Kosatka, which admittedly wasn't that much, indicated that it was a peaceful star system, with a colony planted several years earlier and growing at a rapid pace as humanity spread across Kosatka's primary world just as it was spreading through neighboring stars.

Which was why Rob Geary wasn't surprised when *Squall* left jump space and encountered no one guarding the spot. Ships serving as sentries at jump points happened in the Old Colonies, usually using spacecraft whose primary mission was customs enforcement rather than war, but it wasn't something that star systems diverted resources to in the new colonies.

The peaceful façade of Kosatka crumbled as soon they picked up a local newscast. Rob watched the reports in disbelief, seeing the images of battered Lares, the unmistakable craters from orbital bombardment pocking the surface, the craters surrounded by tangled wreckage that had once been a fast-rising new city for a new colony.

"Who did that?" Danielle Martel asked, sounding as shocked as Rob. "That ship they're showing is not one of the warships that Scatha has. And Lares is jumps away from Scatha."

"This is old news here," Rob said. "Kosatka heard about this weeks ago. These reports are just rehashing the original information and speculating."

"What do we do?" Drake Porter asked. "Shouldn't we go back to Glenlyon right away? What if that ship shows up at our star system?"

Rob felt the fear racing through his crew and knew he had to bring it to a halt. "We have a job here that is about protecting Glenlyon," he said. "We need to do that job. We need to deliver our message and see if we can get a response from Kosatka. Then we will return to Glenlyon and defend it from threats like that. Drake, am I ready to transmit to the primary world? We'd better let them know right away who we are."

That world was, Rob saw, currently over four light hours distant. "Right away" meant Kosatka wouldn't hear his message for four hours, but since they also wouldn't see the arrival of *Squall* for that same period of time, a quick message should reassure Kosatka about *Squall*'s intentions.

"Uh, just a sec. Yeah. You're ready."

Still rattled by the news of what had happened at Lares, Rob composed himself, trying to look both professional and nonthreatening. "This is Lieutenant Robert Geary of the Glenlyon warship *Squall*. We are here on a peaceful mission to request Kosatka's assistance. I repeat, we pose no threat to the people of Kosatka. We urgently request communications with your government, so that I can transmit to them a plea for help from the government of Glenlyon."

He was about to end the transmission when Rob remembered something from the news reports about Lares, about the mystery warship approaching their planet. "To ensure that our peaceful intent is clear, *Squall* will not proceed any closer to your worlds but will remain in the vicinity of this jump point. Geary, out."

"What are we going to do while we wait?" Drake asked.

Rob slumped back, knowing that it would be at least eight hours before he heard anything in reply from Kosatka. "We're going to stay here and wait, just like I said."

After doing what little else could be done, Rob went to his stateroom. He didn't know what local time was at the city on the planet where he had sent his message, but *Squall* had arrived late in the day for the ship.

He couldn't shake the memories of those awful images from Lares. Rob wondered if he would be able to sleep.

* * *

Rob was awakened by an insistent beeping from the comm panel next to his bunk. "Yeah?" He squinted at the time on the ship—0300. Of course. Emergencies always happened at an hour like that.

"We've received some messages from Kosatka," Drake reported. "Sorry. You told me to wake you up when any came in."

"Yeah," Rob repeated, trying to clear the cobwebs from his brain. "Forward them to here, okay?"

"You got it."

Drake's face vanished, replaced by that of a very hard-faced man speaking in very hard tones. "Unknown warship, this is Kosatka. You are forbidden to proceed in-system. Any attempt to approach our worlds will be regarded as a hostile act. Identify yourself immediately!"

It wasn't the nicest greeting that Rob had ever received, but understandable given the circumstances.

He called up the second message, sent soon after the first. This time the man looked slightly less rigid, his voice not quite as threatening. "Lieutenant Geary on the Glenlyon warship *Squall*, this is Kosatka. I have forwarded your message to the First Minister's office. Kosatka appreciates your willingness to remain near the jump point and hopes that you will continue to abide by that promise."

Rob rubbed his face, grimaced, and called up the latest information that *Squall*'s sensors had been able to pick up since arriving at Kosatka.

There was still no sign of any other warship in this star system. No other defenses had been identified. Either Kosatka had done an amazing job of concealing all of its warships and other weaponry, or the threats he had just received had been bluffs.

Not that he was interested in calling those bluffs. Gaining the cooperation of Kosatka wouldn't happen if he played games with their very real fears stoked by what had happened at Lares.

"Lieutenant?" Drake Porter again, looking apologetic. "The guys standing watch on the weapons want to know if they can stand down from that."

Rob almost said yes because he knew from personal experience how tedious combat watches in a nonthreat environment could be.

But he hesitated before giving that order. *Squall* was a warship. And she was on a combat mission. And they were close to a jump point, which was just about the only kind of place within space where a spaceship could be surprised by a sudden new arrival. "No. Drake, I understand it's a pain, but we are in combat status. We have to stay ready if anything shows up. And if anybody complains, I'll remind them that I'm standing those watches, too."

Another reply showed up at 0500 ship time. The speaker this time was a wary-looking woman. "I am Safety Coordinator Sarkozy speaking for Kosatka. Please send your message in reply to this. We want to know more about what is happening at Glenlyon. I have to caution you that Kosatka's resources are currently extremely limited, so our ability to assist you may also be very restricted. Out."

Rob, giving up on getting any more sleep, especially since he was due for a bridge watch at 0600, tabbed reply and attached the message the council of Glenlyon had put together. He paused before hitting SEND, took a few moments to make himself look presentable, then added something to the reply. "This is Lieutenant Geary. Thank you for your willingness to hear the message from the government of Glenlyon. I look forward to your reply. I was asked to notify two individuals who may be in Kosatka of our problems in the hopes that they might offer assistance. Those two are . . . Lochan Nakamura and Carmen Ochoa. Thank you again. Out."

He stood up, yawning, made sure his improvised uniform looked right, and headed for the bridge. The short passageway to the bridge from his stateroom seemed even quieter than usual.

He was almost there when the rapid bong of the general quarters alarm shattered the silence.

11

Already on his way, Rob raced the last few steps and through the hatch onto the bridge. "What is it?"

Drake Porter, in the midst of being relieved from his watch, stared at Rob in confusion.

Rob dropped into his command seat and called up his display. As he was cursing the seconds needed for the display to boot up, Danielle Martel came running onto the bridge and flung herself at the operations watch station.

"Another ship just arrived!" Drake finally got out.

"Shut off the general quarters alarm and pass the word for everyone to get to their battle stations," Rob ordered.

His display finally steadied.

A destroyer?

"A warship arrived at the jump point," Danielle confirmed. "One light minute away. It's . . . sir, it's a Warrior Class destroyer."

It took a moment for that to sink in. "Warrior Class?" Rob questioned. "The same class of ship that bombarded Lares?"

"Yes," Danielle confirmed. "Old, but still dangerous. And he's not broadcasting any identification. Just like the one that hit Lares."

This wasn't his battle. *Squall* wasn't here to defend Kosatka. In fact, Rob's orders didn't even mention what he should do if he encountered a threat.

It took him less than a second to realize that none of that mattered. Rob punched his comm control. "Unknown warship, this is Glenlyon Cutter *Squall*. Identify yourself immediately."

He cut the transmission and turned to Danielle. "Full combat readiness. Get all weapons powered up, shields at maximum, notify engineering that we will need full output from the power core."

"Yes, sir."

While Danielle Martel took care of that, Rob called up the maneuvering display, designated the unknown destroyer, and tapped the intercept command.

A moment later, the solution appeared, a pretty short, pretty flat curve that would bring the *Squall* close to the destroyer in a bow-to-bow pass. Words appeared. EXECUTE INTERCEPT? YES. NO.

"What's our status?" Rob asked Danielle.

"Weapons are ready. Shields are building. Most combat stations ready. Engineering warns that we need to save full draw on the power core until we really need it."

"Understand," Rob said. "Drake, anything from the destroyer?"

"No," Drake said, looking worried. "Not a peep."

Rob took a slow breath, studying what the display told him. Warrior Class destroyer. Nearly a century old. Standard armament included a bombardment launcher, a grapeshot launcher, and a particle beam a generation behind that on the *Squall*.

"It's roughly even odds if we engage him," Danielle said.

"Our sensors say his after shields are degraded."

The destroyer had steadied out on a course aiming in-system, toward the primary world of Kosatka. *Squall*'s maneuvering system automatically updated the intercept solution for Rob.

EXECUTE INTERCEPT? YES. NO.

Squall was the only warship that Glenlyon had. He couldn't afford to get *Squall* too badly damaged.

But the destroyer must also know that this would be a nearly equal fight. And whoever controlled that ship, whichever star system it had come from, surely didn't want to lose it. Especially since examining who and what was on that ship would allow blame to be fixed for the devastation at Lares.

"If we come around in a long approach—" Danielle began.

"I know," Rob said. "But we need to try to win this fight fast, without exchanging fire. Maybe they don't want a fight."

"Maybe they do."

"Then they'll get one. Tell engineering I need full power and make sure forward shields are at full strength."

He reached out and touched YES.

Squall's thrusters fired, pitching her around, then the main propulsion kicked in, hurling *Squall* toward the destroyer. The aging inertial dampers on the cutter whined in protest as the structure of the ship groaned from the stress. Rob hung on to his seat as acceleration forces leaked past the dampers.

The destroyer was moving at point zero three light speed. *Squall* was coming up to point zero four light speed. With just less than a light minute separating them, at a combined velocity of point zero seven light, the two ships would cover the roughly eighteen million kilometers between them in a minute and a half.

"Lock weapons on the destroyer," Rob ordered Danielle. "Set them to fire when we get within range."

"Yes, sir. Getting hits at a relative velocity of point zero seven light speed is outside the capability of our fire control system."

"He may not know that." Still no message from the destroyer. The slim barracuda shape was just off *Squall's* port bow and slightly below, *Squall* aiming for the point where the destroyer would be in another minute and five seconds.

"He should be seeing our course change now," Danielle reported. "Thirty-five seconds to intercept. Sir, you're not giving him much time to react."

"I want him to know that," Rob said. "I want the cowards who bombarded a defenseless city to know that we are coming for them and that they only have a few seconds to decide what to do."

"He's maneuvering!" Danielle said at the same moment as Rob's own display alerted him.

Twenty seconds before the ships came within weapons range of each other. What was the destroyer doing? Altering course to better engage *Squall*?

"He's using full thrust," Danielle reported. "Still coming up and around."

Rob frantically entered new commands, shifting *Squall* to come up and over slightly so she was still aiming to intercept the destroyer.

"He's lighting off main propulsion!"

The destroyer's maneuvers had brought it in a long curve upward, its bow now almost facing back toward the jump point.

Rob had two seconds before intercept as he ordered *Squall* to adjust her own course again.

What would have been a bow-to-bow encounter, with both ships having their strongest shields and weapons facing each other, had changed as the destroyer turned away. With so little time to react, and unable to accelerate out of danger fast enough, the destroyer had ended up presenting her vulnerable stern to *Squall* as the cutter swept past.

Squall lurched as her weapons fired under the control of the automated systems, the moment of closest point of approach coming and going in a tiny fraction of a second too short for human reflexes to have pressed firing commands.

Rob entered another set of maneuvering commands, bringing *Squall* back around to hit the destroyer again, but this time the solution was accompanied by a pulsing red warning message. PLANNED MANEUVER WILL EXCEED HULL STRESS PARAMETERS. EXECUTE ANYWAY? YES. NO.

"Hell," Rob muttered, ordering the new intercept to take place using less extreme maneuvers that wouldn't threaten to destroy *Squall*. The arc of the new intercept doubled, and the time to new intercept grew even more, but he punched approve for the new solution. It made little sense to try to reengage the destroyer at the cost of tearing *Squall* apart.

"We're getting an evaluation of damage," Danielle reported. "Some grapeshot from the destroyer impacted our forward shields, but they held. The destroyer . . . his after shields suffered spot failures! We scored some hits aft on him!"

The crew whooped with triumph, but Rob bent to look at his display. "Our sensors can't evaluate damage to him. What do you think, Danielle?"

"Let me check something." Her hands flew across her display. "His thrust is down to sixty percent maximum for what a ship of that class should be capable of. He demonstrated eighty percent maximum coming out of the jump point."

"We did hurt him," Rob said.

"Yes. Not enough, though."

It didn't take him any thought to realize what Danielle meant. The destroyer had steadied out heading back for the jump point on the quickest possible trajectory. *Squall* was swinging through her long loop to reengage, but the projected intercept was past the jump point.

"What?" Drake Porter asked.

"He's going to get away," Rob explained. "We can't reengage before he jumps out of this star system."

"Huh? But we—"

"It's not possible," Danielle said. "Not with *Squall*'s capability to maneuver. Physics is a bitch. She won't let us."

"We'll stay on this trajectory anyway," Rob said. "If that destroyer changes his mind, we'll be ready."

But whatever the destroyer's mission might have been, it had no desire to continue the fight. Rob watched it reach the jump point and disappear into jump space while still twenty light seconds away from *Squall*. "Secure from battle stations."

"He can't turn around, right?" Drake asked.

"Right," Rob said. "Ships can't turn around in jump space. He'll have to go to whatever star he jumped to, then, if he wants to return, jump back."

"The nearest star accessible from this jump point is five days in jump space distant," Danielle said. "That means a ten-day round-trip, minimum."

"Whew!" Drake said. "I wasn't complaining."

Rob saw Danielle smiling at him. "That was some wild fighting," she told Rob. "I'm impressed."

"Thanks." Rob realized his heart was still pounding. "Uh, I didn't have a chance to grab anything to eat. Could you get me something?"

"I think there's still a pack of donuts left."

"Victory feast!" Drake cried.

"The breakfast of space squids," Danielle agreed with a laugh. "Come on, Drake. Let's get the lieutenant a donut and some coffee to celebrate the Battle of Kosatka."

Rob ordered some sedate maneuvers to get *Squall* back to the region where she had been waiting to hear back from Kosatka, wondering what the people on the planet would think four hours from now when they saw the just-concluded battle take place.

The reply from Kosatka that showed up eight hours later had six people visible. One was spliced in, with an identifier saying "Orbital Facility Chief Operating Officer." The five others were all standing in the same room and included the Safety Coordinator who had sent the last message.

"Lieutenant Geary," the man in the center began. "I am First Minister Hofer of Kosatka. You already know our planetary safety coordinator, and this is Leader Ottone of our House of Peoples' Representatives. And of course Citizens Carmen Ochoa and Lochan Nakamura, who you asked after. We have seen your unhesitating and heroic defense of our star system against what appeared to be the same criminals who struck Lares. Kosatka owes an immense debt to Glenlyon. You had no obligation to defend us, but you risked yourself for us anyway. There are no words of thanks adequate for how we regard you and Glenlyon."

The First Minister paused, looking uncomfortable. "If we had means to assist you, we would provide it. But as you may have already seen, we lack defenses of our own. Citizen Ochoa has offered advice on a solution to that problem that we will be pursuing, but at the moment we cannot even defend ourselves. I understand that the soonest that awful warship can return will be more than a week, and by then we will have improvised some combat capability on one of our freighters. As soon as we have acquired an additional defensive capability, we will endeavor to return a hundredfold the favor you have done us. Please assure the Council of Glenlyon that Kosatka honors her debts."

He gestured toward Lochan Nakamura, who looked slightly bemused. "Lieutenant, I don't know who referred Carmen Ochoa and me to you," Lochan said, "but we were happy to advise Kosatka to assist Glenlyon when possible. Our advice was not necessary to convince them, as it turned out. Your actions did that."

First Minister Hofer spread his hands in a welcoming gesture. "Thank you, Glenlyon. Kosatka, out."

Rob slumped in his stateroom seat, sighing with relief. As the initial glow of victory had faded, he and the rest of those on *Squall* had been getting nervous about having left Glenlyon defenseless in their absence.

He straightened again and tapped reply. "Kosatka, we are honored by your offer of assistance and understand your concerns. Since it appears that Kosatka will have some defense in place before that destroyer could return, we would like to return ourselves to Glenlyon to defend that star system against any similar threat. You may not have detected that we inflicted some damage on the destroyer's propulsion during the fight. He was down to sixty percent of maximum propulsion when he jumped out of this star system and won't be able to work at repairing external damage while the ship is in jump space. I think it unlikely that ship will risk another battle until they have time to repair that damage, which will likely require them to return to the star system that sent them out, whichever one that is.

"Therefore, I intend taking *Squall* back to Glenlyon. I will wait eight more hours after sending this reply to give you the opportunity to tell us if you see a desperate need for us to remain. Otherwise, I will return to Glenlyon to defend it and pass on your reply to my government.

"For Citizens Lochan Nakamura and Carmen Ochoa, I was referred to you by Mele Darcy, the commander of Glenlyon's ground forces. I'm sure she sends you her best wishes. If you have any messages for her, please transmit them as quickly as possible, as *Squall* will leave in eight hours unless Kosatka urgently requires otherwise. Geary, out."

The replies that showed up eight hours later consisted of another wave of thanks from the government of Kosatka, and a joint message from Nakamura and Ochoa for Mele Darcy.

Should he have told them that Mele Darcy had already committed to a hazardous mission? That there was a good chance that she might be killed before *Squall* managed to return to Glenlyon?

No, Rob decided. What good would such knowledge have done them? Better they enjoyed as long as possible the thought of their friend alive and well.

He called the bridge, where Danielle Martel had the watch. "Danielle, head for the jump point. We're starting back for Glenlyon."

That was, he knew, probably the most popular command he had given since leaving home.

Squall trembled as thrusters fired, pushing her onto a direct course for the nearby jump point.

Three and a half weeks. Barely enough time to teach someone how to salute properly. Barely enough time to scrounge together the equipment she would need. But Scatha's base had finished their antiorbital weapon installation today, firing a test blast of charged particles that tore through the atmosphere and into space. Warned of the pending test, Glenlyon had used their satellites' maneuvering capability to switch to orbits out of reach of the weapon, but that meant that Glenlyon could no longer keep track of what Scatha was doing at the base.

Barely enough time, but it was time to go.

"All right, listen up." Mele looked over her best twenty volunteers, who made up the raiding force. Aside from her, only Grant Duncan would be guaranteed reliable in a fight. The others were willing enough but had little idea of what they would be facing. Theory and games and simulations and stress tests were one thing. Actually facing people out to kill you was another. "I've only had time to give you the basics. But we've got a few big advantages. We've been watching Scatha's soldiers, and they are not ready for us. They think they brought in enough firepower that Glenlyon has no choice but to accept the inevitable. And they think if we do try something, it'll be something stupid. But we're going to be smart.

"So," she continued, trying to radiate confidence, "we're going to surprise them, and they won't be ready for it. I'm going to take the lead on a lot of things because I've got the training. Ninja has laid some fantastic groundwork for us. But I need you guys to stay focused and stay sharp. Because you are also one of our big advantages. Scatha never imagined that Glenlyon could put together a group of people like you in such a short time to kick Scathan butt. You've all got important roles to play. If you get confused, use your heads. And remember that we are going to do our best not to kill any civilians at Scatha's base. Only the soldiers are targets. Any questions?"

No one had questions. They looked both nervous and eager, Mele thought. All except Grant, who had the look of a skilled worker about to tackle an ugly job.

She probably looked the same way.

"Everyone who has a weapon is to ensure it is on safe. Check it! All good? Let's board," Mele told them, watching as her twenty filed onto the WinG, then following last.

All of the others except Riley strapped themselves into seats in the passenger deck, while Riley went down and aft to check on the improvised explosives, and Mele went forward to the cockpit. "Everything's aboard?" she asked the pilots.

They nodded, radiating excitement. "I never thought I'd be playing this kind of game," one told Mele.

"It's not a game," she reminded him. "We can't afford any slipups. What about Delta?"

"They'll accompany us partway and set up while you guys are doing your business. Do you think we'll need Delta?"

"Delta is insurance," Mele said. "Let's hope we don't need it, but if we do, we'll really need it."

The other pilot looked back at Mele. "You pretty much improvised all this stuff out of gear designed for other uses. I never knew so much of our equipment could be used for things like this."

"Humans are pretty clever when it comes to figuring out how to kill each other," Mele said.

Riley came forward. "I checked over the bombs. Everything looks fine."

"Should we ask what kind of bombs they are?" one of the pilots said.

"Some are explosives and some are thermite," Mele said.

"Thermite? Are you sure none of those will go off in flight?"

"If one did," Riley offered, "it would just burn its way through the floor and out."

"That's not too reassuring."

"I've got the detonators," Mele said.

"And you're sitting up here right next to us?" the pilot said. "That's not too reassuring, either! Hey. We got a call. There's someone outside wants to see you before we take off."

Grumbling to herself about delays, Mele went back to the passenger hatch.

Waiting next to the WinG was Council Member Leigh Camagan. "Good luck, Major Darcy."

"I guess the rest of the council was busy?" Mele said. "Um, sorry. That wasn't very majorish of me."

"The rest of the council doesn't know how to send men and women off to risk their lives for us," Leigh Camagan said. "They *do* care, Major."

"How is it you know how to do that?" Mele asked.

"I was married once, Major. To a firefighter who went off to help those who needed it, and one of those times did not come back."

Mele straightened to attention. "I'm sorry."

"I know." Leigh Camagan gripped Mele's forearm. "Get it done, Major. And if there are any greater powers watching out for us, I pray that they be with you tonight."

"It never hurts to ask for help," Mele said. She saluted Leigh Camagan in a way that showed she meant the gesture of respect, then went back inside the WinG and sealed the hatch.

The WinG moved forward, rising on its ground-effect cushion of air, accelerating as it headed north and east. The other one of the smaller WinGs paced them for a long time as they raced toward the coming night, the sun falling toward the horizon in the west. Ocean swells rolled a couple of meters beneath them like the backs of monsters of the deep, the water dark and mysterious in the way of all oceans.

That was one of the differences between space and planets with water, Mele realized. Space didn't conceal anything. It was all out there, no matter how far away. You just had to figure out how to spot it across the distances and the vast gulf of years that usually separated humans from the stars and galaxies they studied.

But oceans kept their secrets as long as they could, hiding them beneath waters that might be placid or rough but always enshrouded what lay under the surface. You could look at a star and tell just about everything about it. But looking at an ocean only let you see what the ocean allowed.

Like people, Mele thought. Humans might move among the stars with increasing ease, but they still had much more in common with the seas of worlds where humans could live.

"Why didn't Scatha ever put up a satellite?" one of the pilots finally asked Mele, breaking the silence in the cockpit. "If they had, they would have been able to see us approaching even coming in as low as we are."

"Scatha couldn't while *Squall* was here. Lieutenant Geary would have just shot down their satellite. I guess they didn't expect *Squall* to leave, so they didn't bring any launch capability to put up a small sat if it did."

"They must have left behind a lot of stuff that they would have brought if they had more cargo space available," the second pilot observed. "We understand that! Half the time, people want to load twice as much as we have room for. Scatha must have wanted to bring more ground sensors. Why didn't they put any up on those hills we're going to run in behind?"

"Their sensor fields around the base are thin as it is," Mele said. "I would have put sensors on the hills anyway, but any by-the-book commander would put them all in close until they met the required density for base protection. And from what we've learned from the files we captured on the *Squall*, Scatha is all about punishing people who deviate from instructions. They've been gearing up production at their base of more sensors and we've seen a few more planted, but they're still way behind the curve, so whoever's in charge at that base is playing it safe."

"And by playing it safe, they're actually increasing their risk," the first pilot said with a laugh.

The WinGs moved fast for planetary craft, but the trip to the continent where Scatha had planted its base still took time. Mele, knowing how hard the waiting could be, went back and moved around the passenger deck, talking to her volunteers, trying to project confidence, and going over the plans yet again for anyone who might still be unclear.

Night fell. Glenlyon had two minor moons, which didn't reflect much light, but Mele was still glad when thin, high-level clouds moved in to obscure the moons and the stars.

As they neared a couple of small islands well off the coast of the continent, the WinG accompanying them veered off and headed for the islands.

Alone now, the WinG carrying Mele's raiding force angled north to ensure it would be beneath the curve of the planet's surface as it went past the base location, then swung close to due east as the coastline appeared ahead. Mele was happy to see whitecaps and bands of white foam where waves were thundering against the coast. The waters had grown rougher as they went north and east, and the more noise the ocean was making tonight, the better.

The WinG zipped over a short stretch of gravelly beach and began slowing, dropping a little closer to the thick scrub covering the soil.

"This is it," the lead pilot said to Mele as the WinG slowed even more, touching onto the surface and sliding to a slightly bumpy halt. "You guys be careful."

"Thanks. If we're not back by sunrise, get out of here and head back," Mele said.

The pilots exchanged reluctant glances. "We'd rather wait—"

"If we've gotten picked off, Scatha will be looking to find out how we came in. They'll find you," Mele said. "When the sun rises, head for home. But hopefully we'll be back well before then."

She led her team out of the WinG, walking back to where the big cargo hatch had lowered. It was dark enough out that Mele kept one hand on the side of the WinG for guidance as they walked. When they got to the back, one of the volunteers pulled out a hand control and began punching in commands.

Something stirred in the deeper darkness of the cargo bay, uncoiling and sliding toward them in a way that set Mele's hair on edge. The tunnelpede looked like a massive earthworm with broad tires set along its length, as well as a single line of seats and handholds along the top.

The tunnelpede rolled to where something like a boulder stood out from the ground. The volunteer tapped in more commands, and the boulder turned out to be hiding the rear of the snake that had dug the tunnel. The snake, compressed back into a one-meter diameter, still looked scary as hell to Mele as it slid along the ground and into the WinG's cargo space, coiling itself into a tight curl.

The two-meter-wide opening left behind by the snake angled down into pitch-blackness. The volunteer with the control took the seat on the tunnelpede closest to the front, Mele and the others climbing onto seats behind. "Lay as flat as you can," the volunteer called back in a low voice. "The tunnel is narrow enough that if you sit up, your head might graze the top, and you do not want that to happen because we're going to be traveling pretty fast at times."

The tunnelpede began rolling forward, the motion of the many tires so gentle that it felt as if the device were simply sliding forward. A headlight came on as the vehicle entered the tunnel, showing an eerily round tunnel leading lower before leveling out, the only breaks in the smooth surface ridges of instacrete every half meter or so to provide purchase for feet or wheels. The focused beam provided little scatter of light, so from the front of the tunnelpede back, most of the vehicle traveled in total darkness.

Mele, seated on the tunnelpede with her upper body lying flat, tried to see ahead, but her view was blocked by the driver. She was suddenly glad that the tunnel was unlit because it seemed the primary view of anyone on a tunnelpede would be the butt of the person in front of them.

The location chosen for their base by Scatha must have looked perfect on a map. Foothills to the north and west framed a broad plain sloping gradually downward toward the coast. The hills seemed to offer protection, while the plain served as a wide, open area that any attacker had to cross to reach the base. Comparatively little work at the construction of a breakwater and some dredging close to shore would provide a good harbor for oceangoing ships. A wide river ran between substantial banks nearby and might pose a future flooding threat, but for now guaranteed enough freshwater.

What wasn't obvious from the map was that the low hills, if not occupied, offered concealment for anyone threatening the base. Maybe Scatha planned on occupying those hills as soon as possible, but Mele intended throwing a monkey wrench into Scatha's planning. Whoever had chosen the site had also not taken into account the ground vibrations that the river and the not-far-off wave action would create, allowing Glenlyon's modified snake to tunnel right under ground sensors without being detected.

That ancient Old Earther Sun Tzu had a lot to say about how to attack, but most of his advice came down to figuring out what the enemy expected you to do or wanted you to do, then doing something different. Scatha, with all of the effort put into including that antiorbital weapon in their first wave of equipment, had plainly been looking mostly to defend against attacks from above. The setting of the base had shown that Scatha was also concerned about attacks coming on the surface. Mele had looked at those things, then sought out the mining equipment.

The tunnelpede slowed and halted. "The tunnel angles up from here," the driver whispered back to Mele. "We should be three meters deep."

"Okay. Grant," she called back in a soft voice, "get everyone off the 'pede and lined up. Riley, get up front with me."

Grasping the high-powered hunting rifle she had selected, Mele led Riley up the slope as the tunnel angled toward the surface. The tunnel halted abruptly, ending in a plug of dirt directly overhead that had been left in place by the snake. The scrub roots protruding from the bottom of the dirt revealed that the plug was not very thick.

Mele pulled out the big combat knife sheathed on one of her hips. That had been one of the easiest things to get manufactured on short notice. She placed the tip of the knife near one side of the tunnel, slid the blade into the dirt, and began sawing her way along the edge of the tunnel. The topsoil offered little resistance, but the tangled roots made the work hard and sweaty, and as she worked dirt rained on her.

The plug suddenly tilted down. Mele pushed it to the side of the tunnel, seeing night sky above. The distant roar of the surf could be heard. Grateful for the background noise that would block any errant sounds from her team, Mele checked the time here. "O-Dark Thirty. Perfect. Riley, get up here with Ninja's magic box."

Riley crawled up next to her, cradling the thick epad that Ninja had provided. Mele helped raise an antenna just above ground level as Riley tapped the activate command.

The pad displayed the ancient sign of the hourglass as it worked, strings of code flashing by at the bottom. Mele waited patiently until the hourglass vanished and words appeared. LINK ESTABLISHED. VERIFICATION SUCCESSFUL. INTRUSION UNDER WAY. SUBSTITUTE COUNTERFEIT DATA?

"Here's what Scatha is seeing," Riley whispered, passing another pad to Mele.

She checked the symbology, which didn't quite match that used by Franklin but was close enough to be understandable. One section provided an overview, showing exactly where the current perimeter patrol was located. Another section showed what those patrollers were seeing on their helmet displays. Mele put on an earpiece that would let her hear any orders issued on Scatha's command net or conversations on the patrol net.

A warning symbol popped up on both sections. Apparently one of Scatha's sensors had spotted something odd where Mele had opened the access tunnel.

"Get the false data going," she ordered Riley.

He tapped the YES command, and the warning symbol vanished as Ninja's device scrubbed out the detections from the sensor net.

"What was that?" she heard one of two soldiers on patrol say as the symbol disappeared.

"Another glitch," the other sentry complained.

"Maybe a wabbit. I think I'll take a shot."

Mele gestured to Riley to stay motionless.

The pop of a pulse weapon sounded on the surface. She heard the energy bolt hit somewhere in the scrub, but on the fraudulent display that Ninja's hacking had created the shot didn't appear. Mele tensed to see if either member of the patrol had spotted the discrepancy, but both appeared too bored and uncaring to notice.

"Hit anything?"

"Shut up."

Mele eased her head up enough to see the two members of the patrol, bulky in their battle armor, walking in her direction. Their movements and postures were even more casual than the sentries she had observed while planting the surveillance pickups.

She lowered herself back down into the tunnel and gave Riley a thumbs-up. "They're sloppy as hell," she whispered.

"I don't get it," Riley whispered back. "You told us these Scatha guys are really tough about following rules and doing everything perfect."

"The bosses are," Mele explained. "Funny thing. The harder the bosses are, the tighter they try to control everything their people do, the more likely those people will screw off the minute they're not being watched."

As the patrol ambled along its route, she eased the plug of dirt and plants back into place and waited with growing impatience, depending on the relayed images of their displays to know where they were rather than risk exposing her head again.

The two soldiers from Scatha walked past the tunnel exit, only a few meters from it, but both were discussing how to get their hands on booze rather than paying attention to the landscape around them. Why should they? Nothing had happened since they landed here.

Mele pulled the plug down again, grasped the hunting rifle, and came out of the tunnel silently. The rifle had a newly made silencer screwed onto the end, which probably wouldn't hide all the noise but should work well enough.

One of the soldiers was slightly behind the other. Mele moved like a wraith until she was directly behind the lagging patroller. Her right hand grasped the rifle near the breech, her finger near the trigger. Her left arm came around the front of the soldier from behind, her left fist pushing up the startled soldier's right arm before he could realize what was happening. Jamming the muzzle of the rifle into the soldier's exposed underarm, a place where she knew this type of armor had a major weak spot, she fired.

The soldier jerked as the large caliber bullet tore through his upper chest from side to side. He started to collapse, and Mele let him go and dropped her hunting rifle as well, grabbing the soldier's pulse rifle from unresisting hands.

"What was that—?" the other soldier said, turning to look.

Mele was already raising the pulse rifle. The second soldier only had time to realize she was there before Mele fired into his faceplate, the pulse rifle's muzzle almost touching it.

The faceplates were heavily reinforced, but that wasn't enough to stop an energy pulse at such short range.

The soldier's head jerked back, then his entire body fell backward.

Mele turned back to the first soldier to make sure he was down and saw him jerking on the ground.

Riley came up, staring down at the first soldier. "What's he doing?"

"Dying," Mele said. "Dying in pain."

"W-what can we do?" Riley asked.

"He's only got a couple of minutes left, at best," Mele said, her voice flat. "There's only one thing we can do to stop his pain."

"We should do it then," Riley urged.

"Are you sure?"

"Yes!"

Mele braced herself, put the muzzle of her pulse rifle against the stricken soldier's faceplate, and fired.

She looked up to see Riley staring at her.

"Don't think that was easy," Mele told him. "Or anything I wanted to do. But if it had been me lying there, dying in pain, no hope, no other way to stop it, I'd want someone to end it if they could."

"Th-that wouldn't happen . . . to you . . . would it?"

"It might," Mele said.

The killing had been quick. Much harder was dealing with the emotional aftereffect. Mele paused to breathe deeply, fighting off a sudden feeling of nausea. *Them or me. Them or me. I didn't start this.*

She checked the pad, seeing that according to it the two sentries were continuing their patrol. The alarms that should have sounded when both were killed had been blocked by Ninja's hack of Scatha's systems.

She retrieved the second soldier's pulse rifle and passed it to Grant as he brought everyone else to the surface. "Obi, take my hunting rifle. We're going to head for the command bunker single file. Me in front, Grant behind me. Riley, make sure you're in the middle. Obi, bring up the rear. Only Grant and I should have ready weapons. The rest of you keep yours on safe until I say otherwise. Ninja's hack will prevent the sensors from reporting seeing us, but we can't risk a stray shot being heard by someone."

While the others were lining up, Mele went over the fallen soldiers and removed a pair of grenades from each, stuffing them into the pockets of her short jacket.

She led the column toward the command bunker, which was clearly identified on Scatha's own command net. Mele had to fight down repeated urges to run toward her objective. But if she ran, everyone else would run with her, and too many of her new volunteers might get disoriented in the darkness and do something wrong.

As they got closer, Mele could see the bunker's visual observation periscopes resting in their armored mounts, the lenses blocked by protective shielding that would prevent anyone inside the bunker from actually looking at the outside. Shoddy, careless, and complacent. Standard procedures should have called for visual searches to be performed at random intervals as a backup for the automated system. She felt a surge of anger at the sheer stupidity of Scatha's soldiers, who seemed to be cooperating in their own deaths.

A short ramp led down into the half-buried bunker, a sealed blast door at the end. Mele squinted at the pad in her hand. "Get Riley up here. Hey, how do we open this door?"

Riley brought up a menu, tabbed a submenu, studied the blast door, then tapped something else.

The blast door slid open.

The secondary door behind it was already open, another sloppy violation of standard rules.

Mele gestured to Grant, then went into the bunker fast, her stolen pulse rifle ready.

Two soldiers were sitting at watch stations along a wide set of displays.

One started to turn at the noise of Mele's entry. "What are you guys doing back—?"

She shot that soldier, then put another shot into the head of the other watch-stander.

Mele and Grant paused, their weapons trained toward an internal door. "Sentry rest area," Grant breathed to her. "Hard way or easy way?"

"Let's see if they're awake." Mele edged forward cautiously.

She kept her rifle trained on the door, so that when it suddenly swung open, she was already lined up for a shot.

"What the hell was that noise?" another Scatha soldier demanded, blinking to adjust to the slightly brighter red light in the rest of the bunker.

Mele fired, the bolt hitting the soldier in the chest. As the soldier tumbled backward, Mele yanked one of her stolen grenades from a pocket, primed it, and threw it after the soldier she had shot.

Grant hit the internal wall next to the door and yanked it closed moments before a muffled explosion sounded, and the metal door dented in several places from grenade fragments hitting it.

Grant slammed the door open again while Mele went inside in another rush, her weapon questing for targets.

There had been four other soldiers sleeping in the rest area. The one Mele had shot lay on the floor. The others had died in their bunks.

She backed out, fighting off another surge of queasiness. "Close it," she told Grant.

Mele went back to the entry and gestured the others inside. The bunker had felt roomy, but with twenty men and women plus Mele and the two bodies of the watch-standers it had become crowded.

The dead were hauled away from the displays, Mele gesturing to Riley to sit where one of them had been. He hesitated, then sat down.

"Get going," Mele said.

Riley wasn't as good as Ninja (no one was, he had admitted to Mele), but he was very good. Swiping through control displays, he quickly opened paths to critical systems throughout the Scatha base. "Ninja was right. We're inside everything," he told Mele. "Past all firewalls."

"Plant the malware bombs and be sure the timers for them are all set right."

Riley nodded, dropping a data coin into a slot on the console, extracting the destructive software inside it, and directing the malware into every system within reach of the Scatha command and control net. "One hour? Are you sure that's time enough?"

"It should be," Mele said. "I don't see any signs of problems at the big gun. Make sure their alarms there are disabled and their gates and doors unlocked."

"Got it," Riley said. "The big gun is wide open. Malware bombs planted. Timers are all set. One hour."

"Can you tell who is inside the big gun's site?"

"Hold on." Riley swiped through several more screens, then paused to study an image. "Two people. From their outfits, they're technicians, not soldiers."

"Good. Grant, you stay here with your ten. Make sure nobody shows up early and raises an alarm. Set the explosives we brought to destroy this bunker. Here are the detonators for those. Riley, download every Scatha file you can so we can bring them back with us, and if you spot anywhere else in Scatha's networks we can cause problems, see if you can raise more hell. But make sure none of that hell happens before the malware bombs go off. Obi, you bring your ten with me. There are two techs at the site. Civilians. Make sure we only use shockers on them."

"Wouldn't it be better to kill them, too?" Obi asked. She had the look of someone who had already fallen off a cliff and wasn't trying to pretend otherwise. "Since we've already killed these others? If those techs are alive, they could work against us, maybe help repair the weapon?"

"No," Mele said. "We shock them, haul them out where they'll be safe and unharmed when the site goes up, and the civilians with this camp will know they are safe from us. The soldiers here will know that, too. They'll be mad about their buddies we killed and mad that the civilians didn't get a scratch. That will drive a wedge between the civilians and military even if there wasn't one before.

Besides, there isn't going to be enough left of that weapon for anybody to be able to fix."

"I don't know," another volunteer commented. "We should take them out! Aren't they all enemies? I wouldn't shoot kids, but everyone from Scatha—"

Mele silenced him with an abrupt gesture that held both command and menace. "I don't conduct debates during a combat op. Let's put it this way. If anybody kills one of those civilians, or tries to kill them, *I'll* kill whoever fired. Does anybody want to try dodging *my* shots? No? Then follow orders. Shockers only inside the site. Make sure you've got your bomb packs. Come on."

With the Scatha sensor net and warning systems totally compromised, and in fact under the control of her own people, Mele led her group at a run across the wide stretch of pavement separating the antiorbital site from the command and control bunker. If they were going to take out the big gun and get back to the WinG before daylight, they couldn't waste time. The rest of the base stretched off to the north and west, the buildings housing families visible as well as the low, rounded dome of the main power plant.

The gate in the chain-link fence protecting the site opened when she pulled on it. Sensors that should have reported the gate opening and intruders entering the site remained silent.

The weapon site was an impressive feat of engineering, a massive hexagon with sloping sides of thick multithreat armor. The top was only five meters aboveground, though, because most of the massive particle beam cannon was in big rooms excavated below ground level.

Mele led the way past defensive infantry firing ports that were sealed closed. The gun site could have been a fortress against a ground attack if any soldiers had been inside. And if every lock and alarm hadn't been tied in to a central control system that Mele's people now directed.

She went through a surface blast door that had already slid open, its impressive thickness posing no barrier. Steps led down to another blast door, which also stood open.

The pad Mele held showed the floor plan for the weapon site, so she had little trouble finding the operating room nestled into one side of the armored citadel. The armored hatch that should have sealed off the operating room swung open easily when Mele tried it. Looking inside, Mele saw one tech dozing in her chair while the other watched a vid on a personal pad.

She nodded to four of the volunteers who carried shockers, gesturing for two to target one tech and the other two the remaining one.

Shocks knocked out both techs before either realized they were in trouble. Part of the charge from one shocker hit the personal pad of the vid-viewing tech and fried it.

One of the volunteers had come from Glenlyon's police force and fell to binding the arms and feet of the techs while others wrapped gags around their mouths.

Mele turned to another volunteer. "Hedy?"

Hedy dropped into one of the vacated seats, studying the controls and displays. While not a weapons expert, she knew enough about similar systems to have been able to quickly learn all that Glenlyon's databases had about antiorbital weapons like this one. "Okay. No surprises," Hedy said. "You can plant the bombs. The preplanned spots should work fine."

"Let's go," Mele directed. Most of the remaining team followed her out of the control room. On Mele's pad, locations for each bomb glowed. As they reached each one, a bomb was gingerly removed, placed, then Mele put the detonator in and set the timer.

"We're putting these on the most critical parts of this site," she told the others. "When these thermite bombs ignite, the thermite in them will burn at something over two thousand degrees centigrade, melting right through everything they're on and everything under that."

"Can they put it out?" Obi asked.

"Thermite? Yeah, if they've got the right stuff. There are special powders that can bind with the thermite," Mele said. "Other than that? No. I watched thermite burn out in the shell of a spacecraft once. Full vacuum. It just kept going until the thermite had all oxidized."

Back inside the control room, Mele found Hedy carefully entering some commands. "Can you give me the right time for this? I'm going to power up the cannon so the power storage cells are at peak when the thermite melts into them. The explosion *that* sets off will destroy anything that the thermite hasn't slagged."

"You engineers love doing this kind of thing, don't you?" Mele asked, leaning down to look at the display in front of Hedy. "Your time is good."

"Thanks. Yeah. You know what they say, engineering is like science, only louder." Hedy stood up. "We're ready. It's all on auto. I admit I'm nervous to be inside this site with those thermite bomb timers ticking and the cannon about to power up."

"Then let's get out." Directing the rest of the team to hoist the bound techs and carry them, Mele went last, making sure no one was left behind.

She closed the blast doors as they passed each one, pausing only long enough to fire energy pulses from her rifle into the lock panels so that getting through the doors again would be a major chore for the techs and soldiers from Scatha.

"What is the power plant going to do when that cannon starts drawing power big-time?" Hedy asked Mele. "I didn't think of that."

"It's okay. They'll do one of two things," Mele said. "Either call and ask what's going on, or assume they didn't get told about something and not worry."

"If they call, they won't get any answer."

"As long as they spend another . . . half hour arguing about it before they send anyone, it won't matter."

They were outside again. Scatha's base remained silent, but the quiet now wore at Mele with the feeling that menace lurked unseen and soundless just out of sight. Things had gone too well. Something always went wrong, so what would it be and when?

They dropped off the bound techs, still unconscious, about halfway between the antiorbital weapon site and the command and control bunker, Mele ensuring the two were placed inside a drain culvert to protect them from the mayhem that would soon erupt. Both were still out cold. She made sure the gags didn't obstruct their ability to breathe through their noses.

Obi turned a worried gaze on Mele. "I know we're not hurting them, but what are the guys in charge here going to do to these two once they find out we've done so much damage?"

"All we can do is what we can do," Mele said, not surprised that once Obi had seen the techs as people she had lost any desire to kill them out of hand. "I'm sure not hauling them out of here with us."

At the command bunker, Grant was waiting just outside the front entrance, weapon ready as he scanned his surroundings. "Are we ready?"

"You tell me," Mele said.

"All bombs planted. I just have to set the timer for the fuel-air explosive that will pop the top off this fixer-upper."

"Do it, and get everyone else out here. Obi, start leading them back to the tunnel entrance. You know where it is? Right. Listen up, everyone. Nobody relax yet. Stay in full-alert mode until we get inside that tunnel again and are riding the 'pede back to the WinG."

Mele waited with growing nervousness as the last members of the team left the bunker. As soon as Grant gave her an all clear she waved him off to join the others, then waited, cautiously watching for any sign of alarm. She checked the pad. Ten minutes until both malware bombs at remote sites and physical bombs at the bunker and big gun started going off.

"I cut this a little too close," she muttered, backing away from the bunker, then running to join the others through the deceptively peaceful quiet of the night.

Almost everyone was inside the tunnel when Mele reached them. She waved the last two inside, lowering herself behind them but keeping her eyes on the bunker.

Which was why she saw the ground vehicle pull up at the command bunker. Her lower body already inside the tunnel, Mele laid her upper body on the ground, watching. Three soldiers got out of the vehicle, moving with the slow, casual pace of people who expected no danger. Distant sounds of conversation came to her, too faint to make out but followed by unmistakable laughter.

Five minutes left. If these soldiers from Scatha realized what had happened and acted quickly, they could still disarm some of the bombs.

12

"Obi! Give me back the hunting rifle!" Mele lowered her pulse rifle to those fully in the tunnel and brought up the hunting weapon, loading a round and aiming hastily.

The rifle bucked against her shoulder as she fired.

If it had been an individual soldier, she might well have missed. But the tight group of three made a bigger target. The sound of the shot, soft as it was, caused the three Scatha soldiers to start to turn at the noise, which had been muffled enough by the silencer to not immediately sound like a slug thrower rifle going off.

One of the soldiers fell backward abruptly.

Shouts rang out as the other two soldiers went to ground.

Less than three minutes. "Get everyone seated on the 'pede!" Mele ordered, aiming again.

What would those soldiers do? The bunker was right behind them, where they would expect to find help. But why risk jumping up and running into it when they could call for help? There was a patrol out there, right?

Mele's pad alerted her that signals were being sent. Alerts from comms held by those two soldiers. But Ninja's software was blocking the alerts.

She fired again, aiming for the ground vehicle to be certain her shot would hit something and discourage the remaining two soldiers from rising.

One minute. Some big bombs were about to go off, and she was still way too close.

She aimed and fired again, ready to fall back, but didn't leave enough time.

Ninja's device chirped a warning. "Damn! Stay down!" Mele yelled to her team, dropping her upper body again to lie prone herself.

A titanic crash echoed across the plain. The heavy armor forming the top of the command bunker catapulted into the air from the force of the explosion inside the bunker. Mele caught a glimpse of the ground vehicle that had brought the soldiers to the bunker being flung aside as if slapped by a giant. The two soldiers outside the bunker probably died never knowing what had hit them.

An even more powerful series of blasts erupted from the antiorbital weapon site as thermite reached the maximized power storage cells, and everything let loose at once inside the armored structure. Jagged openings were torn in the protective armor, showers of burning thermite being hurled outward. The massive top of the site sagged downward into the devastation beneath it as the glow of melting metal lit the night.

Mele slid completely into the tunnel, shoving the plug of dirt and vegetation roughly back into place. The outside sounds of panic and destruction faded as the plug blocked and absorbed most of the noise. Anyone searching the field in daylight would spot the sagging place that marked the tunnel entrance, but every delay in Scatha's soldiers finding the tunnel would be important. She expected that Scatha's remaining soldiers would be busy for a little while with other matters, but no sense in making things easier for the enemy.

The 'pede could go back the way they had come simply by being driven from the opposite end. Mele climbed onto the last position of the 'pede, trying to slow herself down and think. "Does everyone have their weapon? Are all weapons on safe? Grant, Obi, is everyone accounted for?"

A chorus of replies assured her that all was as well as could be expected with explosions still rocking Scatha's base, the walls of the tunnel trembling around them in a very disquieting way. Mele thought at this point the new explosions must mark software-controlled equipment suffering destructive failure because of the malware bombs. When she got a chance, she would have to ask Riley about some of the locations those bombs had been sent to.

"We're not safe yet!" Mele called. "Get this thing moving! Maintain the best speed you can! The sooner we get back to WinG, the better!"

"Is this what being a Marine is like?" Obi called back to Mele.

"Part of it," she said, watching tensely for any sign that Scatha's soldiers had spotted the tunnel entrance behind them.

"I like it."

"Then you might be crazy enough to be a Marine," Mele said as the 'pede rolled rapidly through the tunnel. "Listen up everyone! This isn't over! We're still way too close to the hornets' nest that we stirred up at Scatha's camp. They're mad as hell right now, and as soon as they figure out we're responsible, they're going to be looking very hard for us so they can get even!"

As if timed to emphasize her warning, the tunnel reverberated again to a distant vibration as something else big blew up back at the Scatha base.

"What was that?" someone asked.

"I don't know," Mele said.

"Maybe the power plant," Hedy suggested. "There shouldn't be anything left to blow that big at the antiorbital site."

"Could be," Riley agreed, his voice echoing off the tunnel walls. "Several malware bombs were planted in the power plant's operating software. The design wouldn't allow a runaway nuclear reaction, but there could have been a need to dump energy fast that resulted in a regular explosion."

The conversation sounded weird, Mele thought. Hurtling along through the dark tunnel, the glow of the headlight barely visible ahead, and engineers discussing in academic terms what probably just blew up.

"If the power plant blew," Hedy added, "they'll be able to keep basics running using solar, but their manufacturing is going to slow a lot. It's going to hurt them."

"Good," Mele said, worrying about something else. "Riley, did you get any malware bombs into the aerospace craft?"

"I don't know. I think one of them was hooked in, and I was able to get something into it, but that was only one."

Great. That left one aerospace craft as a potential problem.

Mele gasped with relief as the tunnelpede raced up the slope to where the tunnel came to the surface on this end. They rolled completely out of the tunnel and toward where the dark bulk of the WinG still sat.

The bulk of the foothills screening them from view from the Scatha camp didn't block all of the sound coming from there. Mele heard a low murmur that at this distance was the mingled noise of hundreds of people shouting and yelling, mixed in with the roar of equipment and punctuated by occasional crashes and bangs that marked continuing explosions. A slight glow visible over the foothills drew everyone's attention.

"Do you think that's the weapon site still melting down?" Hedy asked Riley.

"Could be. Or the power plant. Most of the structure might have been liquefied by an emergency energy release."

"Move now, talk later!" Mele ordered. "Everyone into the WinG! Except you! Get the 'pede stored aboard as fast as you can!"

She stood watching as the tunnelpede rolled up the cargo hatch, curling up to form its own, smaller coil next to the mining snake. As the cargo hatch swung closed, Mele shoved the 'pede guy toward the WinG's personnel hatch while checking the ground for any equipment left behind or any person not yet aboard. Satisfied, she jumped into the WinG. "Get a head count!" she ordered Grant before racing to the cockpit.

"Are we ready?" the pilot asked. Both pilots looked about as nervous as could be expected after having to sit out here waiting through a long period of silence that had been replaced by the cataclysmic noises as various equipment and buildings in Scatha's camp blew up.

"Still getting a head count," she replied.

Grant came far enough forward to call out. "Everyone accounted for! We're all aboard!"

"Let's go," she told the pilots. "Get us out of here as fast as you can. Stay hidden. One of their warbirds might still be operational."

The WinG's engines powered up. The craft slid forward, rising slightly as the ground effect kicked in, moving faster and faster down to the beach and over the water, curving north to avoid detection as it kept accelerating past five hundred kilometers per hour. The pilots held the altitude down to two meters above the highest swells of the dark ocean passing beneath them.

"Head toward Delta as soon as you think we're outside Scatha's detection range," Mele told them.

"We're already altering course to do that."

An urgent tone sounded, a symbol appearing on the displays before each pilot. "That's not good," one commented.

"We've got company," the other pilot told Mele. "An aerospace craft. It's coming from the direction of Scatha's base."

"Who's faster?" Mele asked.

"He is. And he's pushing it hard to get within weapons range of us."

"I imagine he's pretty upset," Mele said. "Can we get to Delta before he gets to us?"

"Don't know yet. He's still accelerating. It depends what he tops out at."

"Give Delta a call. Tell them that we're coming in hot with a Scatha warbird on our tail," Mele said. "And get every bit of speed you can out of this skimmer."

"We're already trying to go our fastest," the second pilot informed her.

"Sorry," Mele apologized. "It's hard to be a passenger. I did the same thing to fleet sailors."

"Now you're treating me like a sailor? I'm a pilot, not a space squid!

Making me angry isn't going to make this skimmer go any faster."

"Sorry, bird driver." Mele sat for a moment longer, gathering her thoughts, then went back to the passenger deck, where everyone looked at her. She took a deep breath before speaking. "The good news is, we're heading back. The bad news is, Scatha got one warbird up. It's chasing us. We're trying to get to Delta before the warbird catches us."

"How bad is this?" Riley asked Mele.

She shrugged. "If we get to Delta before the warbird gets to us, we'll probably be fine. If the warbird gets to us before we get to Delta, it could be ugly."

"We got the job done," Grant said.

"Yeah," Mele agreed. "We got the job done. Up to a point. Part of my job is getting you guys back. I'll make that happen. I'm going to send an update so the government will know we hit Scatha hard, then if anyone needs me, I'll be in the cockpit."

When she got back to the cockpit, the pilots were looking ahead with grim expressions.

Mele checked their displays. "The warbird should be within range of Delta in half an hour."

"Yup," one the pilots said.

"But the warbird will be within range of us in twenty minutes."

"Yup," the other pilot said.

"Does this skimmer bird have any defenses?" Mele asked, hoping there might be some secret, hidden capability.

"Speed, very low altitude, and our lightning reflexes," the first pilot replied.

"What do you think our odds are?"

"Pretty damn poor."

"He's going to engage with his missiles first, right?" Mele asked.

"Yeah," the pilot agreed. "Most likely missiles with full-spectrum active seekers with backup full-spectrum passive seekers. Even a crate with a state-of-the-art countermeasures system would have trouble dealing with those. Our very low altitude won't help. We can't jink to avoid the missiles faster than they can correct and still hit us. Our only option is to go fast enough that he can't get within range, and that's not possible."

Mele frowned. "I had a gunny once who told me that when anyone says there's only one option, it means there must be another that's not occurring to them."

"A gunny?" the second pilot asked. "A Marine? That's your source of wisdom and inspiration?"

"If you knew gunnies, you wouldn't be skeptical," Mele said. "If— You said all we can do is speed up. Why couldn't we slow down to evade his missiles?"

Both pilots shook their heads. "We can't decelerate fast enough to make a difference," the first said.

"Hold on," the second pilot said. "What if we pancake?"

"At this speed? It'd tear us apart." The first pilot paused in thought. "We could skip. Bounce along the tops of swells. That would slow us a lot faster, much faster than that warbird and the missiles could manage, but not too fast for the bird to handle it."

"If we did it right."

"Well, yeah, if we did it wrong, the bird goes boom."

"If those missiles hit us, the bird goes boom," Mele pointed out.

The first pilot looked at his companion. "If we cut speed fast enough while the missiles are on final, they'll be aiming at a point well ahead of where we are. They'll try to compensate, but they'll be on a downward trajectory and going very fast without much altitude left."

"They'd hit the water," the second pilot said. "Somewhere ahead of us. Hopefully. Of course, then we'd be going a lot slower, with that warbird rocketing up our tail."

"Hmmm." The first pilot studied the data on the pursuing warbird. "He's coming on real fast. If we slow down as much as we're planning on, he won't be able to reengage us before he tears on past."

"Looks like a good bet," the second pilot agreed. "What does he do then?"

"He'd either have to shoot past us and swing back around, or climb almost straight up to shed velocity and tip back down and dive on us. Maybe a full loop if he thinks of that in time, but it would be a big one because of how fast he's going and how much speed he has to lose."

"Do you think he could manage a passing shot?"

"He could try. We're going to be throwing up a lot of spray while we're bouncing off the swells, though, and . . . the missiles aren't going to impact that far ahead of us."

The second pilot grinned. "They go boom, we fly right into a big fountain of spray, and maybe our warbird thinks he hit us. He's going to have trouble figuring out what happened. Only for a few seconds, but at the speed he's chasing us—"

"A few seconds might do the trick." The first pilot grinned. "Want to try?"

"Why the hell not?"

"Why the hell not?" the pilot agreed. "Hey, Marine. If this doesn't work, we'll probably end up cartwheeling across the surface of the ocean, shedding pieces as we go. Since you gave us the idea, I wanted you to know that."

"Thanks," Mele said. "And if it does work, will we be able to get close enough to Delta before the warbird can engage us again?"

"Maybe."

"That's better than no chance," Mele said.

"So it is. Make sure your guys are strapped in back there. In about ten minutes, we're going to see whether we can do this."

Mele passed the word, then returned to the cockpit and strapped into her seat. The pilots were both visibly tense, sweat on their necks as they watched the warbird draw ever closer. She stayed quiet, not wanting to distract them.

An alarm sounded at the same moment as one of the pilots called out. "Incoming! Two of them!"

"Hold on," the other said.

"You going to call it?"

"Uh, yeah. I'll call it."

"I'll cut the engines when you call it."

Mele could see the threat markers that represented the two missiles closing fast on the WinG. The pilots held the WinG on a steady course as the alarm sounded again with more urgency. Red lights flashed. "Danger," a woman's recorded voice said. "Incoming missiles. Recommend evasive action."

"No kidding," the first pilot muttered. "Stand by."

"Ready," the second pilot replied.

"Ten seconds to impact," the woman's voice warned.

"Now!"

The WinG tilted down as the first pilot headed lower and the second pilot cut thrust. Almost immediately, there came a jolt that slammed Mele against the straps holding her in her seat, and the WinG bounced up again. The WinG floated several meters above the waves while the pilots fought to bring her back down, then fell and bounced upward again in another shower of spray.

"Not too hard!" the first pilot yelled to the second as they struggled to bring the WinG down again.

A third jolt, longer this time, the WinG ringing with the sound of the contact with the water.

Mele, looking forward, saw two objects plummet into the water just ahead. An instant later, spray from two explosions blossomed as the WinG reached the impact point. The WinG jolted as the spray hit it under its belly and wings, then steadied out as the pilots goosed the thrust again.

"What's he doing?" the first pilot demanded as he steadied the WinG.

"Already overhead," the second one reported. "He's climbing. Coming up . . . it's a loop. He's coming all the way around."

Mele saw the displays light up with warnings again. She didn't need the pilots to interpret that. The warbird would soon finish his loop and dive at the WinG in a second attack.

"He's either out of missiles," the second pilot said, "or he doesn't want to waste any more. This looks like a gun run."

"It's going to be real close," the first pilot gasped, checking the distance remaining to Delta. "Here he comes. Let's dance!"

The pilots of the WinG jinked the craft wildly as the warbird came boring in, its manta shape making it look malevolent as well as deadly. The WinG pilots lost speed with every maneuver but also created an erratic target whose path the Scatha warbird's fire control system couldn't predict. The warbird's first burst tore up water to the left of the WinG, the second burst pelted the ocean just to the right of the WinG, and the third burst was hitting just in front of the WinG when the warbird finally came into range of Delta.

Two heavy-duty industrial lasers, their output pumped and their operating controls tied to simple optical tracking systems that spanned into infrared and ultraviolet. In daylight, its hull heated by the friction of tearing through the atmosphere at high speed, the warbird was easy for the tracking systems to lock on. And the beams of the lasers moved much, much faster than the bullets fired by the warbird's guns.

The warbird's skin was designed to vaporize when hit to help protect against damage from lasers, but two powerful weapons firing at the fairly close range demanded by their industrial design put out too much energy for that to make much difference.

An explosion in the warbird's right weapons bay tore off the right wing, sending the warbird spinning wildly as it spiraled in an uncontrollable corkscrew across the sky.

Mele saw a symbol appear as the pilot of the warbird ejected, but the symbol vanished an instant after it appeared when the rapidly spinning craft's left wing slapped the ejection module before it could boost clear. The impact turned the ejection module into flying debris and tore off a large part of the left wing, slowing the crippled warbird's tumble a little as it nosed over and rocketed into the ocean. A tall plume of water erupted to mark the destruction of the warbird. As the water settled, nothing could be seen but small fragments of the aerospace craft.

"No way they survived that," the first pilot said somberly.

"No," the second pilot agreed. "Too bad. That pilot was pretty good."

"Yeah." The first pilot looked back at Mele. "It worked."

"I noticed," Mele said. "Next time you meet Marines, buy them a round."

"Fair enough. Shall we tell Delta to pack up and go home?"

"Yes. Do they need us to hang around until they can lift in case Scatha sends someone else?"

"You haven't had enough excitement for one day, Marine?" The second pilot passed on the request, then shook his head at Mele. "Delta says they're already loading their power unit and lasers back on their WinG and they'll be out of there in ten minutes, so there's no need for us to hang around."

Mele kept her eyes on the pilots' displays as they raced past the two islands, watching until she saw Delta's WinG take off and head for home as well.

She sighed, feeling her whole body suddenly overcome with weariness, but unstrapped and went back to her team. "You can relax," she told them. "There's nothing to do now but wait until we get back."

"I'm writing my memoirs," Obi announced. "And I'm going to update my online status from *It's complicated* to *I'm still alive*."

Everyone laughed except Grant. "What's the matter?" Mele asked.

He shrugged, looking embarrassed. "I know he doesn't deserve it, but I'm worried about what must be happening to Spurlick."

"Spurlick?" It took Mele a moment to understand. "Oh, yeah. We figure he told Scatha they had nothing to worry about from me because I was an idiot, and that if Glenlyon did do something, it would be a head-on attack across the open field. That probably contributed to how unprepared they were tonight. No, I don't expect Citizen Spurlick is having much fun right now."

"He's probably already dead," Grant said.

"If he's lucky, he is. The only reason Scatha would keep him alive would be to make him pay for their losses tonight."

Riley spoke up. "I can go through some of the files we downloaded and see if there's anything about Spurlick in there."

"Good idea." Too tired to care much about the fate of someone who had betrayed them, Mele went back to the cockpit, strapped in, and fell asleep.

Glenlyon had gone from tense foreboding to wild celebration. "They think the fight is almost over," Grant remarked to Mele.

They were sitting in the temporary building that Mele had labeled the Supreme Headquarters Complex, in the small office that Mele called the Planetary Defense Command Center. "How many volunteers came in today?" she asked.

"Another ten," Grant said. "That takes us close to two hundred. How large do you think the council will let us go?"

"I'll keep them informed and see when they say stop," Mele said. "We're going to need those warm bodies. And next time, we're going to lose some of them. Scatha still has more than eighty soldiers at that base, and they're not going to be asleep at their watch stations next time we show up." She gestured toward her portable display. "They finally found the surveillance pickups I planted, so no more close-in signal collection for us."

"Too bad we couldn't have hit them again already," Grant remarked. "Their morale must be low enough to walk under closed doors."

"The satellite shows they're running patrols out a lot farther from the base," Mele said.

"Can we take one?"

"Maybe. Their second warbird hasn't lifted since the raid. It might be down, or they might be playing dead." Mele's alert chimed. "Let's see what fan mail the council sent me. Hey, *Squall* is back. Showed up at the jump point four hours ago."

"That's good. We've got top cover again," Grant said. "How'd their mission go?"

"No details. Space squids send status reports as soon as they arrive in a system, right? So the council should know something. They must be worried about people tapping into our network."

"We did do that to Scatha."

"Yeah," Mele said, "but the same people who tapped into Scatha upgraded the defenses on our networks. I'll go over to the council for a face-to-face with Leigh Camagan to find out how *Squall* did and let her know our current strength."

"Sure thing, Major Darcy," Grant said. "Maybe they'll make you a colonel while you're there."

"I'm not sure I'm dumb enough to be a colonel. Maybe they'll just bust me back to sergeant."

Rob Geary had sent a detailed report in to the council as soon as *Squall* arrived back at Glenlyon Star System. He had talked with the council as soon as *Squall* got close enough to the planet for something like real-time conversation. And he had taken a shuttle down for a face-to-face with the council, which had dragged on for some time.

All the while, he had really wanted to meet with someone else.

"Ninja?" Rob asked as he opened the door to Ninja IT Consulting. She was there, smiling at him from her desk.

Mele Darcy was in the office as well, just getting up from a second chair that Ninja had finally acquired. "Hi, Lieutenant Geary. I heard you did some great work."

"Hello, Major Darcy," Rob said. "I guess you outrank me now."

She grinned. "I'm sure you'll get bumped up in rank soon."

He shook his head. "Not likely."

Ninja's glower was obviously aimed at the council, not him. "Why not? Look what you did!"

"I endangered Glenlyon's only warship and may have started hostilities with another star system," Rob said. "Or that's what a good chunk of the council is worried about, anyway."

"What were you supposed to have done? Let that ship bombard Kosatka?"

"The council can't decide what I should have done," Rob said, leaning against the wall. "Or if what I did was done the way I should have done it."

"But you're the one who done it," Mele Darcy observed.

"Right. Speaking of stuff done, you did a real number on Scatha here. We saw the damage from orbit."

"It's going to take more," Mele Darcy said, and he understood the dark undertone to that statement. She clearly feared that "more" would be expensive in terms of casualties. Having worried that Darcy would be strutting around like the savior of Glenlyon, Rob was relieved to see her still acting as levelheaded as his first impression of her had been.

"We're here to help," he said. "Uh, did I interrupt a business meeting?"

"Nope," Darcy said. "Ninja and I were just discussing how vital it is not to put off important stuff when there's shooting going on. You never know when it'll be your last chance to tell somebody something, you know? I'll let you guys catch up."

Ninja gave Mele an exasperated look as she left, then waved Rob to the other seat. "Is the council really mad at you?"

"The council," Rob said as he sat down, "doesn't know what it wants to do. It's been spooked ever since Scatha sent a ship to shake us down, and that's gotten worse as the situation got worse. They're thrilled I've got Kosatka's promise of aid, scared that I might have triggered hostilities with another, unknown star system, glad that I probably saved Kosatka from what happened to Lares, and terrified that what was done to Lares might happen here."

"So what they're mad at is the universe," Ninja said.

"Yes. But they can't take anything out on the universe. I, on the other hand, am right here."

Ninja looked down. "I'm glad you're back."

"Me, too. Are you and Darcy friends now?"

"I need someone to spend time with while you're gallivanting all over the galaxy," Ninja said. "Don't you like her?"

"Mele Darcy? Yeah, I think I do. What she's accomplished against Scatha's base is amazing given what she had to work with. I was worried about her when I left, you know that, but now it seems she's really something."

Ninja cast a very quick glance his way. "If you like that sort of thing," she said in a toneless voice.

"What?"

"Nothing."

"Ninja, I thought you'd be happy to see me. Are you all right?"

"Why wouldn't I be all right? I'm fine. Just don't assume I'll always be sitting around waiting for you to get back from another star," Ninja said.

Rob eyed her, thinking. "I've got a sister, you know."

"Congratulations."

"She told me what it means when a woman says *fine*. It means whatever man she's talking to is in trouble. Why am I in trouble?"

"Look," Ninja said, "I'm sort of busy. If you don't mind, I need to—"

"Ninja, I spent a lot of time thinking about you while I was gone. You're an amazing person. I missed you. But I want to be fair to you."

She kept her eyes on the display before her. "What does that mean?"

Rob had practiced his speech countless times, but now found it hard to say anything. "You already know what my life might be like. Danger, sometimes, and a lot of separation maybe. How could I ask any partner to put up with that?"

"Wouldn't that be up to the partner?" Ninja asked. "If you respect someone, shouldn't you let them weigh in on a decision like that instead of making it yourself?"

"Yeah," Rob said. "I should. You're right."

"That's a good start."

"So?" Rob asked.

"So?" Ninja replied.

"How do you feel about it? Because I'm starting to wonder if I've been imagining things."

She finally looked at him again. "One of the reasons I like you is because you don't mess with people."

"I'm not messing with you," Rob said. "That'd be kind of dangerous, wouldn't it?"

"You have no idea how dangerous it would be," Ninja said.

"Is that what happened to that chief petty officer back in Alfar?"

"Him? Nah. He was just a jerk to everybody. It'll probably be another decade before he gets his public and private records straightened out. Not that I know anything about that, you understand. Just tell me one thing. Are you doing me a favor?" Ninja asked.

Startled by the question, Rob took a moment to answer. "No. I'm doing myself a favor. I'm finally taking a chance on something that . . . could be really special."

"It took you long enough," Ninja said. "Now what?"

He felt awkward, rubbing the back of his neck. "Um . . . what are you doing for dinner?"

Ninja waved toward a bulb of highly caffeinated soda and a pack of candy. "Working meal."

"You wouldn't mind if we went out and got some dinner with actual nutrients in it, would you?"

"You mean like a date? Are you asking me out? Because I have a lot of work to do, and I wouldn't want to waste any time."

He grinned at her. "I've already wasted enough time. Yes, I am asking you out. I just realized how much I've always enjoyed talking to you."

"You just realized that?" She shook her head, looking exasperated again. "You should do it more often, then. Sure. We'll go out and get something *healthy* to eat if that's your thing. Oh, wait, there's something else I need to get out of the way first."

"Will it take long?" Rob asked.

"Nah." Ninja got up, walked the short distance to him, and bent over to kiss Rob, long and gently. When she finished, Ninja straightened and smiled at him. "I've wanted to do that for a while."

"You can do it again if you want," Rob said, his lips still tingling from the touch of hers.

Ninja laughed. "Maybe after dinner."

Scatha had, of course, started planting sensors where they could watch behind the foothills. Mele led a raid in the WinG again, keeping a cautious eye out for the second warbird to lift while they located and destroyed Scatha's remote sensors. They fled again in the WinG before Scatha could send a force to attack them.

Scatha planted more sensors the next day. Mele led another raid to destroy those.

Scatha planted more sensors. This time, not everyone who came on the WinG got back on it to leave. But with the sensors gone again, Scatha had no way of knowing that.

Mele lay as still as she could along the reverse slope of one of the hills. Scatha's base was out of sight on the other side, but sensors planted on the hilltops by Mele's team the night before offered a view of a patrol headed this way.

The patrol had ten soldiers in it. All in battle armor. Two were lugging sensor packs in addition to their normal loads. They were spread out in the proper dispersed formation for a combat patrol, but the way they trudged along didn't speak of high morale or alertness. Behind them, their base was marked by two large craters full of slag where the power plant and the antiorbital weapon had been. Another smaller crater marked the former site of their command bunker.

With Glenlyon's satellites back in place to maintain constant watch from above, Mele knew that large patrols were being sent out every day, wearing down the limited Scathan garrison. And Scatha's soldiers had done this particular task twice already, replacing sensors destroyed by the same raiders who had trashed much of their base. They would replace the sensors a third time, and knew they would do it again as many more times as necessary while their commanders played a game of who-is-more-stubborn with the enemy. But at least while they were out here on the open plain, they didn't have to worry about being attacked by surprise.

Mele sighed, imagining herself among that patrol. It was far too easy to guess what they were feeling and thinking.

The latest data from the satellite had also shown the warbird being worked on, panels removed, systems being replaced. The malware bombs must have torn apart a lot of the warbird's equipment. It shouldn't be rising anytime soon.

She checked the status of the mortars that had been brought in last night and placed behind the hills. Mortar tubes had been very easy to manufacture. The projectiles had been a little harder but nothing really complicated. And the firing calculations had been extremely easy for engineers to program into the control pad that Mele held.

The sensors that her team had planted fed through that control pad as well. A large red outline marked the firing zone that the mortars were set for. No matter what path Scatha's patrol took to the hills, she would know when they were within the firing zone.

Mele gestured to her small team, spread out on either side of her, giving a warning sign. Obi grinned. Grant nodded in reply.

Scatha's patrol began walking into the firing zone as Mele tapped to update the mortars' firing solution.

Mele waited until they were all inside the red lines, then tapped the firing command.

The eight mortar tubes chuffed behind her, their rounds rising over the tops of the hills and plummeting down toward the patrol.

This close, with mortars firing on a low trajectory, there wasn't much warning time. The patrol's battle armor spotted the incoming rounds, of course. With no time to run, all ten soldiers dropped onto their bellies for the only protection available out in the open.

The mortar rounds fell until they were five meters above the patrol, then their warheads detonated, blasting out downward-focused cones of shrapnel.

Mele was already running, her own eight-person team following as she topped the hill and ran down toward the patrol. She saw the mortar rounds detonate, the dirt around the patrol puffing up as the deadly fragments hit at velocities sufficient to penetrate the back of Brahma-made battle armor.

It seemed to take far too long to reach the remains of the patrol. Mele started grabbing pulse rifles and grenades that the Scatha patrol no longer had any use for, passing them to her team as they caught up.

Then they ran again, back toward the hills, the sensors on the hills warning that soldiers were boiling out of Scatha's camp.

Mele brought out the command pad and sent another firing signal.

Eight more mortar tubes chuffed behind the hills in a staggered volley, throwing their rounds much farther than the first eight. The rounds began exploding close to the base, driving back the retaliatory pursuit.

Scatha had mortars, too, the sort of professional military gear that could cause a lot of trouble. At extreme range, they could just hit the front edge of the hills. Mele's command pad chirped to warn that those mortars had fired, aiming to hit her retreating team. "Even numbers, drop the packs!" she yelled to the rest of the team. "Everyone count to five, then run to your left!"

The even-numbered members of the team shrugged off their backpacks, Mele barely waiting until the last one was down before hitting a third command that detonated them. Charges bounded a short distance upward around the team and exploded, throwing out clouds of full-spectrum chaff designed to blind sensors.

Unfortunately, the chaff also made it very hard to see as Mele led her team through the dense fog that was only slowly settling as everyone ran off to the side of their earlier path. Mele heard mortar rounds detonating behind her as Scatha's barrage went off blindly in the chaff.

Another warning. Mele squinted at her control pad as the team ran through thinning chaff. Scatha had fired again, but this time was aiming at the mortar launch sites behind the hill. That was a by-the-books move, to take out the enemy's artillery, but how had they managed the extra range? They must have used vehicles to rapidly move some of their mortars out into the area outside the base enough to gain the extra range. They couldn't leave the mortars out there very long, exposed to whatever trick Glenlyon might hit them with next, but for the moment, Scatha's commanders were mad enough to risk it so they could get in some shots at Mele's force.

But Mele breathed a sigh of relief. Scatha had no way of knowing that Glenlyon's weapons were cheap single-use mortar tubes, and that all had expended their loads. The barrage would be wasted.

Getting up the slope and through low places in the hills took all the endurance that Mele had. She kept pausing, though, to make sure every member of her team was still moving.

Another warning. More Scatha rounds incoming, this time

targeted on the team again. "Odd numbers, drop your packs, everyone jog right on the count of five!"

Once again they stumbled through clouds of chaff, this time uphill.

Coming out of the chaff, Mele only counted seven following her. "Grant! Lead everyone to the pickup point! I've already called the WinG!"

Without waiting for a reply, she plunged back into the cloud, moving slowly enough to search around her.

Mele found Obi lying where she had caught the edge of a mortar blast, one leg a bleeding ruin. Mele knelt to strap a tourniquet on Obi's thigh, took a deep breath, then got under her, rose with Obi draped over her shoulders, and moved at the best pace she could into the hills.

The WinG, which had been waiting just over the horizon, was already sliding to a halt near where the rest of the team waited. Scatha was firing individual mortar rounds blindly over the hills, raising the risk that a round might fall close enough to the WinG to target it. As Mele approached, Grant ordered the others into the WinG and ran back to help Mele carry Obi.

The WinG was already starting to move again when Mele and Grant shoved Obi through the hatch and climbed in after her.

A doctor had volunteered to come along this time. She had them carry Obi to the WinG's emergency bed, while the craft shuddered along the ground and rose a meter into the air, leaving behind Scatha's mortar barrage.

Mele collapsed into a seat nearby as the doctor and the emergency bed's equipment worked to save Obi. Grant took the seat next to her, sweating heavily and breathing hard. "I'm getting too old for this," Grant said.

"You and me both," Mele gasped.

Eventually, the doctor stepped back, rubbing her eyes. "She should live. The leg is gone, though."

"Can you grow her a new one?" Mele asked.

"Maybe. There are still some bugs with that technology. If we can't make it work, there are prosthetics that are almost indistinguishable from the real thing." The doctor sat down, too. "She's not going to be doing this kind of work again anytime soon, though."

"Thanks, Doc."

"It could have been a lot worse," Grant said.

"Next time it probably will be," Mele said.

13

Carmen stopped at the door to her room, tired out from another long day of pretending to be an unofficial representative sent from Old Earth to save the new colonies. She wondered at what point a false story became real because enough people believed in it.

But, tired as she was, Carmen went to check on Lochan Nakamura.

He was still up, blinking wearily at her. "Hi. Is everything okay?"

"Close enough," Carmen said. "Why are you still awake?"

"Going over everything we could find out about Warrior Class destroyers from the databases on Kosatka. I'm not the only person who's been doing that since the news came in from Lares and apparently the same guys tried to do the same to Kosatka." Lochan waved her to a seat, shaking his head. "You won't believe one of the theories that's going around."

Carmen sat down on the couch, yawning. "Try me."

"Did you know that in the later phases of testing the jump drives ships were sent out on long voyages? Multistar jumps as far as they could go before they had to turn back for fuel and food." Lochan gave her a look that conveyed he was telling her the truth. "Two of the ships sent out were Warrior Class destroyers. One of those came back. The other one, which should have jumped to stars in this general region of space, disappeared. It never returned, so eventually the ship was written off as having been lost in an accident. But there isn't any record of wreckage having been found drifting in any star systems or on any planets."

"So it got stuck in jump space? That's awful. What does that—" Carmen stared at him. "Are you serious? People think it's a ghost ship?"

"No," Lochan said. "The theory being floated is that the ship was captured by aliens, and now they're using it to hit human colonies encroaching on their space."

She laughed. She couldn't help it. "The intelligent aliens we still haven't found any trace of? They are out here, still unseen, and using an old human warship to attack us? Wouldn't they have ships of their own?"

"Presumably," Lochan said. "But if they are hiding from us, using one of our own ships would maintain their secrecy." He raised a restraining palm toward Carmen. "I'm not believing this. I'm just telling you what other people are saying. But it's impossible to refute at this point because the mystery ship didn't communicate at all, and of course we couldn't see inside it to see who the crew was."

Carmen leaned back on the sofa, gazing at the ceiling. "That would be comforting, wouldn't it? The idea that the perpetrators of the atrocity at Lares weren't human. Unfortunately, humans have proven themselves capable of worse things than what happened at Lares. And Glenlyon has also been attacked, in their case undeniably by another human-colonized star system."

"Yeah, but why would Scatha have hit star systems this far from it? Apulu isn't that far off, and that Red you captured thinks the ones who hired her might have been from Apulu. If it was humans, Apulu is our number one suspect. That would make two human-colonized star systems out here that are making trouble for their neighbors."

"Kosatka wants me to accompany a delegation heading to Earth," Carmen said. "There is a ship here that we can hop a ride on, then get further transportation as we go up toward the Old Colonies. They want to make sure we get the best deal we can on some former Earth Fleet warships."

Lochan looked at her in surprise, then nodded. "I can understand that. Are you going?"

"Yes. How do you feel about that?"

"Hell, Carmen, why do I have a say?"

"Because we're a team," Carmen said. "We've been a team here on Kosatka, and we've done a good job as a team. But Kosatka would like you to stay here while I go back."

"You can handle Earth, can't you?" Lochan asked. "I'll take care of Kosatka until you get back. Besides, it's about time for another younger woman to show up, tell me I make a great friend, and shove a weapon into my hand."

"Aren't you afraid that the commander of Glenlyon's ground forces wouldn't like that?" Carmen teased, relieved that Lochan would be all right with her being gone for a while.

"Mele Darcy?" Lochan laughed. "Wasn't that amazing news? No, I'm lucky to have Mele as a friend, and I just hope she's not taking on too much for her. You get back to Earth long enough to make sure Kosatka gets its hands on some decent firepower, then come back here and we'll continue trying to save the galaxy."

"I'll watch out for aliens," Carmen said.

Mele Darcy had long ago given up on the idea of sleeping through the night. But it was still irritating to be rousted from sleep after midnight for a very important errand. Much worse was how little she wanted to carry out this particular errand.

Lieutenant Rob Geary wasn't at the apartment listed as his address, which didn't surprise Mele. She suspected that Rob Geary hadn't spent very much time in that apartment since being roped into command of *Squall*. Mele called up her official net interface, entered his locator code, then plugged it into the ground vehicle she was using.

The vehicle stopped at an apartment complex. Mele got out, walked through the predawn stillness to the entry of the building, then followed the locator to Ninja's address. She leaned on the doorbell.

It took a few minutes before a bleary-eyed Ninja stuck her head out. "This had better be important."

"It is. Lieutenant Geary needs to get moving, fast."

"Why are you telling me?"

"Don't be cute, girlfriend. You forgot to hack *his* locator. It says he's here."

Ninja sighed, nodded, and retreated. Mele waited impatiently until Rob Geary appeared at the door, showing every sign of having dressed rapidly. "What's up?" he asked.

"Big trouble has arrived in-system," she said. "The council didn't want to send word to you over the comm net because of worries about snoops. You're needed on your ship. I'll brief you on the way to the shuttle pad."

"Big trouble?" Rob Geary said.

"Yeah." Mele glanced toward Ninja. "Make it a proper good-bye."

He had some idea of what that implied, gazing at Mele for a long moment before turning to Ninja and holding her while he whispered in her ear.

"Take care of yourself," Ninja said. She and Rob Geary kissed, while Mele looked away and tried not to count the seconds ticking by.

Farewells over, Rob followed Mele into the ground vehicle. She punched in the destination, then sat back, her eyes scanning the outside as the vehicle rolled through streets almost deserted at this hour.

"Why did they send you?" Rob asked her.

Mele didn't take her eyes off the outside as she answered. "Based on the news you brought back from Kosatka, the council is worried that Scatha has slipped an assassin or two into Glenlyon. I'm your escort to the shuttle in the military sense as well as the guide sense."

"How bad is this?"

She appreciated that he didn't waste time worrying about a possible assassin threat that she was already handling. "Two more ships showed up four and a half hours ago at one of the jump points. One is a freighter. The other is a warship. They're not broadcasting ID, but the warship matches one in the Scatha databases we've captured. It's a Sword Class destroyer."

"A destroyer?" Rob didn't sound happy. "What are my orders? Did they tell you?"

"Intercept and stop by any means necessary." This time Mele did look away from the outside for a moment, catching his eye to reinforce her words. "The council is worried about what happened at Lares. They don't want it happening here."

"Intercept and stop?" Rob Geary laughed softly, but he didn't sound amused. "I can intercept, probably, but how the hell do I stop him? A Sword Class destroyer outguns and can outmaneuver the *Squall*. How do I beat a ship that is quicker and tougher than my own?"

Mele shrugged. "If you can't outgun them or outmaneuver them, then you have to outthink them."

"Sure. How do I do that?"

"Sorry," Mele said, not happy to be passing on such difficult orders to someone as decent as Rob Geary. "I mean that. I have no idea. Space combat is way outside my skill range. I'm sending some of my people up with you in case you get any boarding action. Grant Duncan's in charge. He's the best I can give you."

"Thanks." Rob Geary stayed quiet for a little while as the vehicle rolled closer to the shuttle pad and silent, mostly dark buildings went by on either side. Mele kept her eyes on the passing structures and the streets. She had no idea who had thought of programming the heavy-construction designs to reflect a variety of architectural styles, but the result was that even though every brand-new building still looked brand-new, the overall impression of the city was of some age, as if it had been built over time as styles changed. Her gaze lingered on one building, imagining what would happen to it if a rock dropped from orbit by the Scatha warship impacted on that site.

"Mele?" Rob said abruptly. "Would you do me a favor?"

"Probably," she said. "Depends what it is, though."

"Keep an eye on Ninja for me. All right?"

"Sure," Mele agreed. "But whether she stays safe will be mostly up to your stopping that destroyer. I can't stop an orbital bombardment."

"I'll stop it," Rob said, looking out the window of the car, the three words sounding like a vow. "But . . . stopping it might cost a lot. If it does . . . please keep an eye on Ninja for me."

"Sure," Mele repeated, trying to put the same sense of a solemn oath into the word. "I keep promises to my battle mates. I'll make sure she's looked after. I'm glad you figured it out in time."

"Figured what out?"

"Figured *who* out. Ninja. You two make a good pair."

Rob paused before answering. "I've known that for longer than I admitted to it. Isn't it funny how someone can be right there, and you don't realize it, and suddenly it hits you like a ten-kilometer-wide asteroid?"

"I'll take your word for it," Mele said as the vehicle rolled up to the new security gate around the shuttle pad.

"It's never happened to you?" Rob Geary asked.

She thought he sounded a little sad at the idea, which was a little annoying, but Mele smiled back anyway. "Nope. Maybe someday. I'm not looking for it."

"Neither was I," Rob said as Mele checked them through security. "At least Ninja and I had the last few weeks."

She walked him the last steps to the shuttle. Council Member Leigh Camagan was waiting beside the entry ramp. "Lieutenant Geary. Have you been told the situation by Major Darcy?"

"Yes," Rob Geary said.

"You have to stop them," Leigh Camagan said. "I hate to send you off with orders like that, but that destroyer cannot be allowed to reach orbit around this planet."

"Is the council aware of what stopping that destroyer might require?" Rob asked, his voice taking on a brittle edge.

"Some of us are all too aware, Lieutenant Geary," Leigh

Camagan said, her voice breaking slightly at the last.

"Take care of yourself," Mele told Rob, wondering if she would ever see him again. "You're the first sailor I actually liked working with."

"And you're the first Marine I ever worked with who wasn't a pain in the neck," Rob replied.

"I'll have to try harder," Mele said. She could see his fatalistic mood and shook her head at him. "This isn't a farewell. Do your job and get your tail back here in one piece, so Ninja can have her happily ever after. Or whatever it is that ninjas have. Hey, I've heard that the council wants its own hackers supporting you instead of hiring Ninja again because she's supposed to be focused on supporting me." Mele glanced at Leigh Camagan as she kept speaking to Rob. "I know that you're a by-the-book guy, and would never do anything you've been told not to do, but if you need that support from Ninja, this is one of those times when the book has to accidentally get deleted."

Rob Geary shook his head. "If the council knows that I went around their instructions—"

Leigh Camagan had turned away, but spoke in a clear voice. "I'm not hearing anything."

"The council is sending you out to face a destroyer with your cutter," Mele said. "I think you have the right to forget those particular instructions and improvise a little if you think you need Ninja at your back." She stepped back and saluted. "Do your ancestors proud."

"Same." Rob returned the salute and walked onto the shuttle.

Mele stood by Leigh Camagan as the shuttle lifted. The council member sighed. "Major Darcy, I have orders for you as well."

"I was worried about that," Mele said, watching the shape of the shuttle dwindle as it rose toward the stars.

"You know the odds that Lieutenant Geary will be facing. No matter how well he does, it may not be good enough to stop that freighter and destroy that warship. Scatha's base must be captured before new soldiers and equipment can be landed."

Mele bit her lip and looked at Leigh Camagan. "Does the council know how lucky we were on the first two operations? It won't be that way if we have to hit that base head-on. We'll lose people. Maybe a lot of people."

"The council understands," Leigh Camagan said in a low voice.

"I've got, what, a week to launch the attack? To make sure we control that base before the ships get here? And while the morale of Scatha's forces at that base has been pretty low, they'll have seen those ships arrive. They'll know that help is on the way. All they have to do is hold out a little while longer."

"Major, if I could give you another week, if I could give you a thousand more soldiers, I would. I can't."

Mele nodded. "At least you feel bad about it."

"Can you do it?"

"I can try," Mele said. "And hopefully not lose too many. Can you do me a favor?"

"If I can," Leigh Camagan said.

"I promised to look after Ninja if Rob Geary didn't come back. If I don't make it back from attacking that base, I need someone to honor my promise."

"I swear to you that I will," Leigh Camagan said. "I hope with all my heart I won't have to. It would be a cruel universe indeed if we sacrificed both you and Rob Geary to save Glenlyon."

Mele gave a short, sharp bark of laughter. "The universe isn't cruel. People are."

She headed off toward her headquarters. There was a lot to do.

Rob Geary felt emotionally numb as the shuttle climbed toward orbit and a rendezvous with *Squall*. Given the situation he was facing and his orders, there was a more than even chance that this would be his last shuttle trip, and that his farewell to Ninja had been the last time he would be with her. He wished there had been time for a formal marriage commitment. Hasty, perhaps, after only a few weeks, but they had known each other longer than that. If only he hadn't waited several weeks to listen to his heart rather than his head.

Which reminded him, ironically, of the times he had counseled young sailors to wait on marriage, that their hearts might be totally sincere and totally committed today but that time had a way of changing hearts sometimes, and that warnings from the head should be listened to. The sailors had always earnestly assured him that they understood that, but that this time was different. And, caught in the same sense that Ninja was the one and the only one, Rob couldn't help also feeling that this time was different.

Certainly if his commitment to Ninja didn't last, it would first and foremost be because he didn't survive this mission.

But there were other people affected by his orders, and he had a responsibility to them. Rob shook himself out of his inner focus. He wasn't alone on the shuttle. Twelve members of *Squall*'s crew also occupied seats, many of them new volunteers inspired by Rob's "victory" at Kosatka and Mele Darcy's strikes against Scatha's base. And there were a half dozen men and women Rob didn't recognize. All six carried weapons, either sidearms or short-barreled rifles.

"Sergeant Grant Duncan," one of the men introduced himself when Rob looked his way.

"Major Darcy told me you were coming," Rob said. "I'm glad to have all of you. Hopefully, your skills won't be needed."

Grant smiled but shrugged. "None of us have that much combat experience, Lieutenant, but we'll do our best."

A Sword Class destroyer carried a normal crew of sixty-four. It could carry more. With the half dozen soldiers that Mele Darcy had lent, Rob would have thirty-one aboard the *Squall*. "Major Darcy said you're good, and given the success you ground fighters have had, I believe her. I'm afraid that the accommodations aboard *Squall* will be a little cramped, though, and the food isn't the best given the limitations of the galley."

"Is there coffee?"

"Yes, Sergeant, there's coffee. No matter what else we may lack, *Squall* keeps a decent supply of that on hand. I won't swear for the quality of it, but we do have quantity."

"Then we'll be good," Grant assured him.

Once aboard *Squall*, Rob threw himself into ensuring that the ship was ready to go. The work kept him from thinking about Ninja and the last moments he had spent with her. There was enough food, the water tanks were full, the recyclers were functioning, and life support was just able to keep up with the burden of thirty-one adult humans inside a ship designed to normally carry a crew of twenty-two. Most of the new volunteers were enthusiastic even if they did have to work off various forms of

Operating Instructions for Dummies as they learned their tasks.

As always, the weakest point was the power core. Rob had hoped that Corbin Torres would finally rise above his bitterness, but the veteran had remained on the surface. The engineering section would do its best but were painfully aware of their own lack of experience. And fuel cells were low. Without an orbital facility to manufacture new cells and with the problems one of the surface facilities had encountered getting fuel cell production ramped up, the ship had been running on what had been captured from Scatha. Whether *Squall* won or lost, there were only enough to get the ship through the next few weeks.

Everyone knew that a destroyer and a freighter from Scatha were on their way to the planet, but only Rob and Danielle Martel knew just how bad that made the odds against *Squall*.

"Let's take it easy on the way out," Rob told Danielle as he settled into the command seat on *Squall*'s bridge. "Aim for an intercept a light hour from the planet."

"If we head out that slow, with Scatha's force limited by the speed of that freighter, it'll take five days," Danielle Martel reported.

"That's fine," Rob said. "We've got a lot of new people doing new tasks and we can use the time for training. I also want to conserve fuel cells. We're going to need them when we close to fight."

"All departments report ready to get under way," Danielle said.

Should he give a speech about the vital necessity of their mission and the need to win at all costs? No, Rob decided. Aside from his own awkwardness at such a thing, the need for an inspirational speech would be when they were about to engage in combat. Save it.

The intercept calculations had already been done, and the maneuvering systems awaited his command.

Rob punched the execute command and *Squall* swung about, accelerating away from the planet.

Late that afternoon ship's time, Danielle Martel stopped by his stateroom, closing the hatch behind her and eyeing him soberly. "You're good enough to know how tough our job is. How are we going to do this?"

"Get close enough for detailed information about the destroyer's status, whether he has any weak shields," Rob said, "or weapon systems that aren't up to strength, and try to work around that."

"Scatha has two destroyers and sent one," Danielle pointed out. "That implies if either of those destroyers had any weaknesses, they sent the better one. They may even have cannibalized parts from the one that didn't come to ensure the one that did is fully operational."

"That had occurred to me," Rob admitted. "What would Earth Fleet do?"

"We'd be still be working on checklists," Danielle said. "Scatha's force does have a vulnerability. That freighter. Unless he forgets his escort job and goes after us, the ability of the destroyer to maneuver will be limited by his need to protect the freighter."

"That still leaves him a lot of room to play with," Rob said. "I figure we'll have to adjust each engagement to take advantage of whichever enemy ship makes the best target and try to wear them both down."

"That might be our best bet," Danielle admitted. "We don't have any real good bets."

Rob nodded. "Can I ask you something personal?"

"You can ask," she said, wary.

"You and Drake Porter. He's obviously interested. He's stayed up on *Squall* with you while other crew members rotated down to the planet."

"Drake is nice," she said. "Yes, we're, um, friendly. And since I lack any official status aboard *Squall* even though you've declared me an ensign, there aren't any rank barriers involved. Are you worried about it?"

"No, not as long as you two stay professional on the bridge."

Danielle nodded. "If it gets that serious, I'll talk to Drake about his transferring to a shore job. I see you have a new picture," she added, nodding toward Rob's desk.

Rob glanced at the image of Ninja. "Yeah."

"Does she understand the deal with this mission?"

"Yeah."

"Sorry."

"We'll beat them," Rob said, not really believing it but trying to will it to happen.

"We'll do our best," Danielle agreed.

"Three days to get everything and everybody assembled," Mele told Council President Chisholm. "One day to load the whole mess on all three WinGs and transport them to the vicinity of Scatha's base. I'm planning on landing the assault force late on the fourth day, but these aren't experienced Marines, and the WinGs aren't combat assault vehicles with armor and defenses. We won't be able to run off the vehicles and hit the base immediately. We'll strike probably early the next day."

Council Members Leigh Camagan, Kim, and Odom looked uncomfortable. Council President Chisholm simply looked unhappy. "That's the fastest you can do it?"

"Yes," Mele said. "The fastest way to do it halfway right. I could just throw people and equipment on the WinGs and hit Scatha's base by the end of the second day, but if I do that it would mean taking something on the order of fifty percent casualties in the assault. We might be able to overwhelm Scatha anyway, but you'd have to be prepared for heavy losses."

"I believe that we should defer to Major Darcy's judgment," Leigh Camagan urged.

"But surely we can move it up at least a day quicker," Kim said.

"Fifty percent," Odom emphasized. "Is a day quicker worth that? How many of that fifty percent would be dead as opposed to wounded?" he asked Mele.

"Since we only have light body armor that's been recently manufactured," Mele said, "and Scatha has some powerful weapons, it would probably be close to an even split. Twenty-five percent dead."

"Thirty-eight or forty dead out of a total force of a hundred and fifty!" Odom said, glaring at Kim. "If Major Darcy isn't being optimistic!"

"Major Darcy has proven her judgment with two highly successful actions," Leigh Camagan said. "If she says she needs that time, she should be given it."

"You regard four days as the necessary minimum?" Chisholm asked Mele.

Mele shook her head, feeling unhappy but determined to say the truth as she knew it. "The necessary minimum is something like a couple of months. We don't have that. It's going to cost us. I need four days to try to keep that cost down."

"Why can't we wait to see if Lieutenant Geary succeeds?" Odom asked. "If he does, the ground assault will not be necessary."

"We cannot assume that Lieutenant Geary will succeed,"

Chisholm said. "And if he does not, it very well could not leave enough time to launch the ground assault before Scatha's reinforcements arrive."

"Taking their base on our planet wouldn't prevent Scatha's warship from bombarding us in the same way Lares was devastated!"

"We'd have the population of their own base as hostages," Leigh Camagan pointed out. "Perhaps Scatha wouldn't care. But at that point, it would be the only tool left to us."

"You have your four days," Council President Chisholm told Mele. "Are you getting the necessary IT support?"

"Lyn Meltzer says Scatha has really clamped down on their transmissions," Mele explained. "She doesn't think she'll be able to break in again in the time we have available, but she's doing her best."

"Ensure that she knows no other tasks should distract her from that assignment!" Chisholm ordered.

Mele glanced at Leigh Camagan, who gazed back at her with apparent bland ignorance on that topic. "I'll make sure that Ninja knows what the council expects," Mele said. "If you'll excuse me now, I need to get things into motion."

Three days remained until intercept, the long, curving tracks of Scatha's ships and that of *Squall* still heading for that spot in space where they would meet. Rob took a break from drilling his crew to listen to a message from Ninja. *Squall* was already far enough from the planet that there were about twenty minutes of time delay, making a conversation very difficult but not impossible.

"I can't find anything accessible," Ninja said, looking drawn with fatigue and worry. "Scatha's ships are locked tight again. Our consolidated sensor picture spotted some visual-spectrum lights blinking on one of the ships, so they're probably using flashing lights to send simple messages back and forth. They'll probably start transmitting once a fight starts, but that'll be too late for me to break in and mess with anything. I'm so sorry. I love you, and I'd do anything to help, but there's nothing I can do right now."

He sent a reply, knowing that she wouldn't see it until forty minutes after she had sent this message. "Ninja, I know you're doing all you can. You gave *Squall* the best protection possible against intrusions, so we know we're safe from Scatha pulling that on us. Do what you can to help Mele Darcy. I love you, too. Please take care of yourself. I can't wait to see you when this is over."

Rob went back to the drills, knowing that if there was any chance of him or anyone else on *Squall* seeing their loved ones again, it would take every trace of skill and luck they could muster.

Mele missed having Grant around to help with things. Obi had actually volunteered to help any way she could from the hospital bed where she was still confined, and the doctor had approved, saying the task and purpose would help Obi recover. But there was only so much a badly wounded woman could do from a hospital bed.

She promoted Riley fast, and what he lacked in experience he made up for in enthusiasm. Mele winnowed out the best one hundred and fifty volunteers from the slightly more than two hundred available, designating those left behind as the city defense garrison so they wouldn't feel useless. Counting the pulse rifles acquired from Scatha's soldiers and weapons being manufactured by facilities whose output had hastily changed, she now had more than one hundred rifles and pistols to equip her soldiers. Most of the weapons were slug throwers, but those had the advantage of simplicity and ease of use. And everyone had the light body armor, which was no match for battle armor but better than no armor at all.

She had twenty more mortars, this time intended for multiple shots, a few dozen chaff packs, and special portable mortars that might be needed.

Mele weighed her assets against the defenses and shook her head. Ninja had picked up indications of at least a few summary executions among Scatha's forces, but Scatha still had around seventy soldiers, all equipped with obsolescent but still-effective armor and weapons. Those soldiers had stayed huddled inside their perimeter since Mele's force had wiped out the patrol, which had prevented further chipping away at their numbers. The mortars that had come out to hit the area behind the hills were once again entrenched inside Scatha's base, ready to bombard anyone approaching. And work had continued on getting the second Scatha warbird able to fly again.

Scatha's base had not responded to any attempt by Glenlyon to negotiate, instead sending out one image, knowing it would be received. Spurlick had clearly taken a while to die. Despite her disdain for Spurlick, Mele had gazed at the image in cold fury at the sort of people who would torture enemies to death. Even though the government tried to censor the image, it still made its way around, generating anger in every part of Glenlyon. If the intent had been to discourage further attacks on Scatha's base, it had backfired badly.

It wasn't that long after the third day had ended, barely after midnight, when Mele's force began embarking on the WinGs and loading equipment.

* * *

Squall would intercept Scatha's ships around noon of this ship's day. Rob Geary made sure he looked his best because sailors picked up on that kind of thing when they were looking for reassurance that their officers knew what they were doing. He made sure the galley served the best breakfast that it could. As the crew mustered, Rob ordered final checks on the survival suits that everyone would put on an hour before the intercept. If part of *Squall* was holed by enemy fire, with atmosphere escaping into space, the only thing the crew in the affected compartments would have to do was seal their head coverings.

There was all too strong a chance that even the bridge, as well protected as any compartment on the ship, would be pierced by charged particles from the destroyer's pulse cannon.

Squall's single lifeboat, which in theory could get survivors back to the planet, would barely hold everyone on the ship if they were packed in tightly. But everyone knew that if *Squall* had to be abandoned at least some of her crew would have died already. No one talked about it, but they knew it. Rob looked over the status on the lifeboat, all systems green, comforting himself with the knowledge that if it came to that no one would be barbaric enough to fire on a lifeboat full of survivors. Humanity had left that sort of atrocity behind.

He stopped by the two weapon stations, encouraging their crews, and went by engineering, where the team seemed more worried about the power core acting up than they did about whatever the enemy would do.

Rob ended up on the bridge. Everyone was already at battle stations before being called.

"One hour to intercept," Danielle Martel said.

"Thank you." Rob rubbed his face, inhaling slowly. The feel of the survival suit he wore reminded him with every movement of the worst that might happen. He shrugged off the foreboding, then tapped his controls to speak to everyone on the ship. "You all know that we're facing a tough fight. You all know how important it is that we stop Scatha. I have no doubt that every single one of you will do their very best. We will defend our homes, we will defeat those who threaten them, and we will be victorious."

Maybe it was just denial, or maybe an outright lie to claim that victory was certain, but the reaction of the crew told Rob that they needed to hear it. And, who knew? Belief had changed certain defeat into incredible victory before in history.

But hopefully luck would be on their side as well.

The biggest WinG and one of the smaller WinGs off-loaded north of Scatha's base behind the foothills. The other smaller WinG dropped a contingent of Mele's force to the south, in the open but out of range of Scatha's mortars. She didn't want Scatha to be able to focus all of its defenses to the north.

Mele had run into some problems organizing the smaller movements of people and equipment, but the difficulties seemed to have gone up at a steep rate as the numbers of both grew. Torn by frustration over the seeming inability of supposedly intelligent men and women to follow simple instructions, and haunted by anxiety over the outcome of the looming battle, Mele had to repeatedly restrain herself from giving her volunteers high-volume demonstrations of Marine profanity. She finally began to understand why the officers and senior enlisted she had dealt with in the past often seemed irritable and short-tempered.

None of which helped get her people into position with the equipment they needed. But eventually she got everything settled despite the sun's setting and growing darkness.

Scatha's base had remained silent throughout the off-loading. Mele's biggest fear had been that Scatha's soldiers would sally out to hit her small southern force while she was still trying to organize the northern force, but there had been no movement from the defenders. Having been badly stung twice by Mele's forces, Scatha's defenders didn't appear inclined to take any chances. They were probably worried that the small force to the south was not simply a diversion but bait to lure them out into the open.

Studying the base through multispectrum binoculars, Mele could catch glimpses of defenders in the entrenchments. No trace of the civilians could be seen. She had worried that Scatha might herd the civilians, including children, into the entrenchments to further serve as human shields and prevent her attack, but that hadn't happened.

Lowering the binoculars, Mele looked back down the slope. One of her new sergeants, Diego, dropped down beside her, gazing cautiously at the base. "Why aren't we going to be attacking while it's dark tonight?" he asked.

"It's too easy for things to go wrong in the dark," Mele explained. "Even with infrared gear, which we don't have enough of. Look how confusing it was just unloading the WinGs. That's why our attack will go in during the first traces of morning twilight, when it's just becoming light enough to see."

"Won't that make us better targets for them?"

Mele remembered asking questions like that to long-suffering superiors. "Not really," she half lied. "Scatha's battle armor helmets have built in infrared, so they'd be able to spot us regardless." That was true as far as it went, but it took good training to use IR gear well, and so far she had seen few signs of good training among Scatha's soldiers. The lack of veterans out in the new colonies had hindered Glenlyon, but apparently it had also made things harder for Scatha.

"Pass the word to try to get some sleep," Mele told Diego. "We'll be rousing everyone at 0100 to prepare for the assault."

Half an hour before *Squall* intercepted Scatha's ships, Drake Porter called out to Rob Geary. "You've got a message. High priority, personal for you."

Rob put on an ear set and tapped the privacy settings to limit the ability of anyone else to see whatever appeared on his display.

Ninja's face appeared, rigid with that desperate attempt to look calm in someone who was actually terrified. "Rob, I know you're too far off to respond. Not even sure you'll get this in time. I've had no luck getting into Scatha's ships. I . . . I know how bad this situation is. I've run simulations here and . . . I wanted you to know I understand what you're doing and why, and hope you come back. I'm actually praying to my ancestors for that, can you believe it? But if you don't, I wanted to be sure you knew that . . . well, that there are going to be people who have you for an ancestor. You and me. And they'll know what you did and why. I'll . . . I'll make sure our kid knows and passes it on. So do your best, and if you don't make it back, know our child will know who you were, and that I'll be thinking of you always until I see you again in the light beyond the dark."

Rob stared at the screen for a moment after the message ended, unable to process any thoughts, then tore his mind back to the present.

If he was ever going to see that child, he needed to focus on what was happening here.

"Was it something important?" Danielle Martel asked as Rob removed the headset.

"Yeah," Rob said. "Very important."

The two ships from Scatha had not altered their trajectory in response to the approach of *Squall*. Glenlyon's sole warship was coming in from slightly below and to one side of Scatha's. But the destroyer had shifted position so that as *Squall* came in she would have to first encounter the enemy warship before being able to fire upon Scatha's freighter. If *Squall* took the time to reposition and come in from a markedly different vector, the destroyer could easily shift to block that new approach as well.

"What sort of tactics does Earth Fleet call for in this kind of situation?" Rob asked Danielle Martel.

"Use two warships in the attack," she said.

"What if you don't have two warships?"

"The tactics all call for two. That's the only answer I've got," she said. "Earth Fleet's answer to the problem of how to do this with one ship is to say you should use two."

Twenty minutes to contact. Rob confirmed that all of *Squall*'s shields were on maximum, both the grapeshot launcher and the pulse particle beam ready. But the shields of the destroyer were strong enough to shrug off the quick blows that the cutter could deal during a lightning-quick firing run, while the destroyer's weapons had enough additional punch to have a chance of getting through *Squall*'s shields.

The freighter would be carrying reinforcements for Scatha's ground forces and probably new heavy weapons. But the destroyer was capable of bombarding the planet.

"Lock weapons on the freighter," Rob directed. "If we can damage it enough, Scatha will either have to withdraw, or the destroyer will have to reduce speed to a crawl to stay with it."

Squall was coming in at point one light speed. Warships today could push double that. The destroyer and freighter were coming toward the planet, still a light hour distant, at point zero three light speed. Anything more than point zero six light speed introduced targeting problems that greatly reduced the chances of a hit.

"Reduce velocity to point zero three light speed," Rob ordered.

Squall pivoted as her thrusters pushed her around, then her main propulsion unit lit off to begin cutting her velocity drastically. The inertial dampers whined in protest but did their job of preventing the forces employed from pulping frail human bodies.

"Revised time to contact, forty minutes," Danielle Martel reported. She had no sooner said that than an alarm sounded. "The destroyer is accelerating. He must want to hit us before we finish braking our velocity."

"Hold it as long as we can," Rob ordered. The destroyer had been lured away from the freighter, but that still left it a serious threat. "Weapons, shift target to the destroyer, then back to the freighter as soon as we've engaged the warship."

"We're not going to maneuver?" Drake Porter asked. "Dodge?"

"*Squall* can't dodge a destroyer," Rob said. "We get in our best shot at it and keep going to hit the freighter before the destroyer can come back to hit us again."

"The freighter is transmitting," Drake reported.

"Probably asking the destroyer why it's running off and leaving them," Danielle commented. "Revised time to contact with destroyer is ten minutes. We'll complete braking maneuver in eight minutes and pivot to face forward for contact."

"Good," Rob said, watching his display. In planetary terms, the destroyer was immensely far away. In space terms, it would be very far away one moment and very close the next before being far away again the moment after, the moment of close approach a tiny fraction of a second. "Input order to accelerate at nine minutes."

"To what velocity?" Danielle asked.

"We'll hold acceleration for thirty seconds, long enough for *Squall* to pick up appreciably more velocity, then cut off. If the destroyer reacts wrongly to our changes in speed and vector, that might mess up his ability to hit us. But we'll still be slow enough to get good hits on that freighter."

Squall's main propulsion cut off, and the ship pivoted once more, bringing her bow to face the oncoming destroyer. "One minute to contact," Danielle reported as *Squall*'s main propulsion suddenly cut in again, this time accelerating the ship rather than slowing it. "The destroyer is adjusting vector to compensate."

Maneuvering systems had automatic safeguards built in to try to avoid collisions with enemy ships when conducting firing passes close enough for weapons to hit and hit hard. But at the velocities warships traveled that was an imprecise calculation, prone to error if either ship bobbled the slightest off its predicted track. Space battles could be very long as warships made repeated passes at each other with long periods to reposition in between, or very, very short as a pass ended in a collision that reduced both warships and their crews to a cloud of gas and dust.

Squall and the enemy destroyer tore past each other in far less than the blink of an eye, *Squall* shuddering from hits as she lined up on the freighter.

Rob saw damage reports pop up on his display. Bow shields had suffered spot failures as a rain of grapeshot slammed into them, and at least one pulse from the destroyer's cannon had hit *Squall*. "Losing atmosphere, compartments sealed off, no critical systems hit, local reports say one dead," Danielle reported. "No damage noted on the destroyer. His shields held."

No damage to the enemy and one dead aboard *Squall*. Rob couldn't spend any time wondering who in his crew had already died. "Make sure we get a good shot at that freighter!"

Squall adjusted course slightly as she came up from just below the freighter, closing the range to the minimum safe distance.

The freighter came and went, there and past, *Squall* jolting slightly as her weapons fired again. This time *Squall* took no damage since the freighter lacked weapons.

"Up two zero zero degrees, come right zero two degrees," Rob ordered to bring *Squall* swinging through a wide arc to hit the freighter again. "Get me a damage report on that ship."

"We lost some sensors on that encounter with the destroyer," Danielle Martel said. "Getting an assessment now. We collapsed his shields on an after quarter. Significant damage. Unable to assess whether propulsion or thrusters were impacted."

Far ahead, Scatha's destroyer was looping about as well, though to the side and up, climbing to meet *Squall* as she dove back at the freighter. "If we hold planned vector," Danielle cautioned, "the destroyer will hit us again right after we hit the freighter."

"Weapons," Rob commanded. "Target the freighter again. Try

to recharge to hit the destroyer afterward, but only after throwing everything we can at the freighter."

The minutes crawled by as the ships shot through space, covering huge distances as they strove to get close enough to each other again to shoot.

This time *Squall* went past the freighter from behind, overtaking it and having slightly longer to shoot. But before they could assess the results of that run, Scatha's destroyer slashed past *Squall* from the side, the cutter bucking from more hits. "Come down zero zero three degrees, port two four zero degrees," Rob ordered.

"We've lost a thruster," Danielle reported. "Compensating. Coming around."

Rob's display popped up an assessment of the damage to the freighter. "Fifty percent loss of main propulsion, damage to entire stern section," Rob said.

"He's changing vector!" Danielle cried.

The freighter was lumbering into a turn that made the warships look like gazelles by comparison. "Any guesses?" Rob pressed her.

"He's definitely turning off the vector for the planet . . . still coming around. I think he's running."

But he would only keep running as long as *Squall* kept after him, Rob knew. How long could he keep that up, with the destroyer swinging back for another attack on *Squall*?

"Lieutenant?" Sergeant Grant Duncan's face wasn't visible on Rob's display, but his voice held the rigid calm of someone who was holding back fear. "That last shot took out the lifeboat."

Rob checked his status screen, seeing the red marker blinking there. "It's gone?"

"No, most of it is still there, but there's a big hole through it. I plugged in and got status on nothing except the escape jet. Every life support system and control system on the pod is showing negative."

"I'm showing damage to the lifeboat," Danielle reported. "A shot from the destroyer went through its bay."

Rob fought off the urge to slump in despair. The odds of surviving this fight had been bad to begin with. Even though he had temporarily turned back the freighter, the destroyer was unmarked and coming back again.

And now, thanks to sheer bad luck that had led a shot from the destroyer through the lifeboat nestled inside the hull of *Squall*, there was no way for anyone on *Squall* to survive if the battle was lost.

14

"Follow me!" Mele Darcy shouted, the one hundred and twenty volunteers with her following Mele over the crest at a fast walk. It wasn't a single line spread out to either side of Mele, but several lines with wide gaps between individuals to prevent creating groups of fighters close together for the enemy to aim at. In the still-dim light before dawn, the farthest figures were almost invisible.

"We're not running?" a volunteer near Mele asked.

"No. It's too far. We'll run at the last."

An incoming message alert annoyed her. If Glenlyon kept distracting her—

"*Squall* began engaging Scatha's ships an hour ago," the message reported. "Outcome remains unknown."

"Could be worse," Mele mumbled to herself. She checked her control pad both for signs of activity at Scatha's base and for the readiness of the mortars behind the hills. Ten minutes earlier, Riley's group of thirty had stepped off, approaching Scatha's base from the south. Scatha had lit off jamming gear, but satellite signals going almost straight up past the jamming and back down on the other side of the base were strong enough to punch through, so Mele could keep track of what was happening.

But her ability to control Riley from this distance was limited by the improvised command and control gear she was using as well as by Mele's need to focus on her own assault force. She couldn't hold back and watch everything. If they were going to break Scatha's defenses, Mele knew she had to literally lead the way.

"Don't get too deep into mortar range!" she sent to Riley. "You want to draw their fire but not get caught by it!"

Mele looked to her right and left, seeing her lines of volunteers spread out to each side, walking steadily forward, grasping their weapons, the sky overhead still too dark to make out their expressions. It was probably just as well that it was too dark for any of them to see her expression, Mele thought.

The satellite far overhead spotted activity around Scatha's mortars, sending an alert to both Mele and Riley. She waited, tense, to see which way the mortars would fire. A moment later the shells started rising, aimed toward the south.

Riley should be ordering his small group, already dispersed, to run back to the south, the southwest, and the southeast, and toss out chaff packs behind them.

Hopefully, not too many of them would die while serving as a diversion.

"Pick it up!" Mele called, raising her gait to a slow jog. She grasped her pulse rifle with hands slick with sweat, imagining every gun in Scatha's defenses aimed at her.

Scatha's mortars fired again, this time aimed to the north, at Mele's force. "Chaff and halt!" Mele ordered.

Her volunteers stumbled to a halt and threw backpacks off before the packs exploded into clouds of improvised chaff. The mortar rounds, aimed to hit where Mele's advancing force should have been, couldn't spot any targets inside the chaff clouds and fell short, the closest rounds tearing up the shrub only a few meters in front of Mele. She hit the command for her own mortars to fire, scrambling to her feet. "Move it! Forward!"

Scatha had fired another volley, aimed at the long, low chaff cloud where Mele's force had been lying. But she was leading them at a run forward, out of the impact area, hoping that Riley was advancing again to draw some fire and wondering just how damned long it would take her own mortar rounds to hit.

The area along the north side of Scatha's defenses facing Mele's advance vanished from sight in a flurry of air detonations of downward-firing fragmentation warheads, followed by a line of improvised chaff clouds bursting to cover the entrenchments and block their view of Mele's force. She hit the command for the aircrews waiting back with the WinGs to reload the mortars with more chaff so they could automatically keep firing.

Another alert pulsed frantically. The second warbird was taking off.

Mele saw Scatha's remaining warbird rising vertically above the chaff, then darting forward toward her lines, cannon fire already blazing toward her volunteers. "Launch air defense!" she shouted.

Gambling that the warbird, if it launched, would be at low altitude and with little warning time, and with some of her volunteers not equipped with other weapons, Mele had equipped them with something one of the engineers had dreamed up. Setting the bottom of portable mortar tubes against the ground, canted toward the warbird zooming at them, they triggered the tubes.

The warbird had automated countermeasures to defeat conventional weapons and skin designed to shrug off hits. It didn't have anything to deal with the mad engineer's design—shells that bloomed into widely spreading nets of woven thermite.

Most of the nets missed, but two partially draped themselves on the warbird as they were igniting. Once on fire, the bird couldn't shake them as the strands of thermite ate their way through its skin and equipment underneath.

The warbird broke off its attack, rolling backward, but it didn't complete the maneuver before parts of its front end and right wing began falling off. As the warbird staggered, the pilot punched out, flying backward and away as the chute rapid-deployed to try to fill before the pilot hit the ground somewhere inside the base. The bird itself rolled wildly, slid sideways, then vanished as it crashed behind the chaff.

"Keep moving!" Mele yelled.

The thermite nets that had fallen to the ground ahead were burning out rapidly, but Scatha's troops were firing now, blindly through the chaff, but they had automatic weapons in entrenchments and could put out a lot of fire. Mele saw some of her volunteers fall, others going to ground in fear, as energy pulses thundered past and slugs snapped by their ears.

The entrenchments weren't that far ahead, but Mele realized she was the only one still charging. Cursing, she dropped as well, the enemy fire ripping by just overhead. Her mortars were firing more chaff, the aircrews reloading as long as they had chaff rounds left. That kept Scatha from targeting Mele and her volunteers, but the volume of unguided fire was heavy enough to make charging farther forward nearly suicidal.

And sooner or later, the supply of chaff rounds would run out, and Scatha's defenders would no longer have trouble spotting the attackers out in the open.

"What are we going to do?" Drake Porter asked Rob Geary.

"We're going to win!" Rob replied, almost yelling. "We're still able to fight, and we'll keep fighting even if all we can do is throw rocks at them!"

"We might as well throw the lifeboat at them," Danielle Martel muttered.

He almost told her to shut up, then paused as her words hung in his mind. *"Throw rocks at them." "Might as well throw the lifeboat."*

"Sergeant Duncan!" Rob called back. "How does the fuel look?"

"The fuel?"

"In the lifeboat. Is its propulsion still charged?"

"Uh, it looks okay, sir," Grant Duncan replied. "Propulsion reads functional, but maneuvering systems show completely out."

"Can the lifeboat still be launched?" Rob demanded, one eye on the curving tracks of *Squall*, the destroyer, and the freighter as they carved separate paths through space.

"I don't know, sir. You need a sailor down here to check on that."

Rob turned. "Drake, get down to the escape pod. It's damaged, but I need to know if it can still be launched, and if we can vector the launch. There should be a limited ability to vector the launch to optimize escape chances. Do you know how to read that?"

Drake shook his head.

"I can read that," Danielle said. "Are you planning what I think you are?"

"Maybe," Rob said. "*If* we can launch that lifeboat."

"I'll find out and get back here as soon as I can. Request permission—"

"Get going!"

"What's going on?" Drake demanded, as Danielle ran aft. "The lifeboat's gone? Useless?"

"No," Rob said. "It may not be useless."

"But if it's been destroyed . . . we can't . . . we have to . . ."

Rob turned to look at everyone on the bridge, seeing the fear springing to life in them. "We have to what?"

"If it's hopeless, you know we can't—" Drake began.

"I'll tell you what I know!" Rob said, hitting the button on his seat to broadcast his words through the entire ship, because he knew reports of the damage would be spreading and fear spreading along with it. "This warship, *Squall*, is the first and only defense our home has against Scatha's ships! If we fail, our homes are left exposed and defenseless against the sort of thing done to Lares. You saw those images from Lares! You saw what ruthless people will do! Do you want that to happen to our home? To the families some of you have there?

"Yes, this is a tough situation. Yes, we may die in this fight. You all knew that when we started out. That leaves one question for everyone to answer. How do you want to be remembered? As the ones who gave up and consigned their world and their homes and their families to the domination of Scatha? As the ones who gave up and had to watch as Scatha bombarded their homes to make way for more settlers from their star? Or as the ones who kept fighting, who gave their all if necessary, to save something much more important than themselves? Do you want to be remembered as the ones who *never gave up* and *saved their world*?"

He paused, waiting, dreading the answer, but they looked back at him, and he saw the answer in them, and it was what he hoped for and perhaps even a little more.

"We won't give up," Drake Porter said. "Not as long as there's any chance at all."

"There is a chance," Rob said as Danielle Martel dashed back onto the bridge.

"We can do it," she said, out of breath. "If we come in at the destroyer from the proper angle, we can kick out the lifeboat on an intercept with them. I should be able to link the launch to the fire control system so that we launch the lifeboat at almost the same moment as our weapons fire."

"Won't it be an easy target?" Drake Porter asked.

"Very easy," Rob said. "That's the whole point. We can't use the lifeboat to escape *Squall*, but we can use it to hit that destroyer, and it'll be accelerating on its launch cycle when it hits."

Danielle Martel strapped back in at the operations station. "When we throw the lifeboat at them, their combat systems are going to have to target it," she added. "They'll probably blow it to pieces, but they won't be able to take out all the pieces. Some of them will be big pieces. When the pieces of the lifeboat hit the destroyer's shields, they will knock them down, which will give us a chance to hit their weapons while they're busy engaging the lifeboat."

"And if we take out the destroyer's weapons," Rob said, "then we can beat it to hell at our leisure." He adjusted *Squall*'s course, bringing her around to aim for intercept with the destroyer, which was already coming for *Squall*, intent on a kill. "Target the destroyer's particle cannons and grapeshot launchers. This will be our only chance, everyone. Give it all you've got."

"Fifteen minutes until we meet the destroyer again," Danielle Martel reported.

A tone told Rob that someone was calling on a private circuit. He donned the ear set.

"Did you run the calculations on this?" Danielle Martel's voice asked in his ear.

"No," Rob said.

"I tried running them. The systems can't give an estimate. Too many uncertainties."

"I'm doing this on my gut," Rob told her.

"It's the best chance we've got. And it ought to work. If it doesn't, we were screwed anyway."

"That's what I thought," Rob said. "Might as well take the chance."

He looked over at where she sat at the operations station. She met his eyes and nodded as her voice murmured in his ear set. "Might as well. I told you that you never would have made it in Earth Fleet. I'm glad I had the chance to sail with you."

"Tell me when we get back to Glenlyon," Rob said.

"Yeah. Sure."

He removed the ear set and watched his display.

"Recommend coming right zero one point two degrees to optimize angle of intercept," Danielle Martel said.

"Come right zero one point two degrees," Rob ordered.

"The lifeboat launch is programmed and linked to the fire control system."

"Thank you, Ensign Martel."

The repeated changes of vector and alterations of speed to intercept each other again quickly had slowed both warships. They rushed together now at a combined velocity of only point zero two light speed. For the fire control systems on the *Squall* and Scatha's destroyer, the targets might as well have been standing still.

As the ships raced past each other, *Squall* jolted from the launch of the lifeboat and the firing of her weapons, the shock of enemy hits striking coming at almost the same instant.

As *Squall* swept up and away, Rob stared at his display as red markers appeared all along it to mark damage to his own ship. He tabbed the command to replay in very slow motion the encounter that had just occurred.

The lifeboat had roared out of the escape bay just prior to meeting the destroyer. Rob watched the destroyer's weapons ignoring the lifeboat, slamming shots into *Squall*, until the last moment, when a hail of grapeshot aimed at *Squall* tore the lifeboat apart just before it impacted the destroyer's shields.

The pieces of the lifeboat crashed into the enemy shields, their mass given tremendous additional energy by the velocity of the impacts. The destroyer's screens completely collapsed under the blows, letting through a destructive rain of fragments from the wreck of the lifeboat as well as the fire from *Squall*'s weapons. The hits pelted the lightly armored destroyer down two-thirds of its length, tearing through the equipment, systems, and crew members unfortunate enough to be under that barrage.

"We beat the hell out of it!" Drake Porter whooped in triumph.

"His weapons avoided targeting the lifeboat," Danielle Martel said in disbelief, followed by growing understanding. "Lieutenant, his fire control systems were set to defaults! And the defaults don't allow shots at lifeboats!"

"We cheated, I guess," Rob said. But his sense of elation died as he stared at the red damage markers covering his display. "How badly off is *Squall*?"

"We can still maneuver," Danielle Martel reported. "But the grapeshot launcher is out. Looks like everyone on that weapons crew was killed."

"Lieutenant!" The call from engineering held overtones of panic. "We got trouble!"

"Give me a report!" Rob demanded.

"Those last hits, we took damage in here, and they destabilized the core. We can't hold it!"

Rob kept his eyes locked on his display, where new information was coming in. Scatha's destroyer was out of action. They had accomplished that much. And the freighter was heading back toward the jump point for all he was worth. But it didn't look like *Squall* would be chasing him. "Engineering, execute emergency shutdown of the power core."

"Emergency shutdown is not an option! The stabilizing routines have flatlined. The core will not shut down."

"What can you do?" Rob asked.

"What can I do? I can keep it from blowing up for a little while. That's what I can do."

"How long do we have?" Rob wasn't sure why he was asking. Why did it matter? With the lifeboat gone, there was no place to flee. No possible refuge out here far from the planet. Scatha's freighter was fleeing, and the enemy destroyer was drifting with no maneuvering control—

The enemy destroyer.

"I don't know!" the engineer repeated. "I don't know how long I can hold it!"

Rob checked the projected course of the *Squall*. "Danielle, can we manage another intercept of the destroyer? Coming to a dead stop relative to it?"

"What? Um . . . wait." She ran the data hastily. "Yes, sir. We should be able to do it. Twenty-five minutes to dead stop relative to the destroyer."

"Engineering? Can you hold the power core for another twenty-five minutes?"

"Twenty-five? I don't know. Why twenty-five?"

"Because if you can hold it for twenty-five minutes, we've still got a chance to get out of this alive! Keep that core from blowing for another twenty-five minutes, do you hear me?" Rob hit the circuit to talk to the entire ship again. "All hands, we are coming back around toward the enemy destroyer. It has been crippled, but our own power core is going unstable. Engineering says they cannot stabilize it and it will blow soon. Our only chance is to board and capture Scatha's destroyer. The boarding team will include the entire crew of the *Squall*. Everyone goes. Draw available weapons, anyone whose survival suit is not yet sealed get it done, and everyone but engineering proceed to the air locks on the, uh, port side."

Rob paused to rub his face. "Ensign Martel, make sure the intercept with the destroyer is locked in and proceed to an air lock. All the rest of you, go now."

"Lieutenant Geary," Danielle Martel said. "Excuse me, *Captain* Geary. We don't want *Squall* exploding next to the destroyer. I recommend we set the ship's maneuvering controls to accelerate at full ten seconds after we enter the command from . . . Air Lock One."

He looked at her, unexpectedly moved by her use of the title of captain for him. Such a small thing in the big scheme of things, with death looming, but the gesture of respect meant a tremendous amount to him at that moment. "I agree. Set the controls to accelerate after the command is entered at Air Lock One. Will that give *Squall* enough time to accelerate so we're out of the destructive blast radius before she blows?"

"I don't know," Danielle Martel said. "*Squall* might blow up before we even reach the destroyer."

"Good point. Get the commands entered, then get to the air lock. I'll join you."

Thrusters fired to swing *Squall* around, the main propulsion lighting off to slow her as well, her path through space altering into a steeply descending curve that swerved into a flat arc next to the stricken enemy destroyer. He remembered a Marine who referred to a combat drop as a roller coaster to hell. This felt like that.

"Done," Danielle Martel reported. "Are you coming?"

"In a second. Get to the air lock," Rob ordered. "All hands! Everyone except those in engineering necessary to manage the power core should be at port air locks by now! If you're not there, get there!"

For a moment, he was alone on the bridge. Rob sat in the command seat, his display a flickering sea of damage warnings, feeling *Squall* trembling as her main propulsion fought to reduce her velocity. It was as if the stricken ship were shaking with fear as she felt the end approaching but still fighting to give her crew a chance, and he felt a strange reluctance to leave her. *Squall* had not been the biggest or greatest ship ever built, but she had been his, and she had fought as bravely as any man or woman could have.

But his crew was waiting for him to lead them. For him to help them gain their last chance at life. And if he fought hard enough, if a miracle happened, he might still make it back to Ninja and a child he would otherwise never see.

Rob checked to ensure his sidearm, the same one taken from the former captain of the *Squall*, was holstered on his hip. He sealed his survival suit as he walked off the bridge, then ran, heading for Air Lock One, hoping the power core would hold together until *Squall* reached the enemy destroyer. At any moment the engineers' desperate efforts could fail, and *Squall* would blow up before her surviving crew could even launch themselves at the destroyer. To some, Rob and his crew would already be considered dead. But they also still lived. He had never before really grasped the old paradox of Schrödinger's cat, neither alive nor dead, something that wasn't supposed to apply at the level of people and their interactions with the universe, but now he finally did. Unfortunately, that was because he was now in the position of that famous cat, waiting to learn whether death or life had been decided.

Rob Geary reached Air Lock One, where Danielle Martel and a cluster of other crew members waited. Like many other parts of the ship, this portion of *Squall* had been holed by damage and had lost air, so the inner air lock door was already open.

"Five more minutes," Danielle Martel reported.

"Engineering!" Rob called. "How does it look?"

"Like it could blow any second! If it happens, you won't know, because we'll all be gone just like that."

Rob switched circuits. "Air locks, report in. Is everybody ready?"

"Air Lock Three ready."

"Air Lock Five ready. Lieutenant, we've got a couple of wounded in emergency evacuation bags. We'll haul them along with us."

"Good," Rob said, not wanting to know how many of the

crew of *Squall* were already dead. "Sergeant, where are you and your people?"

"Air Lock Five, sir."

"Good. We're coming alongside the destroyer oriented to match him. Bow to bow, stern to stern. When you jump, you'll be boarding closer to the destroyer's stern. We need to take the engineering section and ensure the power core is either shut down or operating safely."

"Yes, sir. Is there any chance the destroyer's crew will try to blow the power core themselves?"

"What?" It took Rob a few moments to understand the question. "You mean deliberately overload the power core and destroy their own ship along with us? No, Sergeant. That's crazy. No one would do that."

"Understood, sir. See you on the destroyer after we've wrapped things up."

Sergeant Grant Duncan's calm demeanor partially reassured Rob, who turned to Danielle Martel and clicked over to a private circuit. "What do you think our odds are?"

She shook her head. "It depends. Does the destroyer still have an outside sensor picture that will allow them to see us coming and prepare to defend against boarding? How many of their crew died during that firing run? And just how insanely lucky can we be?"

"So we've got a chance," Rob said.

"Yes, Captain. We've got a chance."

"You don't have to call me captain."

"Yes, sir, I do. You earned it." She checked something on her wrist readout. "Two minutes. We should open the outer hatch so we'll know the moment we can jump."

With the *Squall* decelerating fast, there was no sense in anyone's sticking their head out of the outer hatch to look for the enemy destroyer ahead. It would just be another dot in the endless array of stars and other objects in space.

"Here we go," Danielle Martel warned. "One minute."

"Everyone stand by to jump," Rob ordered. "Engineering? How does the power core look?"

"Bad. Really bad." The engineer's voice held so much fear that it seemed to carry the scent of sweat with it.

"How many of you are still back there?" Rob asked.

"Just me." The engineer paused. "I don't know how long it'll hold when I head for the air lock."

Rob stared in front of him, weighing what to do. Did he sacrifice the engineer to try to give the rest of the crew a better chance? Or did he keep faith with someone who had stayed behind to help his shipmates? "I need a plain and straight answer. Once you leave the core, how long until it blows? Give me a number."

"Within five minutes. That's just a wild guess, but it's the best I got!"

Rob made up his mind. "Leave now and get to the nearest air lock! You've got forty seconds!"

"On my way!"

"We're here!" Danielle Martel called.

Rob looked out of the air lock and saw the barracuda shape of the destroyer suddenly only twenty meters away. *Squall* had exactly matched vectors with Scatha's stricken warship, so that for these few seconds the two ships seemed to be drifting next to each other as if they had been parked in adjacent stalls.

"Boarding party away!" Rob ordered, restraining Danielle from jumping with an extended arm. "All hands jump! Ensign Martel, watch for the last engineer to jump from Air Lock Five, hit the command for *Squall* to get out of here, then follow."

"He'd better jump real soon!" Danielle warned.

Mele Darcy ducked as another wave of fire tore through the thinning chaff shrouding Scatha's entrenchments and the air over her force. Riley had managed to get a signal through that he was trying to push an attack to divert some of the defenders, but she had heard nothing since from him. And there were still entirely too many defenders in front of her, with too many weapons.

She heard a scream to her left and knew another one of her volunteers had been hit.

There wasn't any cover out here. The volunteers hugged the scrub-covered soil and turned desperate looks her way.

She couldn't decide what to do. Holding position seemed hopeless, but trying to retreat would result in many more losses as her volunteers had to raise themselves in order to run. But if she gave up—

"Major Darcy." No image accompanied the voice as the improvised comm link fought to get any signal through. The comm link slid up and down in volume, interspersed by spurts of static as Scatha's electronic countermeasures tried to jam the signals.

"Here," Mele growled, angry at the call.

"Request status."

Mele barely resisted the urge to reply with an obscenity. "Unchanged."

"Do you think you still have a chance to take the base?"

She shook her head at the question. "Maybe."

"You have to take the base, Major. It is our only remaining option."

"What does that mean?" Mele demanded.

"We have been watching the engagement in space. Scatha's warship may have been badly damaged but . . . our ship blew up."

Mele stared toward the enemy positions facing her, only barely aware of the shots flying past just overhead. "Say that again. What happened to *Squall*?"

"The ship . . . *Squall* . . . blew up. An hour ago. We haven't been able to spot the lifeboat. The *Squall* blew up. The . . . entire crew . . . must have died."

Damn. So Grant was gone. The entire crew. And Lieutenant Rob Geary. Mele wondered who would tell Ninja the bad news. She'd have to do it. That was her job now. Honoring her promise to Rob Geary because Rob Geary was certainly dead.

Mele didn't remember scrambling to her feet, didn't remember shouting to her volunteers to follow her, but she was moving forward, charging toward the emplacements where weapons were hurling shots past her, the unaimed fire through the thinning chaff rattling her ears as it tore past, one energy pulse scorching the light armor on her left upper arm, a slug hitting her upper body armor and ricocheting upward, the force of the blow breaking something inside her, but she didn't really notice because Mele was pulling out a grenade and hurling it at a heavy weapons bunker, the grenade going through the firing slit and secondary explosions tearing through the bunker, and suddenly there was a low duracrete barrier before her and soldiers huddled behind it firing into the murk and, shocked, trying to shift aim as Mele appeared; but she was firing, and two soldiers fell to her left, then twisting as she fell prone Mele fired again to her right to kill a third nearby soldier as other defenders' shots tore by over her.

She jumped up again as the enemy fire faltered, ignoring the pain in her collarbone and a sudden pain in her hip, charging down the entrenchment, killing one more, two more, then someone in battle armor ahead was gesturing like a commander so Mele fired two rounds at close range into the faceplate and that soldier fell, too.

Her finger froze on the trigger as one of her volunteers tumbled into the entrenchment and looked around for enemies. More volunteers were appearing, racing past the entrenchment and into the base, firing at individual Scatha soldiers who were dropping their weapons and either running or spreading their open hands in surrender. Mele pivoted slowly, looking around. Where she had first entered the entrenchment, members of her own force were streaming in, taking prisoners and pursuing those defenders still fleeing.

"Enough!" A Scatha soldier's voice cracked as he stumbled toward Mele, his weapons gone and his faceplate open, his eyes wide and dark with dread. "Enough! We are done! No more!"

"Surrender the entire base," Mele said, her voice sounding oddly inhuman and metallic to her. "The entire garrison. Now."

"It is done! I have broadcast the order! No more!"

They had won.

Shouldn't she feel happy about that? Mele abruptly leaned on the edge of the entrenchment as her hip gave way. She looked down at blood running down the outer edge of her leg. "Damn." She wondered why she didn't feel any pain there, why she couldn't feel any emotions even while her own forces cheered as they went about taking control of Scatha's base.

* * *

Rob lined himself up in the air lock and jumped for the destroyer. For a short time, there were no decisions to make, no orders to give as he flew between ships. His thoughts raced. The captain was supposed to be the last to leave the ship. But this wasn't an evacuation, an abandon ship. It was an attack, and he needed to be part of that attack, not bring up the rear. Of course, he'd probably be dead in one way or another in a few minutes anyway, and no one would ever know. All they would know was that he had gone down fighting.

He hoped Ninja would understand.

The destroyer was near when Rob twisted to look back at the *Squall*, looming close like a ticking time bomb. There was a wave of figures in survival suits roughly even with Rob, and two more who had just jumped from *Squall*, one from Air Lock One forward and one from Air Lock Five aft.

He twisted back around, seeing the fast-approaching side of the destroyer suddenly lit by the flare from *Squall*'s main propulsion as the warship accelerated away from her fleeing crew and the enemy destroyer that was their last remaining chance.

Rob experienced that odd disorienting feeling that he was falling onto the destroyer right in front of him, then he hit hard enough to drive the breath from him. He had remembered to keep his open hands extended so the gecko gloves on them would grip the enemy hull and keep him from being hurled back into space by the rebound. Rob held there for a second, the sound of his breathing harsh in his ears.

Two members of *Squall*'s crew had landed nearby, one carrying a heavy-duty portable cutting torch. As the other sailor steadied the one with the torch, it flared to life and swiftly cut an access through the destroyer's lightly armored hull.

Rob was about to pull himself inside when light flared again, this time much brighter, as if a tiny sun had sprung to life somewhere ahead of the destroyer.

Squall was gone. But she had held together long enough to give her crew a chance.

Rob drew his sidearm and swung inside, staring around the interior of the destroyer. Vibrations rolled through the ship from somewhere aft. Sergeant Duncan must have gotten inside back there.

Figures in survival suits appeared, coming fast from forward, all of them carrying hand weapons. Rob, the best armed in his group, stood sideways to them, leveled his pistol, and began firing as if on a range, trying not to think about what he was doing.

Caught by surprise, two of the defenders fell from Rob's shots before the others tried to return fire. He kept shooting, drawing their fire, while the rest of his group charged into the defenders. He felt the destroyer lurch, heard more vibrations transmitted through the hull, and knew the shock wave from *Squall's* death throes had reached the destroyer.

The impact of a hit knocked Rob back, leaving him dazed. He got to his feet, staring at the red warning symbol on the limited display of his survival suit. Danielle Martel had joined his group and slapped duct tape over the hole in his suit. "Important damage control tool," she said to Rob. "Can you keep going?"

"I don't . . . I . . . yes." Rob shook his head, gathered his wits, and followed Danielle into the welter of figures struggling in the passageway ahead.

The defending crew of the destroyer had already been rattled by the massive damage done to their ship and had suffered serious losses. The attacking crew of the *Squall* were driven by desperation that gave them a ferocity the crew from Scatha's ship couldn't match. Rob shot another defender, then a fourth, as his crew killed several more. One of Rob's remaining crew died in the struggle before the defenders fled.

"Stay on them!" Danielle Martel yelled. "Don't let them recover and regroup!" She led the attack, racing ahead with most of the other boarders behind her, one of the others staying to help Rob keep moving.

As Danielle ran past a hatch it swung open, giving her enough time to realize the danger but not enough to turn or dodge. A shot hit her and knocked Danielle across the passageway.

The crew member of the destroyer who had shot Danielle made the mistake of jumping out, not realizing she had been a little in advance of more attackers. Before he could fire again, one of Rob's crew had triggered the torch and burned a hole through the defender's survival suit and completely through the chest of the defender.

Someone stopped to help Danielle Martel. Drake, Rob thought, and despite the urgency of the attack did not order him to leave her.

"Keep going!" he ordered the others. "Keep heading forward!"

There had been ten or twelve of the boarding party with Rob when they started out. He thought there might be only a few left with him by the time they reached the bridge of the destroyer. Darkness split by beams of radiance from emergency lights filled the passageway outside the bridge. A hole in the overhead matched another hole in the bulkhead near the deck where a piece of something, probably the lifeboat, had torn through the destroyer. Rob attempted to catch his breath as he tried to recover from the run. He felt weaker than he should have and became aware that something wet was spreading inside his suit from the place where the shot had struck him.

The hatch was sealed. Rob, his thoughts wandering, wondered if Ninja could help them through again. No. She was back on the planet. A light hour away. "Torch! Get through to the bridge. You, are you one of Sergeant Duncan's? Have you got a grenade left?"

The torch made very short work of cutting out a piece of bulkhead. As it fell free to access the bridge, the soldier tossed in a grenade.

They went through in the wake of the grenade's explosion, finding a mess of battered equipment and injured defenders. Two more defenders died before the bridge crew surrendered.

Rob was helped into the captain's seat, once more trying to breathe as he wondered why his chest felt so tight and his thoughts were so hard to focus. Someone was talking to him.

"Lieutenant? We've captured engineering. We think there are still a few of the destroyer's crew out there, but the ones who are left all seem to be surrendering."

He had trouble focusing on the woman who had brought the report. "Where's Sergeant Duncan? Have you heard from him?"

"He's . . . he's dead. But we have the ship. We control this destroyer."

Damn. Rob tried to concentrate. What did he need to do? "I need a comm circuit. We need to let Glenlyon know that we took this ship and they are safe."

Someone offered him a link. Voice only, but that was fine. "Glenlyon, this is . . . Lieutenant . . . Geary. Our ship . . . *Squall* . . . was lost but . . . we have, uh, captured the enemy destroyer. The . . . destroyer is crippled, but we . . . should be able to survive until . . .

rescue can reach us. Get another . . . another ship here. To take us in tow." Just saying "out" felt wrong. Disrespectful. Shouldn't he say something else? Something to mark what his crew had done? There was a phrase he had heard recently. Maybe something like that would do. "My crew fought in a manner . . . that honored their ancestors . . . honored their ancestors," he repeated, feeling increasingly dizzy. "Geary, out."

"Sir? Lieutenant? He's in bad shape! Didn't you guys notice the hole in his suit? Get that medic we captured up here!"

Rob wasn't sure what the voices were saying, and he was too tired to care any longer. He felt a darkness deeper than space filling him and finally gave in to it.

Mele sat on top of a bunker, watching with a dull lack of interest as her volunteers searched the Scathan soldiers who had been taken prisoner, ensuring none had any weapons hidden. Scatha had lost a dozen more soldiers in the attack, meaning the original hundred were down to close to fifty. They stared at her through the open faceplates of their battle armor like men and women who were watching a dragon that had devoured their friends.

"Major," Riley said. His ready smile wasn't there anymore, replaced by a grim seriousness. "It looks like we have ten killed and a dozen wounded. I'll have to pull another muster to be sure."

"Thanks. I appreciate it," Mele said. "That's . . . better than I expected. You did a great job."

Riley looked puzzled and on the verge of crying. "Tina and Rolf died."

They had been in his diversion force, Mele remembered. "You did your best," she told him.

"It hurts," he said, sounding like a confused child.

"It's going to hurt," she said. "It won't stop hurting ever. But you can live with it. We both can. We'll both have to."

"Yes." He straightened and saluted her.

She remembered how absurdly proud Riley had been of learning how to salute properly. Mele, grimacing from the pain of her hip wound and moving awkwardly from the field bandage on it, came to her feet, tried to return the salute with her right hand, grimaced again as her broken collarbone protested, and settled for rendering the best return salute she could with her left hand. "You did good," she told Riley.

"Major? Major!" Mele looked toward her control pad as she heard the thin sound, and with a third grimace, this one of annoyance, reached for the headset. "Major!" Council President Chisholm, calling from Glenlyon, sounded elated.

"Yeah," she said, feeling exhausted from the fight and the casualties sustained, and angry that anyone so far from the fight would feel entitled to celebrate the victory. "What is it?"

"We just heard from Lieutenant Geary on the enemy ship! The crew of the *Squall* captured the enemy destroyer before their own ship blew up!"

She blinked, thinking that she must have misheard. "They're alive?"

"Most of them," Chisholm said, her enthusiasm faltering a little. "I think. Some . . . died. But they captured the enemy warship and damaged the enemy freighter, and it is fleeing back to the jump point. We won in space as well as on the land! What a glorious day for the people of Glenlyon!"

"How the hell . . ." Mele looked upward, where a few clouds

barely blocked the blue of the noon sky, trying to grasp the news. "Rob Geary is alive? His ship was about to blow up, so he captured the enemy ship?"

"Yes, Major, that is what we think happened."

Mele started laughing. She couldn't help it, gazing up at where the stars hid behind the sky of day. "He should have been a Marine."

"What?"

"Lieutenant Geary. He's crazier than I am. He should have been a Marine." She took a deep breath. "Tell him I said that. And tell Ninja he made it."

"Why would Ninja—?"

"Never mind. I can do it. Can you patch me into the city comm net?" That would have been impossible when Scatha's forces were jamming signals, but now it should be easy to do.

"Uh, yes, Major, I'm told that can be done. Voice only. Congratulations again from the council and people of Glenlyon! Wait. All right. You can call."

Mele tabbed the contact and waited until Ninja answered.

"I already heard," Ninja said in a voice devoid of feeling. "I was listening in on the official comms."

"No, you didn't hear," Mele said. "No, you heard wrong. That's it. Your boy is okay, Ninja. He made it."

"The ship—" Ninja began, her voice suddenly faint.

"Yeah, it blew up. But he captured the enemy ship before it did. I guess he wanted to get back here pretty badly, huh?"

"He . . . he . . ." Ninja couldn't speak for a moment. "How about you?"

"I'm all right," Mele said. "A little banged up. We won here, too. What kind of hacker are you that I have to tell you everything?"

"Mele Darcy, if you are lying to me—"

"It's all true, Ninja." Mele looked out across Scatha's base at the ranks of surrendered soldiers. "I guess somebody likes us."

"I guess," Ninja said. "Excuse me . . . I have to go light a candle."

15

Something didn't seem right. Rob blinked his eyes. He was in a bed. No, not just a bed. A medical unit was strapped across his abdomen, status lights glowing softly. Someone had been smart enough to design the unit so that every light facing him was a reassuring green.

What was wrong? Aside from his being in a hospital.

He wasn't on a ship. This was a building. Hadn't he been on a ship?

"Hey."

Rob looked over to see Ninja beside his bed. She appeared to be exhausted, but she was smiling. "You look awful," Rob blurted out, his thoughts still fuzzy.

"You ought to see yourself. And I wouldn't look like this if I hadn't spent the last few days sitting by this bed, waiting for you to wake up."

He stared at her. "What happened? How did I get here?"

"They managed to get you into a medical hibernation unit long enough for the ship from Kosatka——"

"What ship from Kosatka?"

"The ship from Kosatka," Ninja repeated, smiling at him indulgently. "It jumped in several hours after you'd captured the destroyer. Just an armed freighter, but Kosatka sent help just as soon as they could spare it. To return the favor to Glenlyon for the heroic actions of the heroic Lieutenant Rob Geary who saved Kosatka. Once they'd intercepted you, they towed the destroyer into orbit, and a shuttle brought you down to see if we could save your reckless life despite all your attempts to throw it away."

It was a bit much to take in. Rob closed his eyes, then opened them again quickly, afraid that this time Ninja wouldn't be there. But she was real, not a hallucination. "I don't know how many people we lost. From the crew of *Squall*. Did we lose a lot?"

Ninja looked down, biting her lip. "I can get the names for you. Later."

"Danielle Martel. I saw her get hit."

"Yeah. Um . . . you also have to think about how many you saved. From your crew and here on the ground by stopping that destroyer. That's really big, Rob. How many you saved." She met his gaze again, trying to smile as she patted her lower abdomen. "And you need to think about our little fork here, who is going to have both of us around. That's kind of important, right?"

"I wouldn't have wanted you guys to be alone," Rob said. "I was afraid that . . . that . . ." He suddenly had trouble speaking, unable to get any words out as emotions and memories of recent events blocked his throat.

"Hey, hey," Ninja said, looking distressed as she reassured him. "We're okay now. We're safe. Glenlyon is safe. And Mele's okay. Did you know that? She captured Scatha's base. Mele says she's going to make you an honorary Marine."

He did his best to smile in return even though he didn't feel like it. "I guess that's better than any medal, though Glenlyon doesn't have any medals to hand out."

"They need to make some, so they can give you one."

"No." Rob shook his head at Ninja, his heart pounding and breath feeling short as he relived in his mind the assault on the destroyer, the men and women on both sides falling, the fears and emotions he had tried to wall off during the actual events. "I don't deserve any medal. Those should go to people like Sergeant Grant Duncan. Oh, hell. Somebody told me he was killed. And Danielle, if she's . . . They deserve medals."

The lights flickered on the medical unit and Rob felt a wave of drowsiness.

"It's giving you sedation," Ninja said. "To keep you from overexerting. Relax. You've earned the rest."

He didn't fight the sleep, surrendering gladly, happy that Ninja was here, and he was here, and not wanting to think about those who weren't.

Drake Porter stopped by the next day, anxious over Rob's injuries but also unmistakably carrying a heavy load of personal sorrow. "I wanted to make sure you were okay, Rob."

"I'll live," Rob said, not knowing how to ask the question he probably already knew the answer to.

Drake looked down, his voice roughening. "Uh . . . Danielle . . . died. I don't know if anyone's told you."

He felt a wave of darkness press down on his mind. "No. Damn. I am so sorry, Drake."

"Yeah," Drake Porter said, still keeping his face averted. Drake didn't say anything for a couple of moments, trying to compose himself, then nodded toward Rob. "I wanted you to know I'm not going to stay on with the volunteer crew. I mean, there's no ship anymore unless they get that destroyer fixed up, but even if they do I . . . I don't want to go up again. I'm going to go back to working the kind of job I signed up for with the colony."

"I understand," Rob said, feeling helpless in the face of Drake's distress. "You've already done a tremendous job, and you've . . . taken a serious loss. No one could ask more of you. If you ever need anything, Drake, you just let me know. Anything. We'll always be shipmates."

"Sure," Drake Porter said, finally looking back at Rob. "You, too. You saved us, you know. We'd have all died out there, and Glenlyon would've been helpless. All of us who were out there know that. Hell, I was ready to give up. I know if you could've, you would have saved . . . everyone. If you ever need me, you just tell me. Deal?"

"Deal." Rob watched Drake Porter walk out alone, wishing that somehow he could've done things just enough differently that Danielle Martel was walking out beside Drake. But, perhaps, in a way, she always would be beside Drake Porter, a memory of a future that never was that would always haunt Drake no matter what else happened in his life.

Much later, he woke up to see Council Member Leigh Camagan standing in the room. "Please sit down."

Leigh Camagan sat down next to Rob's bed. For the first time he could recall, she looked openly angry.

"Did I do something?" Rob asked.

"Everything you should have and more," she replied. "I have

some news from the council. The council has voted to formally thank you for your heroism in repelling the attack on this star system by Scatha. The resolution expressing their thanks will be made part of the public record for the star system of Glenlyon."

"Thank you," Rob said, not knowing what to say but thinking that he needed to say something.

"For what?" Leigh Camagan asked. "It was the least they could do. I mean that literally. They did the least possible. There will be no tangible sign of their thanks. Nothing that would have incurred any expense on their part."

Rob blinked several times, tried to shrug, found it difficult with the med unit still on his abdomen, and settled for nodding to her. "I didn't do anything hoping for some reward," he said, and that much was true. He did feel some disappointment but refused to openly admit to it because he had never liked those who actively sought awards. "Why do I think there's another shoe about to drop?"

"Another ship has arrived at Glenlyon," Leigh Camagan said. "It included among its passengers a representative of individuals on Old Earth. He carried with him offers for star systems here in the down and out. If Glenlyon was willing to employ former officers and sailors of Earth Fleet, they would themselves arrange the purchase of their former warships, decommissioned destroyers, and enter the service of Glenlyon."

That was good, wasn't it? Rob tried to shrug again and gave it up. "Why are you saying that like you're giving me bad news?"

"As part of the agreement, a Commodore Hopkins will become head of Glenlyon's new fleet. He has glowing fitness reports from Earth Fleet."

"That's . . . nice. I guess I've been expecting something like that,"

Rob said. And he had been because, after all, he had only been a lieutenant in the fleet of Alfar and couldn't expect to vault to higher rank and responsibilities. But it still didn't feel great. "What are they offering me?"

Leigh Camagan didn't answer, looking away.

"Council Member Camagan," Rob said, "aren't they offering me something? I mean, I think I did a good job on *Squall*."

Leigh Camagan met his gaze. "You did an amazing job on *Squall*. That creates problems for those worried about the impact of professional militaries on a free society and whether or not military heroes might reach for political power."

"What?" Rob felt as confused as he had after being shot.

"The representative of the former Earth Fleet crews made it clear that all officer positions on the ships were to be considered taken since the former Earth Fleet commanders wanted people they knew. The council accepted that condition over my objection."

"Oh. Only your objection? I thought Council Member Kim would—"

"Council Member Kim saw an opportunity to quickly acquire two warships for Glenlyon. Council Member Kim is perfectly willing to sacrifice other individuals in pursuit of what he considers worthy goals," Leigh Camagan said. "Bellicose people tend to be like that. Sticking up for you would have meant creating problems with the deal to get the warships. He was already eager to send you into life-and-death situations. Why would he hesitate to sacrifice your career?"

Rob, his thoughts swirling, could only nod again. "What's happening to me, then?"

"The council is willing, in light of your past service to

Glenlyon, to offer you a position in fleet support."

"Fleet support?"

"Liaison for military matters." Leigh Camagan paused. "Liaison from fleet staff to council staff. Duties to be defined."

"They want to make me a gofer?" Rob asked, too stunned to think clearly. "That's it? The guy who gets the coffee at meetings?"

"I'm sure you would assist the commodore in matters such as making sure he had his coffee," Leigh Camagan confirmed. "Rob, I'm sorry. I fought this as hard as I could but, unlike you and Mele Darcy, I lost. The only redeeming aspect of the deal is that the position you're being offered would finally formalize your rank as a lieutenant but make you junior to every new officer being brought in from Earth."

"You have got to be kidding me."

"I wish I were."

"So, as of now," Rob said, "*even now*, I'm still not yet officially, formally, a lieutenant in Glenlyon's fleet? I'd only get that rank if I agree to that assignment?"

"Yes. It's not as if there is a ship for you to command before the former Earth Fleet warships get here. That destroyer you captured is hopelessly damaged."

Rob heard himself laugh. "And my reward for defeating that attack on this star system is for me to be given a position as sort of a junior intern to the Earth Fleet officers coming in?"

"Yes."

He remembered Danielle Martel, Earth Fleet veteran, choosing . . . *choosing* . . . to call him captain. Rob's thoughts steadied, showing two clear vectors he could take away from this moment. He had no trouble deciding on the one he wanted to take.

"Council Member Camagan, can you please inform the council for me that they can go to hell? I hereby, formally and officially, resign any informal assignment I had with the council. They can take their official offer and stick it somewhere uncomfortable."

Leigh Camagan nodded to him. "I expected you would say that. And, to be honest, I was hoping you would. You got outmaneuvered politically, Rob. There's no shame in that. And considerable pride in knowing what you accomplished with the most minimal of resources. I assure you that you will always have at least one true friend on the council as long as I am a member."

"Thank you. What about people like Danielle and the others who died?"

"That's still being debated," Leigh Camagan said. "They'll probably get a monument, a memorial, in a prominent place. I'm going to insist on pensions for surviving family members."

"Good," Rob said, and meant it. "They deserve that. But Danielle Martel didn't have any family members here."

Leigh Camagan sighed. "I don't know what else we can do for her. She died fighting for us, which should count far more than anything else about her. If someone can break the codes protecting Danielle Martel's personal files, they might at least learn who we should tell on Old Earth."

"I'll ask Ninja to do that. Danielle Martel was . . . *important*. I don't just mean in the things she did. Also in what she talked to me about. I didn't understand how important my example might be, but she made me think about that. Glenlyon will be the better for it."

Leigh Camagan nodded to him, her eyes thoughtful. "The official histories may not note her contribution. They may not note yours since they'll be written by a military bureaucracy yet to come into existence. I encourage you to do what you can to keep the memory of her role alive. And as for you, Rob Geary, you still have your life and a future to chart your own course, and that means more than any monument, as I'm sure you realize. Glenlyon owes a lot to you even if it prefers at the moment to brush under the rug just how badly you were supported and equipped while saving everyone else. If you need *anything*, let me know. I'll pull whatever strings I can."

He was lying in bed, staring at the ceiling, when the door opened again to reveal Ninja and Mele Darcy. "Hi, Ninja," he said, feeling better just seeing her once more.

"I've only been gone an hour," Ninja said, smiling as she leaned over to kiss him.

Rob returned the kiss. "Leigh Camagan stopped by."

"I already heard," Ninja said.

Rob looked at Mele Darcy, who was favoring one leg and had a light cast on her upper right body and arm. "I haven't seen you since my shuttle lifted for *Squall*. How are you, Major?"

"Are you talking to me?" Mele Darcy looked behind her as if in search of whoever Rob had spoken to. "I don't see any majors around here."

"What?" Rob stared at her as Ninja sat down next to him and reached out to grasp his hand with hers. "You, too? Are they hiring Marines from Earth Fleet?"

"Nope," Mele Darcy said. "Mind if I sit down? It just seems a simple former enlisted Marine like me ain't up to the job of running anything big, especially since what Glenlyon is standing up will be ground forces, and not Marines, who are a real pain in the neck sometimes, or so I've been told. There were some complaints that I ran a little roughshod over people while trying to get that big assault on Scatha's base done in a few days like I'd been ordered to do."

"What the hell were you thinking?" Rob asked, surprised that he could joke about it.

"Beats me," Mele said, feigning bafflement. "Apparently, some of the time and effort I spent trying to defeat Scatha should have been lavished on sucking up to council members and being polite to production managers."

"I guess I should have been doing that, too. Did they offer you anything?"

"Oh, yeah," she replied disdainfully. "They're planning on hiring veteran officers from Brahma and Amaterasu, but those officers are going to need support. So they offered to make me a sergeant again. A junior sergeant, of course," Mele added. "In a support role."

"Getting coffee for the boss?"

"You got it. What about you?"

Rob flipped a dismissive hand. "Coffee gofer. With a rank of lieutenant, but otherwise pretty much the same deal offered to you."

Mele Darcy snorted as if uncaring, but Rob could hear from the sharpness of the sound that there was anger underneath the nonchalance. "We should have expected it. The gratitude of kings and all that. Still sucks, though."

"I'm really sorry," Rob told her. "You deserved better."

"You both did," Ninja said. "If someone had broken into private discussions among members of the council, she would have learned that a lot of them thought that they should have defended Glenlyon and weren't happy that someone else had done the heavy lifting. Making too big a deal of what you two did would just emphasize how little the council had prepared and how little you had to work with. That'd be awkward, you know? And other members were arguing that Scatha just shows what happens when people with certain mind-sets become too powerful, or too popular, which should be a lesson to Glenlyon. The fact that you accepted Danielle, who had been working for Scatha, was being waved about as proof that all of you are just the same under your uniforms. Or so I've heard," Ninja added.

"I'm glad that *you* didn't break into those discussions," Rob said.

"Yeah," Ninja agreed, not even cracking a trace of a smile. "That would've been illegal."

"Why do they trust the people they're hiring from Old Earth and the Old Colonies?" Mele Darcy asked. "Did you, uh, hear anything about that from whoever might have broken into those conversations?"

"As a matter of fact, I did," Ninja said. "It seems Earth Fleet has these long-standing traditions about being obedient to government decisions and blah, blah, blah. And so do the Old Colonies."

"Just where do they think Rob Geary and I came from?" Mele Darcy asked.

"Somewhere dark and dangerous, I guess."

"Danielle Martel lectured me about how important it was to support the government," Rob said, feeling bitterness rising again. "But they slam her memory, in private anyway. Oh, Ninja, I turned down the offer from the council. I'm currently unemployed."

"Really?" Ninja raised her hands in mock despair. "Whatever will we do if I'm the only one hauling in paychecks?"

Rob glanced at Mele Darcy. "All right, I can tell you two are not saying something. What is it?"

Mele Darcy grinned. "While you and I were positioning ourselves for those great job offers, your Lady Ninja here was working on something that might help take the sting away."

Ninja gave Rob a wide smile. "The contracts are being let for operating the main orbital facility. The biggest pieces of it are being towed in after being built at a shipyard at Franklin and should show up within the month. I'm on the inside. That facility is going to need an officer to run the dockyard and repair section. And guess what? You played by far the biggest role in saving the people on the ground here who represent the corporation that will be finishing construction on the complex and running it. And those people know that."

"It seems they'll also need someone to run a security force," Mele Darcy said. "Council Member Camagan has told the corporate recruiters that if they hire me, they won't be sorry. And they like that you and I have proven we can work together. Apparently that's not a given with sailors and Marines."

"Really?" Rob asked.

"That's what I hear," Mele said. "So, we not only get to do honest work, but the officers from Old Earth and Brahma and other places who took our military jobs are going to have to ask us for our help and cooperation on a frequent basis."

Rob hadn't thought he would be smiling again anytime soon, but he did as he thought about that. "It's a good thing I'm not too vindictive."

"I can be vindictive enough for both of us," Mele Darcy said.

"Don't burn too many bridges, you two," Ninja cautioned. "Glenlyon thinks it's done with you. But I think Glenlyon is wrong. This part of space is still a mess. You guys gave Scatha a bloody nose, but Scatha is still out there. And that Apulu Star

System that gave you a hard time, Mele. Not to mention whoever bombarded Lares and threatened Kosatka, and whoever was stirring up other trouble on Kosatka, and other star systems that could be trouble that we haven't even heard of yet. Glenlyon is going to need you again."

"So what if they do?" Rob asked. "Why should we care if they need us again? Don't you think I've learned my lesson?"

"You'll care," Ninja said. "You'll care because that's who you are. No matter how many times you get screwed over doing the right thing, you'll still care. You and this grunt, both. They'll need you badly, and you'll step up."

Mele shook her head. "Do you think I'm some kind of idealist? I'll bet you a twenty, right here and now, that never happens."

Three years later, Senior Dock Officer Rob Geary looked over from his display as the door to his office on the orbital facility opened, expecting to see another fleet officer either demanding or begging for priority at a repair dock.

Instead, Captain Mele Darcy of the Security Division stood there, holding out her universal wallet. "I owe Ninja a twenty."

"What? Why do you owe my wife a twenty?"

"Haven't you heard? The *Claymore* was blown apart, along with Commodore Hopkins and half the crew. All hell is breaking loose. And guess who the council is asking for help?"

ACKNOWLEDGMENTS

I remain indebted to my agent, Joshua Bilmes, for his ever-inspired suggestions and assistance, and to my editor, Anne Sowards, for her support and editing. Thanks also to Robert Chase, Carolyn Ives Gilman, J. G. (Huck) Huckenpohler, Simcha Kuritzky, Michael LaViolette, Aly Parsons, Bud Sparhawk, and Constance A. Warner for their suggestions, comments, and recommendations.